LOVE, KENNEDY

Her life was like a love letter to each of us

JASON & HEATHER HANSEN

Plain Sight Publishing
An Imprint of Cedar Fort, inc.
Springville, Utah

This is not an official publication of The Church of Jesus Christ of Latter-day Saints. The opinions and views expressed herein belong solely to the author and do not necessarily represent the opinions or views of Cedar Fort, Inc. Permission for the use of sources, graphics, and photos is also solely the responsibility of the author.

Chapters that utilize Facebook posts have their pertinent links and QR codes at the end of each chapter.

ISBN 13: 978-1-4621-2159-5

Published by Plain Sight Publishing, an imprint of Cedar Fort, Inc.
2373 W. 700 S., Springville, UT 84663
Distributed by Cedar Fort, Inc., www.cedarfort.com

LIBRARY OF CONGRESS CATALOGING-IN-PUBLICATION DATA

Names: Hansen, Jason, 1975- author. | Hansen, Heather, 1975- author.
Title: Kennedy's hugs / Jason and Heather Hansen.
Description: Springville, Utah : Plain Sight Publishing, an imprint of Cedar Fort, Inc., [2016] | Includes bibliographical references and index.
Identifiers: LCCN 2016035548 (print) | LCCN 2016037954 (ebook) | ISBN 9781462119707 (perfect bound : alk. paper) | ISBN 9781462127429 (epub, pdf, mobi)
Subjects: LCSH: Hansen, Kennedy Ann, 1997-2014. | Neuronal ceroid-lipofuscinosis--Patients--Biography.
Classification: LCC RC632.N47 H36 2016 (print) | LCC RC632.N47 (ebook) | DDC 616.8/3--dc23
LC record available at https://lccn.loc.gov/2016035548

Cover design by Jeff Harvey

Edited and typeset by Deborah Spencer

Printed in the United States of America

10 9 8 7 6 5 4 3 2 1

Printed on acid-free paper

Dad, I think you should write a book. You and Mom have some things to do, so continue to share my story with the world. I promise that you will not tire from it and you will long to see me again, every day for the rest of your life. We did it, Mom and Dad, we did it! Dedicate my story to my family, my best friends, neighbors, grandparents, uncles, aunts, cousins, and the cheerleaders. But, most important, dedicate it to my Father in Heaven, who will help my story be told. Dad, I chose this. Do not ever forget that. I have to go now but will be waiting with open arms for you, Mom, Anna, and Beau. Give a giant Hug to the world Dad—a Kennedy's Hug.

love Kennedy

Praise for *Love, Kennedy*

"The Hansen Family allows us an intimate view into their gut-wrenching struggle as they prepare[d] to lose a child to Batten disease. This inspiring story is told in such a raw and personal style. You can't help feel like a member of their family and share in the losses, victories, and celebration of the life of Kennedy. Their inspiring account will prompt you to hug and hold those near to your heart."

–Jasen Wade, award-winning actor from films such as *The Cokeville Miracle*, *17 Miracles*, and *Miracle Maker*

"Jason and Heather Hansen do a terrific job of telling a true story of eternal significance—the life and premature death of their teenage daughter. Although Kennedy only lived 16 years, she impacted many people. Her wisdom and influence were greater than most who live a lifetime. This is a miraculous and touching story worth knowing."

–Ron Tanner, award-winning producer of *17 Miracles*, *The Cokeville Miracle*, and *Ephraim's Rescue*

"This book goes far beyond our movie [about Kennedy] and will bring a great insight into all of the lessons we can learn from the life of Kennedy Hansen."

–T. C. Christensen, award-winning director of *The Cokeville Miracle*, *17 Miracles*, and *Ephraim's Rescue*

CONTENTS

The Story Behind the Book and Movie ix
Prologue 1
Chapter 1: The Keys 2
Chapter 2: You're Kinda Cute 5
Chapter 3: The Castle 10
Chapter 4: Nice Mower 13
Chapter 5: Touch and Go 15
Chapter 6: The Chair 19
Chapter 7: The Dress 22
Chapter 8: Little Anna 26
Chapter 9: Little Stinker 29
Chapter 10: The Dandelions 32
Chapter 11: We're Home 36
Chapter 12: No More Children? 39
Chapter 13: Broken Glasses 41
Chapter 14: Going Blind 44
Chapter 15: The Tool Belt 49
Chapter 16: The Zip Line 53
Chapter 17: Worse than Death 57
Chapter 18: What's Wrong? 61

Chapter 19: Walk, Don't Run! 64
Chapter 20: All Alone. 69
Chapter 21: The Changing Day 72
Chapter 22: You Have to Accept This. 78
Chapter 23: You Can't Have Her Yet 83
Chapter 24: She Knew 88
Chapter 25: The Battlefield. 93
Chapter 26: The Tide 96
Chapter 27: Tickle Me, Daddy, Tickle Me 102
Chapter 28: June 5, 2013 106
Chapter 29: Daddy, You're Home! 112
Chapter 30: The Promise 115
Chapter 31: The Violin 118
Chapter 32: The Dance. 120
Chapter 33: Any Wish in the World. 126
Chapter 34: She Could Only Smile 130
Chapter 35: Sand and the Trust of an Uncle's Hand. 132
Chapter 36: Surfing and the TRUE FIREWORK 135
Chapter 37: Who Are Those Men, Daddy, and Goodbye. 138
Chapter 38: The Front Page 141
Chapter 39: The UNSPOKEN CONNECTION .143
Chapter 40: The Pinky Promise 146
Chapter 41: The GATEKEEPER 149
Chapter 42: The Rally. 151
Chapter 43: The Bubblegum Pink Wheelchair 153
Chapter 44: The First Day, the Last Day 156
Chapter 45: The Miracle Walk 160
Chapter 46: Move Over, Cinderella 163
Chapter 47: Cheer On, Kennedy, Cheer On 167
Chapter 48: Imagine–Touching the Hearts of Imagine Dragons! 172
Chapter 49: The Start of Something New. 176

Chapter 50: Party or Preparation? 181
Chapter 51: Letting Her Be Happy? 186
Chapter 52: The Choice to Ignore 190
Chapter 53: I Believe 194
Chapter 54: An Awakening 195
Chapter 55: Our Time 200
Chapter 56: And Then . . . There's Jaden 203
Chapter 57: Seeing Is Believing 205
Chapter 58: Celebrating Her Tragedy 208
Chapter 59: Unaware 211
Chapter 60: Surreal 213
Chapter 61: It Will All Work Out 216
Chapter 62: Fremont's Angel, the Miracle of Cheerleading & the Storybook Ending 220
Chapter 63: My Girl, My Heart 224
Chapter 64: Twitterpation and Love 226
Chapter 65: Rolling with the Punches 230
Chapter 66: The Loss of an Angel 233
Chapter 67: Angels and Demons 236
Chapter 68: Every Little Bit 242
Chapter 69: Understanding Last Moments 246
Chapter 70: Legs Broken 249
Chapter 71: What She Sees 251
Chapter 72: Not Much Time 255
Chapter 73: The Last Cheer 257
Chapter 74: Lucky 260
Chapter 75: The Comforter 265
Chapter 76: The Last Ride 269
Chapter 77: It's All Real 272
Chapter 78: Kennedy's Hugs 277
Chapter 79: The Ride Is Not Over 287

THE STORY BEHIND THE BOOK AND MOVIE

In life, we all have a story. It is human nature to treat our life as a storybook full of different chapters that portray our lives. My family's story began with a dream. A dream that was given to me that all now makes sense. In that dream, I was shown my family, my story, and what was to come. I then lived that dream, and my wife and I were blessed with our beautiful Kennedy, Anna, and Beau. What more could trump the beauty of our children? And yet, what could also destroy that beauty? Unfortunately, part of our dream and a chapter in our lives was losing our beloved Kennedy. Yet, through losing her, we also gained her. We gained her through coming to realize that when hard things come, we could be positive, understanding, and provide an array of love to all of those around us. Those hard things have allowed us to grow as a family and share the deepest parts of our souls and the hardest parts of our minds and hearts. And with that sharing, we were promised by Kennedy that if we told her story openly, lovingly, and aggressively with faith that it would be shared with the world. She asked that a book be written by her dad, and that if done, she promised it would be successful. So successful that she would say, "Have to calm things down." That happened. And with that happening came the great opportunity and blessing of a movie. What more success in sharing her life's story could come than from that opportunity?

Yet Kennedy's story could not just be shared by anyone. It needed to be shared by someone who was not be afraid to tell the truth about her life. T.C. Christensen is that someone. He took to heart the rawness, reality, and authenticity of Kennedy, our family, and the experiences that we endured. He spent time reading, pondering, questioning, and asking. He did nothing hastily, yet did everything perfectly. He wanted to make sure that if he was going to tell her story, that the most important parts were shared. And guess what? He did that!

When you see the film, you will see that he nailed all of the components of her message. She loved boys (especially Jaden), and you will see that. She loved her family, and the movie shows the special relationships that she has with each of her family members. She loved cheerleading and music and always dreamed of being normal, and you will see that. And lastly, she loved her Savior and Heavenly Father with perfect faith, which in turn allowed her to love *everyone* whom she met. If I could relive my life with her again with what I know now, I would simply give her the new nickname that T.C. so perfectly nailed: L. K., standing for Love, Kennedy. As the movie was made and came to its conclusion, it seemed that it was not really work for everyone, but love. We have become so close to the cast, T.C., and his crew. We have a new family. A family called Love, Kennedy, which consists of multiple letters written to us from the people who made the movie possible, reminding me of the letters that Kennedy would write to us. Truly, the movie slogan, "Her Life Was Like a Letter to Us All," could not be more appropriate.

And so now, here we are. The movie is done, the book is around the world, and we sit with our hearts still hurting, yet now beating with excitement for Kennedy's dream and prediction that has come true.

So, you see, we all have a story. But, in our case, like T.C. stated, our story is one that was written and planned long ago. Planned by a little girl, who simply wrote the letter, stored it away, gave everything she had from her heart, and then simply signed, "Love, Kennedy."

Love, Kennedy's dad

PROLOGUE

Right after I graduated high school, I had a dream. In that dream, I saw my beautiful wife, Heather, driving a black-colored SUV. She pulled up to a place I had never seen before but that I recognized many things about. It was an older home that had a nice lawn that gently sloped toward the street. It was sloped just enough that if an SUV were to park at the bottom of it, you could open the door and be face-to-face with whomever was seated in the back of it. In this dream, I ran down the grass, and I was so, so excited—but I did not know why. I opened the back door to see the cutest little girl with pigtail braids sitting in her car seat. Her big brown powerful eyes penetrated mine, and my entire body filled with an excitement and feeling unlike any I had ever experienced. And then, the little girl reached out and *hugged* me. She hugged me, embraced me, and squeezed me so tight that it felt as if I was right there with her in physical form. The hug was unlike any that I had ever received before. Who was this little girl? Who was this beautiful blonde-haired woman who I assumed was her mother? That little girl, that little squeeze, was Kennedy. Kennedy Ann Hansen, my future daughter, my only flesh and blood, princess to a queen and the daughter of a Heavenly King. That queen, that perfect mother, that amazing woman was Heather, my wife and Kennedy's earthly guardian angel. And that black SUV, that house, and that lawn were ours. It was where it all started, where it all began. And as for me, well I was an eighteen-year-old kid who woke up in a cold sweat, confused, yet so excited. For I was the first to have received a Kennedy's Hug™.

CHAPTER 1

THE KEYS

I thought a lot about that dream for the next three years of my life. I grew up in Bountiful, Utah, and had a dreamlike childhood, in my estimation. I had three older brothers and a little sister, and we had the time of our lives. Our mom probably loved us too much and still does. I think that is probably where Kennedy learned and inherited so much love from. We grew up hugging. A HUG before you go to bed, a HUG before you went to school, a HUG even when your buddies were watching and you were getting dropped off to baseball practice! And then, there was our quiet but gentle giant of a dad. A man who demanded respect, but did it with love. He taught us how to work, own up to our mistakes, and respect women to the utmost. He taught us to have good values, and more important, he taught us boys that you can be a tough guy and still provide a HUG to anyone anytime if it was so needed. His idea and teaching was, *"You always listen to the Spirit, which is a higher power, and if you do, you will know exactly what to do."* I took that advice to the deepest parts of my heart, mind, and soul. And in 1981, at the young age of six, I experienced this firsthand. I will never forget one day as a young boy, watching my mother in a panic. At that time, she was working graveyards as an RN and would return each morning to raise five kids under the age of twelve, running us all over the place in her brown station wagon. Simply put, she was stressed. On this particular day, we were in a hurry to get out the door, but she had lost her keys to the station wagon.

We looked everywhere. She was in such a panic and we all were worried. I cannot remember where we needed to be, only that it was important. We looked for over an hour. We looked everywhere! After searching and searching and searching, I will never forget my beautiful mother gathering us all and dropping to her knees right there in the kitchen. She prayed. She pleaded with every ounce within her soul, "Father, please, please, help us find these keys. Father, we need these keys and we need to find them now." The prayer ended and my oldest brother, Greg, immediately rose to his feet and went to the back door, where in the dead bolt he found the keys, right where our mother had left them, hanging within the lock. "How did you know to look there?" my mother asked.

"I listened to the Spirit and it told me EXACTLY what to do," Greg said. He had not put those keys there, and he had not seen them or had any clue that they were there. The SPIRIT told him and he trusted. From that moment on, I never questioned the SPIRIT. And from that time on, I began searching, building, and growing a different set of keys. Keys that would be given to me from our Heavenly Father to be able to listen, follow, and know EXACTLY what to do at specific times, without hesitation, question, or any knowledge of what was to come. These keys were spiritual and would be so important throughout Kennedy's journey, which would require us to drop to our knees and seek answers to many keys that seemed lost, but soon would be found.

Kennedy's mother, Heather, had a childhood much like mine—full of laughter and fun. She had two older sisters and two little brothers, also coming from a family of five children. She had hardworking parents and a loving home. Her father has told me many times, "There is no guile, hatred, or mean bones in Heather. She is the sweetest spirit I have ever known. From the time she was born, she was the peacemaker." And to this day as her husband I could not say it any better. Heather has a way of calming your soul, of making you feel special, and more than anything, of accepting all. I believe that these traits were inherited and given to her from her mother, a mother who gave her all to her family and, at the age of forty-two, gave her all to a two-year battle with cancer that ultimately took her life. Heather was devastated. She was lost, confused, and bewildered. Her hero, her godsend, her mommy . . . gone. This loss, so deep, so tough, and so gut wrenching, would become one of the greatest blessings ever to enter her life, and yet she had no idea—no idea that a little girl just like herself would be coming to her world, a little girl that would be hers for a minute on earth, but an eternity in heaven. And without knowing loss, without knowing care, without knowing pain, Heather could and would never have been able to make it through the journey of raising an eternal princess from an eternal queen. Taken too early, but taken for a purpose, Heather's mother was key in getting Kennedy to us and would become more key as time went on. She was a guardian angel that in the end, we know, came for Kennedy and to this day is with her, being able to receive a HUG that she watched and waited so long for. The keys begin to fit, many on one key chain. All have a purpose, all have a keyhole, and all have their role. Our families each held a key on this key ring and opened the doors for Heather and me to meet. A meeting that, once again, brought a new key to a new keyhole and one where the SPIRIT told me EXACTLY what to do . . . to marry Heather Ann Humpherys.

CHAPTER 2

You're Kinda Cute

When I first met Heather in 1996, she was strikingly beautiful! I never thought in a million years that she would be interested in me. I had seen Heather only one time in high school. I attended Woods Cross High School in Bountiful, Utah, and she attended Clearfield High School in Clearfield, Utah. The two cities and schools are separated by a short twenty miles of I-15 concrete and maybe thirty minutes of drive time. We were both the same age, held many of the same interests, and loved high school. She was a beauty queen and was nominated as such many times. She had to quit cheerleading and dance due to finances with the passing of her mother, but she was involved deeply with the school. She was very social and loved to participate in everything. She was very popular and to this day, there are still men who tell me how lucky I am and ask, "Do you know what you really got?"

I too loved high school. I played some sports and was very involved in every social aspect known to the school. Friends came easy because I tried to just love everyone. I was not perfect at it, but I tried. I was a hugger and I felt very comfortable doing so. I had a great group of friends; we called ourselves "The Boyz." We hung out and did things that were unimportant, but we thought they were important. My senior year, I did an impersonation of Neil Diamond's song "Coming to America," silver suit and all, and now twenty years later, my classmates still have me perform it at every reunion. By the end of my Senior Night as I graduated, I accomplished my goal of being able to name every graduating senior by name. People were my passion and I think I got that from my dad.

I was always out doing something. One night in 1993, at the beck and call of my buddies, we attended a multi school "Stomp" dance at Clearfield High. And that is where I saw her; man, was she striking! I had always seemed to ask and date the girls I wanted to. Not saying I wasn't turned down a time or two, but if I wanted to date them . . . well, I was persistent. But when I saw Heather for that tiny moment at this dance, I was intimidated. How could a girl like that exist? I told my buddy that I was going to ask her to dance. He simply said, "Good luck." I watched one by one as multiple guys danced with her. I could not take my eyes off of her for a solid ten minutes and then she vanished. It was the only time I ever saw her in high school.

Fast forward a few years. I was fresh off of serving a two-year mission for the LDS church (The Church of Jesus Christ of Latter-day Saints). As LDS missionaries, we were not allowed to date for those two years in order to focus on the message that we were sharing. While serving that mission, I remember kneeling down every night to say my prayers. I would pray for so many things: my family at home, the investigators we were meeting with, and my fellow missionaries. But a big part, a HUGE part, was praying for my future wife. I would pray for her that she was out there underneath that big tapestry of stars preparing herself for me as I was preparing myself for her. Many times I would feel of her, not knowing who she was or what she was doing. It was during these times that I knew that she was out there doing the same. I was assigned to serve in San Jose, California, and halfway across the ocean, Heather was attending college in Hawaii. She was still grieving the loss of her mother and trying to figure out how to cope. Her father had remarried (to an amazing woman) and Heather was adjusting to it all. She went to college in Hawaii for one semester and then returned home to Ogden, Utah, to attend Weber State University. At one point, she even got engaged to someone, but it did not feel right. She just did not feel she had met the man she felt she should marry yet.

So when I ran into her in college at the gym, I immediately knew who she was. Her friend introduced me to her and after seeing her again, I told myself that I was not going to let my chance get away this time. My heart seized upon being introduced to her. She was more stunning, more beautiful, and more awe striking now that a couple years had passed. I had to get her number—I just had to. She had gone to the girls' locker room, so I ran up the stairs to the entrance. There was a girl at a check-in table in those days who would check out towels and lockers if you wanted them. I asked her if a blonde had just gone into the locker room.

She said, "Yes." I said, "You have to go and get her for me. It is very important." She looked at me with a look like I was crazy. She said, "What is so important that I go and get her for?" I thought for a moment and just said, "This is an emergency. You have to go and get her. Just tell her it is an emergency." Flustered and frustrated, she got up from behind her desk and said, "This had better be important. I have no idea why I am doing this for you." She came back after about five minutes and told me that Heather was not in the locker room and was gone. Feeling lost as she was talking, I looked out the window to the hallway exiting the building. There was Heather, walking in the parking lot toward her car! I ran out the door; I was not going to let Heather get away this time. And what happened next was that feeling, the same one that I had in my dream with Kennedy after high school and the same feeling my dad had taught me. It hit me like a ton of bricks. *"You always listen to the Spirit, which is a higher power, and if you do, you will know exactly what to do."* This came into my mind three times as I ran up behind Heather. She was sticking her key into her car door when I suddenly came up behind her and all I could muster up was this. "You're kinda cute," I said.

She jumped. "You scared me!" she said. "And what did you say?" She was now chuckling, "That I am kinda cute?"

"Ummm, yeahhh," I muttered. "You are kinda cute."

"Ok. . . . Is there anything else you want? It's Jason, right? We met in the gym."

Oh man, did I feel stupid. Immediately, I could tell that she definitely thought I was a weirdo. "Yes, it's Jason and I do want something else. . . . I want your phone number and I want to go out with you this Friday night." Heather stood thinking for a minute and looking at me with a look like "what should I say to this guy?"

Hesitantly, she replied, "Ok, it's a date. What time do you want to go?"

It just felt so right; it felt so real. Before leaving her at her car, I did something that made her uncomfortable, but looking back, I now know that it came from Kennedy. I reached out and pulled her toward me and hugged her. Heather awkwardly hugged back. She really did not know how to respond to that Hug. But it came from somewhere within and as I walked back to my car, I could not help but feel an intense interest in this girl. A girl who, through a Hug, I just felt so connected to.

As the week wore on, I saw Heather a couple of times at the gym. We worked out a little bit together and I could not get my eyeballs off of her!

She was beautiful inside and out. As the week neared Friday, I received a phone message to call Heather. I called her and she proceeded to tell me that she had forgotten about another date that she had already set up for that night. *Forgotten?* I thought. *Forgotten?* Yeah right! I have to admit that I was ticked off and upset. So just like that I told myself that there was no way she would ever be interested in me. But something inside of me could not get my mind off of Heather. It kept pushing, urging, and nudging at me. *You have to take that Heather girl out, you just have to.*

A few days later, I saw her in the gym again. We began to work out together every single day. I was still dating another girl and Heather was dating others as well. I could not help but continuously think about her. I would wait for classes to get out just so I could go and work out, or more or less see and be with Heather. And each day, I would Hug her. She got used to these Hugs and she got used to me telling her all about my serious girlfriend. One day while working out, she began to tell me about a date that she had been on that weekend. She told me that she had been soooooo interested in this guy and so excited to go out with him. They went to a concert of a rock band that Heather thought she would like. When they got to the concert, though, Heather felt so uncomfortable. Everyone was partying, drinking, and drugging, and the environment was dark and dreary. Heather told her date she wanted to go home, but he would not listen. As she told me this, I was infuriated. I felt a defense mechanism inside of me. And the bad part about it was that he worked out in the same gym we were in. I saw him running around the track as we were talking. I immediately jumped up and ran right next to him. I was loud and clear that if he ever wanted to breathe out of his nose normally again, he owed Heather an apology. He then asked if I was her boyfriend. I responded, "Something like that." I watched as this guy finished running around the track and reluctantly walked up to Heather and apologized to her. Heather turned bright red and was shocked, surprised, and also frustrated. I walked back over to her and she instantly asked, "Why did you do that? I can handle myself . . . but . . . thanks."

"I did that because I care about you. No one, and I repeat, no one will ever disrespect you on my watch again," I said.

"On your watch? What do you mean? Your watch? You have never even taken me out on a date and you have zero interest in me. Why have you not asked me out? The way you just defended me and nearly attacked that guy, you would have thought you were my boyfriend!"

I looked at her and at that moment, right there and then, I knew that

I loved her. I reached out and hugged her and held her so tight. "Heather, fine, fine you win. Let's go out right now."

"Right now?" she asked.

"Yes, right now." I said. The date was May 9, 1996. We left that gym and drove to a diner and ate lunch together. Everything changed from that moment on. We stared into each other's eyes and could not seem to stay apart. And since that day, we have never left each other's side. Our love bonded us deeply and another key was added to the key chain. The key of marriage. I never knew I could love anyone that much. But little did I know what was to come. We thought we were in love. We thought we had it all. But Kennedy, yes, Kennedy, would and did change all of that. She would take our love to a whole new level. A level that would have to be opened up with the key that she would provide to unlock a lifetime door to sixteen wonderful years of amazing blessings with her.

CHAPTER 3

The Castle

We looked up at the ceiling of our 1952 small brick rambler home. We could see all the way through the torn-up wood floor into the upstairs from the basement where we slept. This was our first night in our home together. We had been married just under a week and had just returned from our honeymoon. We had purchased this home from a friend and had begun to tear the entire house apart from wall to wall. The house had no plumbing, no fridge, and no electricity. But we insisted on staying in it. We had purchased a new mattress that we laid on the floor, and we had a Coleman camp light, along with a cooler with ice and our food in it. We knelt on the side of our bed and prayed that night. We blessed our home, we blessed our marriage, and we blessed our future children who would come to us. This was our first night in our home together as a little family, and although this sounds odd, we felt as if we were not alone. We held each other tightly and we laughed. "Am I ever going to have a floor, a toilet, or a fridge?" Heather asked.

"I promise you will have it soon," I said. We could not stop laughing, because we had to go to the neighbor's house to shower and use the bathroom. It was actually funny, but embarrassing. But we wanted our little piece of heaven. We cherished it, we adored it, and we worked hard at taking care of it. We spent the next couple of months finishing our little 900-square-foot castle. Heather got her fridge, she got her electricity, and she even got her new toilet. I would go to school from 7 a.m. until noon and sell windows for homes from 1 p.m. until 9 p.m. at night. I would come home, do homework for an hour, and then work on the house from 10:30 p.m. until 2 a.m. every night. Heather did the same, but she worked at her uncle's orthodontic office. We put everything into that little home that we called our castle. We were poor, we had little, but we were happy. On Friday nights, we would walk to a video rental store and we could get two for $2.00. This was two VHS videos and two bags of microwave popcorn. We would invite friends over every weekend. We thought we were living the big life!

Heather kept that home immaculate (as she has all of our homes!). We were happy, so, so happy, and oh, how we were busy. We had purchased the home in September, so we did not have a lot of time to work on the yard. Wintertime came and we continued to work on the inside of our castle. We would talk every night about our future family, dreams, and aspirations. We had decided that we would wait a year to begin our quest of having children. With such demanding schedules, we wanted to finish school, the house, and just spend time together.

So . . . you can imagine our shock, our surprise, and of course, our excitement when in March of 1997, just six short months after being married, Heather began to tell me that she did not feel right. She was feeling lethargic, tired, and kind of wheezy in the mornings. I begged Heather to go to the doctor, but she refused. There was NO WAY that she could be pregnant. We had been preventing this in order to get through school and adjust to life. I will never forget the feelings I had as I said my prayers the day we found out that she was pregnant. I was kneeling by the side of my bed and praying to Heavenly Father. It was nighttime and she was in the bathroom feeling sick. As I prayed, that same feeling that I had received so, so many times that I have mentioned came over me. *"You always listen to the Spirit, which is a higher power, and if you do, you will know exactly what to do."* As I was praying, that SPIRIT from a higher power gently whispered to my mind, "Heather is pregnant." I was so excited that I jumped to my feet, ran to the bathroom, and through the closed door, I screamed, "You're pregnant, you're pregnant!"

She opened the door and looked at me with that same look that she gave me when we first had met. A look like "you are a weirdo!" I quickly ran and got my keys and sped to the grocery store a short mile away to purchase a pregnancy test. Upon returning, I pleaded with her to just take it. Once again, I found myself outside the bathroom door as Heather caved in and agreed to take the test. I heard the toilet flush. I heard water running. Heather reluctantly opened the door, tears streaming down her face. She held the test in her hands. . . . IT WAS POSITIVE! I was elated! I screamed with joy and hugged her. But she—she was not elated.

She looked at me and said, "I am not ready for this. How is this possible? I am not supposed to be pregnant yet."

I took her by the hand and said, "I promise, Heather, that there is a reason. God would not bless us with this miracle unless it was meant to be. How are you pregnant? Well, I do not really know. But you are and we will give this baby the best life that this child could ever have. I promise." We went to bed that night and I slept like a baby, thinking, *A father, dad, daddy. Will it be a girl? Will it be a boy? Wow. . . . I cannot wait!* But what was to come in the next nine months, what was about to happen, would change all of this.

CHAPTER 4

Nice Mower

Heather would not let me tell anyone about her being pregnant for another month. Heather has always been much wiser than myself. It had been a couple of weeks and Heather had gone from devastated to animated. She was getting excited. "I don't want to find out what we are having until the baby comes," she told me.

"What?" I said. "Are you serious? That is the fun part of technology now, to know, to plan, to prepare."

"It will be such a great surprise. . . . I promise," she said. Well, I was not too happy about this, so with it being spring, I went outside to mow the lawn and begin working on the yard of The Castle. We had not even touched the yard yet. I fired up the ancient lawn mower that had been sold with the place. As I came down the slope, I suddenly heard a *boom*! The mower started making a weird sound and smoke began spilling out of the side of its exhaust. I hurried and shut it off thinking, *I hope this thing does not explode!* I waited for the smoke to clear as I kneeled down next to it to assess the damage. As I knelt down and the smoke cleared, I looked down the gentle slope of grass ahead of me and saw it once again. The dream—the dream from high school all came back to me. I quickly sat down on the grass and was overcome with the thought and memory again of this dream. It repeated again in my mind as follows, "The place was an older home that had a nice lawn that gently sloped toward the street. Just enough that if an SUV were to park at the bottom of it, you could open the door and be face-to-face with whomever was seated in the back of it." I was overcome with emotion. I was overcome with passion to be the best father, the best provider, and the best husband in the world. It was as if my mind had left and was in another place, another realm, another world. And then . . . "Jay, Jay, Jay, you all right? What happened?" Heather had heard the explosion from the mower and had seen all of the smoke. She was by my side and was concerned, but she was laughing. "Nice mower, wow. Came with the house, huh?" So she sat down, we laughed, we hugged, and she looked at me and said, "I love you so much, Jason Hansen!"

"I love you too," I said. She had no idea what I had seen, what had just happened. And I did not want to tell her, because I was afraid of being wrong. As we sat there laughing, something changed. Heather became pale, and she instantly looked weak. She got up and ran to the house. I followed her, where I found her draped over the toilet throwing up. She threw up hard that day—the first of every day for the rest of her pregnancy. It would be "touch and go" for the next eight months. The hardest eight months of our lives to get our angel here. Eight months that physically would prepare Heather to help Kennedy endure her last Eight months, sixteen years down the road, where pain, suffering, throwing up, and physical limitation would become everyday life as Kennedy would be in a "touch and go" state.

CHAPTER 5

Touch and Go

The doctor peered at me with eyes full of concern. "The baby is getting stronger, but your wife is getting weaker. We need to hospitalize her immediately," he said. Heather was only three months pregnant and she could not keep any food down. They needed to get IVs hooked up to her quickly. She was dehydrated, lethargic, and so, so tired. "How long are we talking?" I asked.

"Oh, maybe a week," he said. Almost one month later, we brought Heather home for good for the rest of the pregnancy. There was no reason, syndrome, or medical answer for why she was so sick. The only thought that kept coming to my mind was how strong this baby was. The baby was growing and getting big, healthy, and perfect within Heather. I will never forget how worried I was after we got her home. The doctor had been clear that we needed to have her lay down and rest all day until she got better. The words "got better" never occurred in Heather's experience. Poor Heather would throw up from dawn until dusk it seemed. And the forceful nature of this made her sore, frustrated, and so, so weak.

Ultimately, we were able to get an in-home nurse that would visit us once a day to help change out Heather's IV and check her vitals. Heather still could eat, so I did everything I could to make her happy. I would rub her back, tickle her arm, and stroke my fingers through her hair. One night I asked her what she wanted to eat. "Chinese stir fry," she responded. "Ok, Chinese stir fry coming right up." I quickly whipped this together and brought it to her. She looked at it and was excited, but the minute the flavor hit her mouth and the aroma penetrated her nostrils, she began throwing up. I took the plate away and sought out my backup plan. Well . . . two burritos, spaghetti, and a sandwich later, I gave up. Nothing could pacify her nausea or sickness to food. Man, was this frustrating! So, what did we do? We did the best with what we had to work with. In the end, about the only thing that she could hold down was popcorn. . . . Yes, popcorn. So, I bought it by the case and made it frequently. We are confident that is why Kennedy ate and loved it so much! Kennedy could blow through a large bowl of popcorn in a matter of minutes and even until just days before her passing, she would motion and request popcorn more than anything.

By the end of the pregnancy, Heather was just ready—so ready to get this baby out of her and into this world. She also was more than ready to not be sick anymore. I was fortunate, having a sales job, to be at home when necessary and help Heather throughout the pregnancy. There were so many growing moments during those nine months. So many discussions, dreams, and plans. The nursery amidst it all was completed by Heather and was absolutely wonderful. She completed all of the bedding for the crib, the drapes, and the diaper table. She made a blanket and still stuck to the colors of blue along with neutrality of design. She wanted the sex of this baby to be a surprise. But the highlight of the room was the rocking chair. Heather's mom had rocked all of her babies in this chair, and it was now passed onto Heather. It sat quietly waiting for the arrival of the baby. The chair had a unique creek sound to it that to this day is still present.

Nine long months finally came to an end. I will never forget how tough of a wife I finally realized that I had. Heather was past her due date and ready to pop. I had a study group over at our home for a big project going on at school. Heather simply came out to our living room and said, "I am going to go and take a bath, and then I am going to bed. Good night all of you." She went to the bathroom and it was not but three minutes later that I could feel something was not right. I kept studying and ignored the feeling. Finally, I could not handle it anymore. As I stood up to go check on Heather, she beat me to the punch. She was standing in the living room with her robe on and a surprised look. "I think that the baby is coming!" I immediately went to her aid and had her sit down. Her contractions were very close together and she was definitely in labor. A few hours later, we sat in the hospital where we discussed names again for the millionth time for our baby. "If it is a boy, Corbin," we said. "If it is a girl . . . Kennedy."

To our surprise, our little eight-plus pound bundle of joy came racing into life with more black hair then most six-month-olds have. At first I screamed, "It's a boy, boy. . . . No, no, it's a girl!" The doctor confirmed it was a girl. I kissed Heather and was so ready to hold the baby. I knew without hesitation and without a doubt from my dreams that this would be a girl. A girl that would give me great satisfaction and stop me dead in my tracks at the peep of her voice. As I held her in my arms and stared into those big brown eyes, my heart melted. She gave a little whimper and then produced a smile. This little girl was ours, she was ours forever. We were going to have so much fun, do so much together, and live life to the fullest. I could not help but feel the greatest responsibility of my life within my arms. I fast forwarded my mind to her as a toddler, teenager, bride, and mother. I was so ready, so amped for this to happen.

As I was standing, daydreaming, and thinking of this moment, my mind immediately shifted as Heather blurted out, "I want a steak! A big steak, a potato, gravy, and a Coke! I am not sick anymore!" We both laughed and blamed her sickness on Kennedy. That little stinker! The minute she left her mom, her mom felt great! So I left the hospital, got the steak, and came back to my little family. Heather ate it furiously and did not throw up. She had a grin from here to Texas. She finally could eat again! And she would need to, for we were in for the time of our lives with this little bundle of joy. And after all of the nurses, doctors, grandparents, friends, and family left the room, we huddled together as a little family and we Hugged. Yes, we Hugged. I will never forget the feeling in that room. We Hugged and then I cried. I was so proud, so happy. I contained my emotions and then knelt by Heather's bedside. She held Kennedy in her arms, and I held her hand and Kennedy's little hand. I offered a prayer of thanks to our Heavenly Father. I thanked him for saving my wife and my baby and for allowing me to have this little family. It was all I could do to not want to cry again. It had been "touch and go" for that nine months. But, somehow, someway, we made it. Financially, emotionally, spiritually, and physically. We made it through that short little journey thinking at times we might not. I thanked Heavenly Father for this and then fell asleep. I was exhausted. I was tired. But the castle, the lawn, the black SUV, and her room were all in order. We were ready and we were happy. How little did we know the happiness that was to come, along with the sorrow of losing part of it in sixteen short years. For in sixteen years, our world would change again. We would once again kneel by a bedside, this time Kennedy's bedside, and once again hand in hand we would offer another prayer. A prayer of thanks for giving us this angel and for saving her for so long. For sixteen years later, we would be seasoned at making it through the journey of touch and go—helping Kennedy "touch the world and then allowing her to go."

CHAPTER 6

THE CHAIR

Each and every night, the creaking of the chair would echo in The Castle. Heather was in heaven and Kennedy was her heaven. She would rock her every night and would never miss this moment. I would lay on the ground and just stare. Time seemed to stand still as I would look, reflect, and relish in what was before me. My queen and my princess! At times, I felt it might be too perfect. Kennedy was so easy! She slept all night from day one, and I will never forget the magical first week of caring for her in The Castle. You could have blown up the neighborhood and we never would have known. We were so happy to be a little family.

The chair became a bit annoying to me, and I would always tell Heather, "We need to fix that thing. It is so old and rickety!" Heather would tell me, "That is exactly how I like it and want it. The rickets, the sounds, the creaks, they all have meaning, Jason. They bring me back to my childhood, my mom, and my memories. This chair is all I have left of her and I love it." I had thought many times about refinishing it, but I was so worried about ruining those sounds. Oh, those sounds. I learned to love those sounds, and after one short year in our home together, we decided that we were going to try for another baby, so we needed a bigger home. We were bursting at the seams. I had begun to work from home more and more and more. That little room was so full of love, but so crowded. I could not work, study, and so on without getting in trouble. "Kennedy's taking a nap," "We need to rock her," or "She has a dirty diaper" would all become standard and more important phrases than anything else. So we bought another home: a five-level split with plenty of room. Our plan was to have five kids, and this home would most definitely do the job. The basement was not finished, but four bedrooms and three baths were. Heather was elated! I was stressed. More responsibility, more money, more work! But . . . it felt right and when we visited that home, we both felt that same feeling: *"You always listen to the Spirit, which is a higher power, and if you do, you will know exactly what to do."* Heather had really felt this and so it was time. We put The Castle up for sale and we moved.

Heather had so much fun choosing the carpet, floors, and direction for decor for the home. She immediately went to work on Kennedy's room. She painted a white picket fence that went around the entire border of the room, and she painted flowers, greenery, and bright beaming plants and bushes. Kennedy's room felt like a garden for a princess. This was Heather's love, to make her daughter feel loved. By the time Kennedy started walking, Heather was deep into her life. She was a stay-at-home mom and spent every minute with her. And every night, oh every night, you could hear the chair: creaking and playing its music. It was like clockwork. By 7 p.m., the creaking began and a book would be selected to read to Kennedy. By the time Kennedy began talking, we were having a ball. She said so many funny things, but her first word was "meat?" We think she said this because she loved to eat jerky.

One night, I could not sleep. Heather's mother was heavy on my mind. I always have and still do wonder if she would have accepted me to be worthy of her daughter. It was 1 a.m. and I got up and left the upstairs to go down to the kitchen. I sat at the kitchen table and began reading. As I was reading, I suddenly heard Kennedy cry. I immediately stood up to go to her aide. But I heard the sweet creaking of the rocking chair begin. *Aw,* I thought, *Heather will calm her down with the chair.* The creaking went on for a solid two or three minutes and then stopped. It was at that moment that I felt a presence. The presence of Heather's mother, Ramona. It was strong; it was real. I could not help but accept that she was there. And the message was one of love and acceptance for me. I was so excited about this that I had to tell Heather. I rushed to Kennedy's room thinking I would find Heather asleep in the chair. She had already got up and left. So I wandered to our room and found her asleep. This was odd, only because it seemed to me that she would be awake with rocking Kennedy back to sleep. I woke her up and began to tell her of what I had felt. As I was telling her about my experience, she sat up in bed, turned on her lamp, and became emotional, but serious.

Part of what I relayed to her was how I had heard her rocking Kennedy in her chair. And this is why Heather was so serious. "Jason, I never got up and rocked Kennedy." At this point, I was now concerned, as was Heather. We went to Kennedy's room. We opened the closet doors and we looked around the room. We wanted to make sure that no one was in that room! I searched the house and then realized that our security alarm was set on our home. There was no way that anyone could have come into the home. No way! But, the crazy thing was we both were at peace, we both knew that Heather's mom had come and rocked that little girl . . . we just knew it.

The next morning, little Kennedy woke up and came downstairs. We were eating breakfast. She was about two and a half and could speak well. We had not said much about Heather's mom to her. She walked into the kitchen and came over and hugged Heather. Then she walked over and hugged me. Suddenly she blurted out, "Grandma Mona came and rocked me last night." We both stood still. Now there was no doubting, no questioning, no hesitating that Kennedy was very special and her grandma was very near. Once again, we became emotional and were also a bit shell-shocked at what had happened.

The chair then became sacred. It became more important; it became more meaningful. Many times as a young girl, Kennedy would tell us that she had seen, been rocked, or visited by her grandma Mona. By the time Kennedy's sweet sixteen birthday came around in the last year of her life, this chair still was used. Used by a mother who could not give up rocking her daughter, for she knew that the rocking would soon come to an end.

The chair let us learn really how in tune Kennedy is and was. We knew from this first moment and up until the last rock with her and Heather that Kennedy had a gift. The gift of being in tune with those from the other side. A gift that would serve all of us well as we battled and struggled throughout her journey. And although you may not believe, you may not accept or even talk about life after death, I testify to you that it is real. It is around us and we learned this through another mortal side. The side of receiving one of Kennedy's Hugs.

http://goo.gl/w17UN6

Scan to view post

CHAPTER 7

THE DRESS

I think that one of the reasons Heather loves sparkly things so much is because she has seen them her whole life. Every time she looks in the mirror, she sees the most amazing sea of blue dancing before herself. Her eyes. Those blue eyes. Each morning as these two beauties would get ready for the day, Kennedy would grab her mom's cheeks with her little tiny hands, pull her toward her, and stare into her eyes. "Your eyes sparkle!" she would say. "They are so sparkly! I love your eyes, Mama!" Kennedy would constantly look at her mom and describe her. "Her skin, Daddy, is so, so soft. Her hair is so long and shiny! You look like a Barbie!" It seemed that Kennedy was enthralled with more than just her mom, but with beauty. Heather had been blessed with beauty. Yes, I am biased but it's true. In 2000, this beauty was proven through the dress. A dress that would bring great satisfaction, answers, and blessings to Heather.

Heather was very shy when we first met. So shy that it was very difficult for her to give a presentation in a college class, or talk amongst a small crowd of new people. She did not like this and wanted to overcome this. I was in complete shock when she told me in 1999 that she wanted to compete in the Mrs. Utah America pageant. Heather was determined. She was dead set on doing this. She competed and did incredible. We were so proud of Heather and how she presented herself. She had no fear and presented herself so well. When she finished, I took a big breath of fresh air, knowing that the experience was over and the expenses were gone (because those dresses are pricey). I was happy to get back into normal life.

After the pageant, Heather kept talking about how much she loved the experience. She kept telling me how much good she felt she could do in helping other mothers around our state if she were to win. She did not care about the crown or the notoriety as much as she wanted to help. I, on the other hand, was a bit flustered. Another pageant? More time, more money, more training, more practice . . . awww! But Heather did not let it go. The pageant is always held in June, so by the time Christmas rolled around, Heather was dead set on getting ready and competing in the historic millennial Mrs. Utah America 2000 pageant. "Are you in?" she asked me. "I need to do this, I can feel it," she told me. "Are you in?"

I really struggled. I really had to think about this. This was a very big commitment and we had committed to always be at each other's side on everything. I was being selfish. I wanted to buy a four-wheeler, to go fishing and camping. I wanted to take us on trips or just hang out together. At first, I really did not want to do this. But then it happened again. I was sitting in my office at home, and Heather and I had just had a heated discussion about the pageant. I was being negative about it. I had shut the door to my office and just wanted to be alone. A little knock came at the door. I got up thinking it was Heather, but looked to see Kennedy at my door. She reached out and hugged me. She looked at me and said, "You stop being mean to Mommy and let her do the pageant. She'll win! I love you, Daddy!" And she walked off. My emotions burst. My heart melted, and my body quivered. That Hug, that little girl, and that moment was exactly like my dream so long ago. This little girl was the only thing that could soften her dad, make me wake up, and allow me to realize that life was about much more than me and much more than my little world.

The decision was made and Heather went to work. She was determined to win and wanted to do it for all of the right reasons. For some reason though, Heather kept feeling like her evening gown was not the right one. She felt inspired to trust those very close to her and to allow them to help her find the dress. She also felt that the dress needed to be exceptionally modest. Heather went to her knees and asked God for help.

The following is recorded from her journal on June 11, 2000: "I was told that I should find a more modest dress and that this decision effects Eternity. I won't understand why right now. Where 'Much is Given, Much is Required.'"

Little did Heather know the impact, the role, and the miracle that dress would play fourteen years down the road. A dress so important, so planned, and so needed. A dress that would clothe her daughter in a spiritual cocoon of love so deep that Heather would understand the message from God, "Where much is given, much is required."

Heather found the dress. The dress required quite a bit of work and Heather's sister Lisa lovingly helped her alter and change it to fit Heather just right. I will never forget as she walked down our stairs with just less than one day to spare as the dress was completed. Utter amazement! She looked like an angel. She was so powerful that I began to cry. Cry over a dress? None of us knew why. The dress had something special about it.

Heather was told the dress she had found was too long, too modest, too unorthodox, and too different. She did not care. As she walked out on that stage that night and we sat in the crowd cheering, I will never forget the piece of heaven that entered that room. It stopped . . . literally stopped. Little Kennedy, just two and a half years old, reached up around my neck and hugged me so tight! The evening came to a close and the announcer did announce Heather as the winner of the Mrs. Utah America 2000 pageant.

By 2014, the dress was still stored securely, lovingly, and properly in a safe place within Heather's closet. "I, wwwwannnt toooo gettt mmmmmaried in that dress," Kennedy blurted out one day. Heather had Kennedy put the dress on and she displayed it so beautifully. Although she could not see, she could remember it, and her spirit was remembering. The dress fit her 5-foot-8-inch, 130-pound frame like a glove. It was perfect! She shimmered, she glowed. An emulation of perfection! As I came home from work, I found Heather sitting and looking at the dress. Tears were streaming down her face and her look was one of great sadness and concern. "I now knew why we needed this dress. This will be the dress we will bury Kennedy in. I know it, I just know it."

As we met with the mortuary, we were told that she would need to have a dress high enough around the neckline to cover any work done by the mortician and that she would need a dress with wrist-length sleeves. The work had already been done. The dress was ready, the sacredness done. As Kennedy was presented at her viewing, many asked about the dress. It fit perfect, was completely angelic, and bonded Kennedy and her mother together even more.

As I had my moment alone with Kennedy at the side of her casket on her burial day, I gently stroked my hand down the beautiful fabric that the dress contained. I said many things to her at that moment and no one was in the room. One of the things I told her was that she finally got to wear the dress. "You wanted it, you got it," I told her. "Now we have to wait a bit longer and the next time I see you in it, will be at your wedding. I promise, Kennedy, I will live the best I can so that after the Resurrection and in the next life, I will see you the next time in the dress."

http://goo.gl/U2S6Eg

Scan to view post

CHAPTER 8

Little Anna

It was February 2002, and we had been trying to have another baby for over three years. We were so ready to expand our family. The key chain had been filling up with different keys, but it was time to fit the key of another child into the keyhole of expanding our family. Each and every night, Kennedy would kneel down by her bed and pray so hard for a sister. At times, she would pray so long and so fervently for a sister that we would have to help her along to finish her prayer so we could go to bed! Her faith was developing and was incredibly strong at the young age of four. Over time, however, she began to question . . . why. "Why is Mommy not having a baby? Why are we not getting answers to this prayer? I really, really want a sister!" she would say. And it did not matter where we were or what wishing well we would come upon, if Kennedy had an opportunity for a wish, it was for a sister. In fact, I do believe that for both her 3rd and 4th birthday wishes, that is what she wished for.

As parents, we were and were not in a hurry for more children. We wanted them, we were not preventing, but we were becoming increasingly concerned. Heather began to see a fertility doctor who, at that point, said everything looked normal. So we did not worry and just kept living our lives. However, something changed, something began to tug, something began to pull at us deeply. This feeling, this tugging, this grabbing inside of us was to adopt a little girl. We both were feeling it, we both knew it, and we both could not deny it. "Adopt a little girl?" We both would ask ourselves. Yes, adopt a little girl. We began to talk, pray, and investigate this option. We were struggling to have another baby, but we had not even thought of adoption.

We knew nothing about adoption. And then it happened. Heather and I were sitting in our church listening to an amazing talk on adoption, families, and the blessings that come from it. The longer we listened, the more we knew. It became so powerful that we both produced tears. We clasped each other's hands and the feeling overwhelmed us that this was exactly the path we were supposed to take.

We took the necessary steps to get approved with the state of Utah in order to be approved for the Foster Election to Adopt program. After nine long months of classes, training, and approvals, our door swung open and the cutest little blonde-haired girl named Anna bounced into our home. She immediately saw me and ran and jumped into my arms and said, "Hi, Daddy." My heart again melted, my soul filled a bit more, and I instantly felt another key be added to the chain. I did not even know her name yet. I did not even know her story. All I knew was that Kennedy's constant prayers had been answered. Her pleas were finally met and instantly I looked for her. She did not know what to say. So instead she stepped forward reached out and hugged Anna. She hugged her so tight that Anna giggled. Kennedy took her by the hand and said, "Come with me." They ran up the stairs to Kennedy's room, where instantly Kennedy began to pull out ALL of her dolls, her toys, and her most precious items. We stood in the doorway and watched as Kennedy so lovingly began to not share but GIVE these items to Anna. They began to play and we stood in the doorway in tears. Heather still had not even been able to talk with this new little stranger, who was not a stranger. Somehow, someway, she had been sent to us. And her sending was a gift, one that was asked for for years by Kennedy and now was being unwrapped before our eyes. Christmas was ever so present. That day, that feeling was special. It was real, it was amazing.

We gave Anna the security that she needed and longed for, but Kennedy gave her something else. Kennedy gave her the sense of love that she needed and had longed to have in her life for so long. The two of them were inseparable, and Kennedy did give her half of everything she had. A room had been prepared for Anna, but Kennedy would have nothing to do with that. Kennedy announced that we needed to buy matching beds and bedding for their room. Toys, clothes, hair bows, and treats were immediately given to Anna. The two of them could not stop hugging each other. By the end of the first month, we began to see Anna develop into areas that she never knew existed.

The task of fighting in the courts to adopt Anna became quite extensive, expensive, and worrying. Heather would pray so hard that we would be able to have a final adoption. What if it did not go through? What if she was taken back to her home? What if the last one-plus year of our lives became nothing more than a memory? As these emotions sank deep and became a daily trial of our faith, Kennedy became stronger than ever. "Mom and Dad, what are you worried about? I prayed for a sister and Heavenly Father gave me her. Why would he take that away?" Her faith was so simple, so perfect, so real. The road became bumpy as we were told that we would have Anna and then we would not. We would, we would not. Forces were being fought in order to get her back with her family. But the circumstances for her return were too devastating to her future, so we fought hard. Ultimately, the decision was made to go to trial for her custody battle. We won! But just know that every night, every day, and every minute a little girl named Kennedy was right by little Anna's side, praying constantly that all would work out. That she would become her sister forever and that the two of them could be sealed as one. As the court date came and we were able to finalize her adoption to our family, it was one of the few times that I ever saw Kennedy produce tears of joy. She was only five and a half years old, yet she understood the great blessing, miracle, and gift she had been given. She cried in the courtroom that day and laid her little head on my shoulder. "Daddy, my heart is so happy. My heart feels so happy, Daddy. I have Anna forever now. Forever, Daddy."

Another key had been added to the key chain, another blessing, another keyhole filled. A hole that Kennedy would fill for the next few vital years of Anna's life and would be refilled by Anna in the remaining years of Kennedy's. And a key that fit perfectly due to constant faith, prayers, and lots of Kennedy's Hugs.

http://goo.gl/dHQtaC

Scan to view post

CHAPTER 9

LITTLE STINKER

Kennedy wanted you to remember her and to never forget who she was or what she was about. Her way of telling you was typically not through words, but through actions. And those actions would play through the rest of her life right up until the day that she died.

Actions like the day that she decided to draw a beautiful picture so bright and vibrant on the wall Heather had just painted in our master bedroom. The picture was apparently of our family, the bright sun, and her dog Poppy. It was drawn with a sharpie marker and there was no denial on her end. At first Heather was furious, but ultimately we laughed and were also proud that she would tell the truth. Heather painted over that picture, but for the rest of the time we lived in that home, you could see where the paint had covered the perfect tapestry Kennedy had worked so hard on. "Why did you paint over my beautiful picture?" Kennedy asked. She just could not understand why such things were wrong, bad, or not allowed. Her idea of life was so simple and her joys came in very simple things. All she was trying to do was draw us a beautiful picture.

As she and Anna began to grow, play, and spend time together, it seemed that Kennedy was always the instigator of something. One day, while getting ready to leave, Heather needed to run back into the house to get something she had forgotten. The car was running and both girls were buckled in their seats. "Let's drive the car, Anna!" Kennedy said. "Mom's gone. . . . Let's drive the car!" Anna instantly said, "No, no, Kennedy, Dad will kill us, and you do not know how to drive!" Well that did not stop Kennedy. She unbuckled herself and somehow found her way to the floor with one hand on the brake and the other on the shifter. She shifted the car into reverse and yep, you got it, the little stinker took her and Anna on a ride. Anna was screaming, and Kennedy was laughing. The car, thank goodness, shifted into reverse and instantly began to travel across the street. Kennedy kept laughing and Anna could not stop screaming! The vehicle traveled across the street where it slammed into the curb and stopped. Kennedy hurried and jumped back into her car seat, and rebuckled herself. At the time, I was in my office working, so I had no idea what was going on. As Heather walked back outside, her heart sank and she went into a panic. From her view, she could only see that the car was gone! She ran back into the house and screamed, "Jay, Jay, come quick, come quick. The car is gone. The girls, the car, hurry!" I had never heard concern come from her voice like that before. It was so deep, so serious, and so stressed. I pretty much jumped to the bottom of the stairs, swung the front door open from a different viewpoint from where Heather was at in the garage. As I swung the door open, I could see Heather's car with one tire up on the curb and the other resting against it. I sprinted as fast as I could toward that car. I swung open the back door to make sure our babies were in that backseat.

Please, Heavenly Father, I prayed in my mind, *please make sure they are ok and there.* I could not see them until I opened the door because the windows were tinted. As that door swung open, my eyes met Heather's as she opened the other door and we were greeted by a "screaming bloody murder at the top of her lungs" Anna and a "Ha ha, giggling, 'I gotcha' laughing" Kennedy. Are you kidding me? I immediately jumped into the driver seat and put the vehicle in park. "What happened? What on earth happened?" we asked. "We went for a drive, Mommy! It was fun!" Kennedy said. As we looked at Anna, she continued to scream at the top of her lungs. She could not stop. She was so scared, so shocked, and so upset. We unbuckled her and held her in our arms. We let her know it was ok. We then had to reluctantly discipline Kennedy and let her know to never, ever, do that again. "But, it was fun, so fun, Daddy!" I brought her back into the house and I set her down on a chair in my office. After scolding her a bit and figuring out what happened and how in the world she reached the pedals, I looked into those big brown eyes. They glistened, they glowed, and they penetrated me as usual. I could not get mad at her. I could not yell or scream or become angry. I walked over and set her on my lap and told her, "You little stinker! You little stinker!" She leaned her head against me and hugged me. "I love you so much, Daddy, and I cannot wait to drive and date and have fun! Are you going to let me drive the truck, Daddy, when I get big?" she asked. My lip quivered, my mind was settled, but my heart exploded.

"Of course I will, you little stinker, of course I will." As the moment ended, once again her embrace subdued my spirit and a Kennedy's Hug fixed the moment. But, for me, deep, deep, deep inside, I began to realize and began to question whether she was just too good to be here.

CHAPTER 10

The Dandelions

She nudged up closer to the TV than she ever had before. "That is too close, honey. Please back away." Heather would say. "But, I cannot see it good, Mama!" Kennedy seemed to feel comfortable at about 4–5 feet away from the TV. She was in kindergarten and was having the time of her life. All of her dreams were coming true. Her love for dance was shown by the hours that she would turn on music in our home and dance with Anna. When they were really little, Kennedy seemed to be right on step, right in tune, and right on beat. Her teachers would always tell us how obedient and how in sync Kennedy was. They would tell us that she could and would have a great future in dance or cheerleading or whatever she decided to pursue. Her biggest strength was her love. Kennedy always seemed to take a girl under her wing, one who maybe was more quiet, did not have a friend, or was struggling.

Sports was also a big part of these girls' lives, and although Kennedy was athletic, it took awhile for her to see it. When we first enrolled her in soccer, the first game she was down on her hands and knees picking a beautiful dandelion. Anna was charging up the field and proceeded to score a goal. After the goal was scored, I took to the field and asked Kennedy what on earth she was doing. "Daddy, look at it, look at it. It is so beautiful!" she told me. I coached their soccer team and they were six years old. I wanted to pull my hair out and yell at the top of my lungs to have Kennedy run up the field and quit looking at a weed flower. As I approached her, she looked up at me with those begging eyes, those darts that could hit the bull's-eye every single time. "Daddy, isn't it beautiful?" she said. Instead of getting mad, I picked her up, took her out of the game, and let her go and pick dandelions while the rest of the team played.

It was during this time in her life that she really wanted to have alone time with Heather and me. I traveled to Las Vegas once a month to sell nutritional supplements to stores there. I had purchased a truck and travel trailer. To cut down on expenses, I would haul products to Las Vegas and stay in the travel trailer versus a hotel. Anna was so easygoing that it did not really matter to her when I would leave. She knew that I would be coming back. But, Kennedy. . . . Well, Kennedy felt differently. She would cry and hug me and run outside and wave and cry and wave again and again and again. I would leave for one week at a time and then come home for a week. This traveling went on for almost eighteen months and although it was necessary, it pained Kennedy deeply. She would always beg me not to go and just wanted to be with her daddy. I would tell her that it was just too hard to bring her and that she would be bored. "I have to work the whole time, honey. You will just be sitting there." I would say.

"I do not care, I just want to be with you, Daddy," she would tell me.

On one occasion, I returned home and loaded up Kennedy for our weekly Saturday ride to the gas station. You see, when Kennedy was about three and a half, I bought my first truck. She named the truck "Trucky" and she loved to hear the roar of its engine. The truck was a black GMC Duramax Diesel and the sound of the diesel engine would for some reason ignite her spirit. She would beg me to go on truck rides. So each and every Saturday she and I would load up and go to the gas station in "Trucky" to get a Coke. We would laugh and scream and she would tell me to go "faster, Daddy, faster!" It seemed that this became a weekly sacred ritual with the two of us. So after arriving home and loading up in the truck for a ride, it only seemed appropriate to play this new song that reminded me so much of her. As we drove, she quickly picked up on the song. As these rides continued on over the years, each and every time it seemed they became more and more meaningful. Eventually, everyone just kinda knew to get out of the way if Kennedy and Dad were hopping in the truck. Even her mom accepted the fact that this was just our thing, our special thing, and one that to this day keeps me going in my darkest of moments.

It was on one particularly hard week that Kennedy's pleas to go to Las Vegas with me hit home. She begged so hard and so long that it almost became annoying. This trip was going to be a very busy one because I would be demoing products in a new chain of stores for an entire week. It would be a lot of work and little play. There was no way that I could drag a little girl along with me. As I pulled out of the driveway and swallowed the lump in my throat, I could see Kennedy on the front porch with her mom and Anna. Heather and Anna were fine, but Kennedy was sobbing. She began waving and suddenly I heard her say, "Who's your daddy? Who's your baby? Who's your buddy?" This was the line from our favorite song. I slammed the brakes. I could not take it anymore. I put the truck in park and swung open the door. It was during the fall, the girls were in kindergarten, and the school year had just gotten underway. In my mind, there was no way that Kennedy could be able to miss school, let alone get the permission from her mother. I ran to Kennedy and she ran to me. She was crying and I was running late. But I stopped, picked her up, and swung her around in the air. I looked at her and together we continued to sing, "Who's the one guy that you come running to, when your love life starts tumbling?" I looked at her mom and said, "Pack her bags, we're going to Vegas!"

I think that Anna was more than ok with this. She really is a survivor and also, in her mind, she understood that the relationship between Kennedy and me was different. It required different types of attention that would make much more sense later on. Kennedy was ecstatic. She jumped out of my arms and ran to her room. I think she packed her bag in less than a minute, but her mom, of course, had to repack.

That trip will forevermore go down as some of the greatest times my daughter and I ever had together. I do not think we listened to anything else other than our favorite album and the same two songs for the entire drive to and from Las Vegas. Kennedy was anything but a bother. If anything, she was the best little helper in the world! We would demo products in stores all day and then hit the town at night. It was interesting because I had no idea how to do her hair, other than I could whip out a braid. So I braided her hair each and every morning and then off we went. She looked at this big city with all of its good and bad. The lights and the glimmer, the gambling, the smut, the rides, and Circus Circus. She quickly identified, and would let me know, what was good and what was bad. What we should look at and what we should not. And what we should go do and what we should not go do. As this process evolved, she could not help but beg to go and ride the Stratosphere. "Let's go and ride that one!" I was in shock. *Seriously?* I thought.

I said, "Kennedy, do you know how high up that is?"

"Yep, and I want to ride it. I want to prove to you I am a big girl and to have fun!" We rode that roller coaster and the Drop Zone ride at the Stratosphere. Kennedy was so brave and had so much fun. By the end of the night, she was beat. I carried her in my arms back to the truck. She fell asleep on my shoulder and I remember holding her and just feeling of her. I loved her sooooo much. I did not want that night or our week to end. As we worked in stores that week, everyone fell in love with her. She would ask them all to sample our protein drinks, and who could say no to her? Our sales skyrocketed that week! One night we went to Circus Circus and saw a couple of kids shows. We ate at buffets and we watched movies. At night, she slept in my bed, which was a big no, no at home. She would snuggle up so tight to me and rub my head and sing me songs. We had the time of our lives.

On the drive home, I remember thinking, *These moments will end, these moments will end.* Just as the dandelion produces a beautiful yellow flower that blooms and eventually dies, so was the time on earth for Kennedy and our family. She was in full bloom, yet eventually her dandelion would wither physically. Just as the wind blows the petals away and leaves nothing but a dead straw on the dandelion, we would watch Kennedy as her bloom would wither and her body would change, suffer, and eventually be blown away from us. But Kennedy being blown away is different. Her seeds would create new dandelions that would flood the earth and become so powerful that nothing could kill them and many would stop and see. Seeing dandelions is something that I believe will forever be engrained in our family. The weeds in our lives become constant and the ability to kill them, remove them, or shut them out is sometimes impossible, but the greatest ability to watch them bloom is the most important and the most possible. It is the way to live through making something so annoying become so wonderful.

CHAPTER 11

We're Home

I sat outside the home peering into its large back windows illuminated with light from within. The moon beamed brightly and the stars were shimmering. A beautiful pasture with horses and a riding arena groomed perfectly sat between myself and this home. A nicely built barn, along with amazing landscaping lights graced the backyard. This could be the biggest decision of our lives. This home, this lot, this place. We had decided that while the real estate market was hot in Utah, it was time to sell our home and to purchase another. We wanted more land and we wanted a place for horses. Kennedy had begun to beg for them. As I sat in that car, I bowed my head and once again found myself praying. I was hoping that the neighborhood and the current family who owned the home had not or would not notice me sitting there, sometimes for up to an hour at a time, looking, praying, and pondering at this magnificent dream home. We had finally sold our home and had made a tentative offer on the place, just to see what would happen. As I sat there on that summer night in 2004, it happened again. I was praying out loud and pleading to know if this was right. I was feeling overwhelmed with the decision and trying to make it all work out in my mind when I felt it. *"You always listen to the Spirit, which is a higher power, and if you do, you will know exactly what to do."* This spirit, this higher power, seemed to explode all at once, and as clear as the typing on this paper reads, I was told, "Buy the home, buy the home." So . . . you got it, we bought it.

Our initial plan was to own the home for five years and sell it. At the rate the market was progressing, that would give us enough funds to pay cash for another home and move into a very good financial position. We moved into the home in October 2004. The girls had been in first grade for just about a month, so starting a new school wouldn't be that bad of a transition. I will never forget, as we were moving in, how several of the people helping us commented on how wide the doorways and hallways in the home were. Years later we would find out the great significance of this.

Anna and Kennedy instantly became involved in the neighborhood, making several friends and having the time of their lives. There were so many little girls their age and they fit right in. The neighborhood that we had moved from only had one other girl their age, so this was a prayer answered for us and for the other families in this new neighborhood.

We would drive home and into the driveway and say to ourselves, "Is this house really ours?" I began to fear the financial burden and questioned our decision. One night as I was worrying about this in my office, I looked down to see a beautiful painting of Jesus Christ and a little note attached to it. It simply said, "Dad, remember who you are! Love, your kid, Kennedy." This hit me hard, right between the eyes. Kennedy was so in tune and she knew I was worried. But she wanted me to remember who I was, what I was about, and that my experiences and trust in a higher power were enough to give us, and especially myself, the answers that we needed. As I sat pondering about this, I just wanted to hug her, be by her, and love her for being her.

I went to her room, where I laid down next to her and stroked her head and kissed her little chubby cheeks. She woke up and looked at me. She then hugged me and asked, "Did you get my note?" I told her that I did and how much it meant to me. She proceeded to ask me if I was ok and why I was so worried. So, I began to spill my guts out to my six-year-old. She listened as she stroked my cheek and looked up at me with those eyes bigger than any planet in the universe. I proceeded to ask Kennedy if we had made the right choice. She simply smiled, looked at me, and put her little hands up in the air and said, "We're home! Daddy, we're home." That is all I had to hear. This was our home and we "were home." This home would prove to be a massive key in the key chain in our lives. So many keys would come from this home that would open door after door and experience after experience for Kennedy's journey, life, and, ultimately, death. This home would prove to be the place where Kennedy would spend the majority of her life. Where she would live, laugh, love, and dream. A home where all associated with her would spend hours, days, weeks, and even months of their lives watching our family eventually lose Kennedy but accept the fact that Kennedy taught us that in the end "we're home."

CHAPTER 12

No More Children?

It was 2005 and life was moving fast. I mean fast! I was working a full-time job selling windows and doors for homes and also running our nutritional supplement business full time. The two together were exhausting. The girls were so busy with dance, music lessons, school, church, and friends. It seemed that every day would race by like a Lamborghini that you rarely see and once you do see it, it is gone before you even have a chance to enjoy its beauty.

We were home and ready for more brothers and sisters. Each and every night once again, Kennedy's little prayers would shine forth to heaven. "Please, Heavenly Father, send us a little brother now. Please send him as soon as you can." Anna also would pray for this, and the two little rascals together would nonstop ask why Mom was not getting a baby in her tummy. They were confused.

Internally and behind closed doors, Heather and I were doing everything and I mean everything that we could do in order to grow our family. We had seen and were seeing every expert we knew how in order to try and get Heather pregnant. The girls were seven years old and we both knew that this was quite a spread in age. It seemed that as we would pray the answers would not come. We would ask, we would search, but nothing seemed to happen. I will never forget sitting down with doctors and ultimately receiving the devastating news that I would never be able to give Heather children nor would she be able to bear them. What had we done wrong? We asked the doctors how in the world we were able to ever have Kennedy. They simply said, "She is a miracle. There is no reasonable medical explanation." This burden was now fully ours. It was hard. It was real. How in the world were we going to tell Kennedy and Anna the news? How were we going to grow our family, and what would our future look like?

It was an extremely hot summer day when we received this news and I just went for a walk. I called my dad. As he answered the phone, I blurted out, "Dad, Dad, I will never be able to have more kids. Dad, what am I going to do? We wanted kids so, so bad!" There was a pause on the other end of the line and silence seemed to seal the air. Suddenly my dad spoke and simply said, "Jason, you have been blessed. You have been given the greatest blessing that anyone could ever have. You have already been given the gift of fatherhood. And now that we know this news, you have to consider yourself lucky. You have to consider yourself blessed beyond measure. For you, my son, are in the midst of an angel. A miracle. A walking, breathing princess that is your flesh and blood. A little girl named Kennedy. You also have been given another miracle named Anna. Together, these two will and have blessed your life. Now, move forward, not backward. Do not fear. I promise you as your dad, that you and Heather will know exactly what to do." The reality of no more children became nothing more than a myth, because Kennedy would teach us that children come in all different ways and in all different shapes, sizes, colors, and forms. They are sent to us when needed. She would teach us why she came when she did and why she left us when and how she did. And the fear of no more children would be answered because of her and from her in a way that none of us wanted, but all of us would have to accept. It would come with miracles that would occur and a life that would prove nothing short of her being simply a miracle in our lives.

CHAPTER 13

BROKEN GLASSES

The key chain was getting full and it seemed that with each key we were given, the burden of carrying the keys became overwhelming! I thought I was tired from these keys that hung invisibly around our necks. Keys that opened up great doors at the time, yet we did not even realize it. I thought we had challenges. I thought we had trials, struggles, and lots of hard things going on. Boy . . . how I long for those times now. Those times were great times in comparison to what we have now endured. Yet, many doors had been opened by different keys, and it seemed that we were well on our way to the last major door that would begin to open up new experiences, journeys, and times.

Kennedy and Anna were full swing into soccer and dance. We went to so many dance performances, practices, and shows. We really did love it and the girls were in heaven. We complemented dancing with soccer. It kept the girls in shape and, more than anything, kept them on their toes, literally. Anna was becoming quite the player. Scoring goals, leading the team, and running all over the place. Kennedy was content with playing defense and protecting the goal. "Go harder, Kennedy, go harder!" I would scream. "You have to get more aggressive!" Kennedy was wearing glasses and had worn them since kindergarten. She was now in 3rd grade and one of the tallest girls in her class. So, on the soccer field, I pushed her hard. I was helping to coach the girls team and I was working a lot. But I so looked forward to those practices. To those times of watching my girls.

One summer day we were playing a game. The game was tight and we had to score to win. There was another girl on the other team who was playing dirty. I pulled Kennedy aside and I told her that she needed to push this girl back. To get aggressive and not be afraid. To stand up to her. It was time to put an end to this bully-type madness. As I told Kennedy this, she simply looked up at me through her dirty glasses and said, "Daddy, why not just love her?" I did not quite understand and this made me mad. I wanted her to stop the other girl, to get mean, and to fight back. Kennedy was the only girl on the team that physically had the size and speed to do this.

The next half started and things got worse. This girl was going head on into Kennedy. Finally, the fireworks exploded as this girl back-handed Kennedy to the face, knocking her glasses to the ground along with Kennedy. Kennedy simply recovered her glasses and got back up. She was crying. However, Kennedy's tears were from sadness. She could not handle contention or problems of any sort. Kennedy was always the peacemaker. By this time, parents were screaming and Anna was ready to go to blows in defense of her sister. How could they let that player get away with this? As we were all acting like children, the only person who seemed to be calm and collected was of course Kennedy. She had gotten up from this backhand and was crying silently. I offered to take her out with the substitution, but she refused. The game continued. Within two minutes of play, one of our players went head to head with this girl and took her out. The girl screamed in pain as she became injured. And then it happened. Kennedy walked from one side of the field clear over to the other. She simply made her way to this other player, where she reached down and helped her stand up. She then said the words we would hear so many times in the next seven years of her life. "You ok?" she asked. The girl looked as confused as all of us. But she nodded her head. Then Kennedy reached out, put her arms around her, and hugged her. She gave her a Kennedy's Hug. As this moment ended, the game came to a close. We rode home in silence. I was in shock due to what had happened and Kennedy was as happy as ever, looking out the windows, singing, and asking if we could go and get a Coke.

My mind drifted and slowed for a bit following this game. The administration of her actions were incredible, yet the Hug seemed to stop time. I really did not know what to think or how to handle it all. I am sure I was as confused as that other player was. Where did that come from? Why did Kennedy do that? And what type of experiences lay ahead for us? As we drove, I remember her saying, "Dad, Dad, hello, Dad . . . earth to Daddy. You ok, Dad?" I had gone into such deep thought that I did not even hear her talking. "Did you hear what I said?" she asked. "Did Jesus Christ ever get mad at anyone? Even those who hurt him?"

"No," I responded. "No. No, He was perfect and could have, but He did not."

"Good, because all I could think of was Him as I hugged and helped that girl. I had already forgiven her for being mean, Daddy. But, we have a problem. . . . My glasses are bent." I looked in the rearview mirror to see her holding up her glasses. They were bent all right and I knew that we would probably have to get a new pair. But what I did not know, what I did not realize, was that not too far in the near future, we would not even need those glasses. They would become extinct in her life, thrown to the curb and completely useless. Her ability to see was well on its way out the door, but her ability to feel had opened up a new door. And the key had been given and hung on our key chain of continual Hugs. For from that day forward, our little girl would officially go out of her way to Hug anyone and everyone who would come into her path. Good, bad. Tall, short. It did not matter. The only thing that mattered were Hugs. Hugs would become the official definition and language of her love. A love that even without physical sight would merit so much more in spiritual sight.

This spiritual sight would carry all of us through Hugs—those constant Hugs. Hugs that to this day now pass around the world as one person Hugs another and another and another. The Hugs that Kennedy longed to pass around the world.

CHAPTER 14

Going Blind

She fell hard, Jason . . . hard!" Heather exclaimed. "Look at her face, look at her lip, her eyes, and her nose. This is serious. I am worried, very worried. She has been falling a lot lately. And this fall was on flat ground. She could not even see the curb in front of her!" It was 2007 and Kennedy seemed out of balance. Tripping, falling, and starting to put things closer to her face were all too normal for Kennedy. She was in the 4th grade and this most recent fall had come while playing at recess. She was just trying to be a normal kid, yet things were changing. "I am sure that she just needs new glasses." I said to Heather. "Just go and get her eyes checked again. Everything is fine. She just needs a new prescription. She will be fine." There have been and are times in our marriage when I have known that Heather is completely serious or concerned or both. And the look, the concern, and the care in her eyes was one of these times. "This feels different," she told me. "I think there is something else wrong."

I did not feel this or lose much sleep over Kennedy on this one. My mind was so occupied with work and providing for our family. And that is how a good marriage works. Many times we have carried one another in different ways. This was one of those times where the key of blindness was being placed around Heather's neck. She would become Kennedy's eyes, guide, and light in a dark new world of understanding and adjusting to life without color, without shapes, and without the ability of sight. Heather would become her earthly guardian angel that would save her and literally carry her so many times through the deep dark gulch of pain, sorrow, and hardships that Kennedy would discover she had to endure due to no fault of her own.

"The optometrist needs to meet with us face-to-face. He says this is serious, very serious. I knew that there was something wrong, I just knew it." Heather said. A family friend was Kennedy's optometrist, and he was the one who had done her testing and administered all of her prescriptions for her sight since kindergarten. We arrived at his office and he asked to have Kennedy sit outside. We sat down and he looked directly at us with a very serious yet concerned look on his face. He stood up and closed his office door. He sat down and his hands began to tremble a bit. He proceeded to ask us if we had ever hit Kennedy. "Hit her?" I asked. "Are you kidding me? Of course we have never hit her! Why are you asking us this? What is wrong? What is going on?" He proceeded to tell us that the pictures from Kennedy's eyes had so much trauma that he had never seen anything like it before. "I have never seen trauma like this behind the retina before. The only other time I have seen anything like this is from a hard blow to the head or from massive trauma to the eyes. I do not know what this is. All I know is that it is serious and is well beyond my pay grade. I am going to send you down to another professional eye center in Salt Lake City. You also need to know that the decline in Kennedy's sight is severe and rapid. I do not know what is going on. All I know is that it needs to be addressed quickly. I have never seen so much stress on a set of eyes like that before." Heather's hand slid slowly into mine. She gripped it tightly and nodded her head up and down. "We will do whatever it takes to find out what is wrong with Kennedy. Whatever it takes," she said.

I remember driving home. Kennedy asked about her eyes. She asked if she would be getting new glasses. She asked why she did not meet with the doctor. "Mom, Dad . . . ummm, what is going on? Please tell me what in the heck is going on. Why are you both so worried? Why are you not saying anything?" The feeling in that car was the first of many feelings to come of the unknown. The grueling number of tests, doctor visits, therapy visits, and so on that would occur over the next few years. That feeling of wanting to know, but not knowing. We explained to Kennedy that we did not know the results of her eye tests well enough to have an answer. However, we were honest with her. We were always honest with her. So we let her know that her doctor felt it was serious enough to have more tests done at another eye center. Our doctor had given us Kennedy's pictures of her eyes and, to say the least, they looked scary! We sat down at home with Kennedy that day and we showed her those pictures. We included her in everything. We wanted her to know that there were no secrets and we would be by her side the entire way. As she looked at those pictures and looked up at us, all she could say was, "You ok? Mom and Dad . . . are you ok?" We told her yes and she hugged both of us. She reassured us that everything would be ok. And that her eyes would be ok.

Close to one month later, we sat eagerly in the waiting room of the office of the doctor at the new eye center. Many tests, and I mean mmm-mmannny, had been done on Kennedy. These tests were not all fun. Some were annoying, some were standard, and others, well, others hurt a little bit. After these tests were done, we had to wait for a few more weeks in order to meet with one of the best specialists in the world. As we waited for what seemed like an eternity, I will never forget Kennedy laying her head down on my lap. I stroked her head and her mother held her hand. Kennedy was nervous. We assured her now that everything was going to be fine. Finally, the nurse called us back to meet with the doctor. We entered the room where he had us sit down and had Kennedy sit in a patient chair. He quickly took out his tools and began to look into her eyes. As he did, he began to talk into a tape recorder about Kennedy. He did not even say hello to us or really acknowledge us as human beings. He simply kept talking and talking. This went on for about three minutes. Finally, I could not take it any longer. We were there to find out about Kennedy. "Excuse me, excuse me," I said. "Umm, Doctor, I do not mean to interrupt, but can we ask you a few questions and get some answers about Kennedy?" He stood up and walked to the back of the room where he proceeded to talk into his tape recorder. This now went on for another couple of minutes or so until he left the room. He came back and kept talking. Ultimately, I stood up and walked over to him again. This time, he shut off the tape recorder and looked at me.

"What do you want?" he asked.

"We just want some answers to what is going on, that is all." I said.

"Well, I am trying to record this, just listen to what I say in the recorder," he blurted.

Listen to what he was saying? I thought. Half of the words I did not understand and the other half were so foreign that I thought I was in China. Kennedy was looking around the room like "what is going on?" Heather was getting more and more concerned. The doctor kept saying the word "Stargardts, stargardts" into his tape recorder. He finally sat down and said, "Ok, here are the results of the tests for Kennedy." He began once again talking into his tape recorder. None of us knew what he was talking about until the words came out, "Macular Degenaration . . . blindness."

"Hold on, hold on!" I said. "Doctor, hold on. Did you say blindness?" "Yes," he said. "What are you talking about? Please talk to us like we are human beings! Turn off your dang recorder and talk to us!" He did not stop. He kept talking into his recorder. Finally, I was done. Kennedy was crying, and Heather was pleading with him, "What does she have? Doctor, are you even listening to me? What about blindness? Please, please just tell us!" He suddenly stopped, looked at us, and said, "Kennedy has Stargardts: a form of childhood blindness. She will go completely blind by her teenage years if not into her early twenties. There, is that the answer you wanted to hear?" I felt my blood boil and I grit my teeth. Kennedy began to sob. "Blind, blind?" she screamed out. "I am going to go blind?" Heather consoled her and put her arm around her. I told Heather to take Kennedy outside of the room. I was hot. Really hot. I reached over, took the tape recorder out of the doctor's hands, and pushed stop. I slammed it down on the table. "You listen here, Doctor, and you listen real good."

"How dare you take my tape recorder, Mr. Hansen! Give it back!" he replied.

"Do you have kids? How would you like it if a doctor told you your child was going blind into a dang tape recorder?" I fumed.

"Leave my office!" he said.

"Oh believe me, I will."

I stormed out of that office and into the lobby where, through tear-stained glasses, Kennedy looked up at me. "What is wrong with me, Daddy? What is wrong?" I picked her up out of Heather's lap and said, "Nothing, honey. You, my little princess, are perfect. But, we got the answers that we needed. Let's go home." As we began walking away, the nurse from the doctor's office came running down the hallway. She reached out and grabbed my arm. "Mr. Hansen, wait. I just wanted to thank you."

"Thank me for what?" I asked.

"Thank you for finally standing up to the doctor. I have watched for too long the way he treats his patients. You were the first parent to ever go right at him. I know you do not want anything to do with him, but how can I help? I can get you the results and I know another doctor that

I would highly recommend." We thanked her and accepted her offer. We all walked back to the car. I remember feeling so mad and then the reality hit. The tears came. I was crying, Heather was crying, and Kennedy sat in the middle of us holding our hands. We got in the car. I could not even put the keys in the ignition. As we cried, Kennedy suddenly leaned forward from the backseat and simply said, "Mommy, Daddy, it's ok. Heavenly Father and Jesus will heal my eyes when I go to heaven." She was smiling. In fact she was glowing! She did not say, "Heal my eyes on earth." She said, "Heal my eyes when I go to heaven." There was a spirit in that car that I want to always remember and yet I want to forget. Who wants to be told that their nine-year-old girl is going to go blind? Who wants to accept that and all that comes with it? I think the only other day that we felt more pain and sorrow than that would be on June 5, 2013. This was the day we would receive the devastating news that Kennedy was diagnosed with Terminal Juvenile Batten disease. And that experience with the eye center, yes, that is how we found out that Kennedy would be going blind. No great explanation, no caring team or a group of candle light vigil consoling nurses.

After Kennedy's statement, I yelled out, "Let's go and get ice cream! It fixes everything!" We went and got ice cream. Kennedy was ok. But Heather and I, well, Heather and I were not. We kept looking at each other. We kept staring into each other's eyes and we knew that we had our hands full and would have them very full with this new chapter in our lives. The key chain had received this key. Yet it opened up a devastating door. One that would be so hard for our family, yet so easy for Kennedy. Kennedy would endure six grueling years of going completely blind, losing the ability to see everything that she loved. Yet, in her heart and in her mind she would see in her array of beautiful colors that she would display on her personality rainbow. She would never, and I mean never, complain, or even hint at complaining about going blind.

CHAPTER 15

THE TOOL BELT

A broken key was definitely added to the key chain. As Kennedy's father, I was going to fix this key. No one, nothing, and nobody was going to cause my little Kennedy to not have a wonderful life. Fourth grade came to a close and Kennedy ended with solid grades and with a great year. Looking back, I will admit that as parents we were in denial. The school was coming back with declines in her core tests, which in our minds were now invalid, because Kennedy's grades were fine and her life was fine. We decided to just move forward and have fun.

We began to arm ourselves with a tool belt full of tools to combat reality. We would tell ourselves, Kennedy can dance, waterski, run, laugh, play soccer, and jump on the trampoline. She can read books and she can type on the computer. She can sing songs and take care of her cat and dog. We began to fill our tool belt with all of the things that she could do. And we began to hammer down nails into large blocks of cement we considered would be road blocks that led to the reality we so denied.

The truth was Kennedy took a turn for the worse that summer. Her sight officially began to slide rapidly. Her speech began to change. She would speak suddenly and words began to be broken up. It was not necessarily stuttering, yet different. She would repeat words and it was odd. But oh how we would reach in our tool belt to sand off the rough edges and make everything look clean, smooth, and all right. We began justifying that it was just her changing. Maybe it was puberty? Maybe it was the social anxieties of going blind? Maybe it was just the shy nature that she possessed? Either way, we still had a great summer.

We owned a cabin at the time and we ended up spending quite a bit of time there. Kennedy would always beg to rise early in the morning and take her dog Sunny on hikes. Her mom and Anna liked to sleep in, so we had some great alone time on these hikes. She would stop and look at everything from the lily pads in the pond to the dead bark on the trees. And with her diagnosis of Stargardts disease, I would let these hikes go on as long as necessary. I wanted to make sure that she could see everything that this world had to offer and that it possessed and produced. She would be blind, fully blind one day, and I wanted her memory to be full.

On one of these hikes, we saw a large log that was hollowed out from years of decay. While still walking, we noticed some movement from one side of the opening of the log. And then a small family of baby skunks came literally tumbling out of the opening of that log stumbling over the top of each other. Our dog began running toward them. *Oh, no, no, no!* I thought. I immediately retrieved her and held her collar tight. That is one animal we and our dog Sunny had already learned a lesson from long ago. Kennedy screamed out, "Daddy, baby skunkies, baby skunkies!" There were three little babies and then the mother followed. They were only about twenty feet from us. I told Kennedy to hold still, be quiet, and watch. The mother took all of these little ones under her care. She lined them up and scolded them a bit and then pushed them on their little merry way. They were squealing a little bit and she hissed a hiss like "Knock it off, let's go!" We sat there and watched them for probably fifteen minutes as they walked through that forest. They were well cared for and the mother knew we were there. She did not mind us much because we gave her her space. But she did not keep her eyes off of us either. She never threatened us because she never felt threatened. But she kept looking around and at us with a spray that would knock us to Mars if necessary. Little Kennedy wanted to go and pet them so, so badly.

As we hiked back to the cabin that morning, I thought about the scenario. The baby skunks needed nurturing, care, and protection. But on the other hand, they had protection and also had a self-protecting mechanism allowing them to be able to survive, flourish, and have a much better chance of a long, great life. I looked at my beautiful Kennedy with her long brown hair, stretching her legs and hiking so gracefully. *"You always listen to the Spirit, which is a higher power, and if you do, you will know exactly what to do."* I felt a bit like the mother of those little skunks.

I could sense that something was wrong with Kennedy and needed to be more aware. I felt like she was helpless as she was jumping into life without us at school, play, and extra activities. She was and would be experiencing life blindly, literally, very soon and I knew the Spirit was whispering to me to get prepared. There was no tool on my tool belt that could fix her eyes. I wanted to so, so, so bad. As I arrived back at the cabin, Kennedy could not stop talking about her adventure and hike. It was as if she had been on the greatest trip of her life. I remember seeing Heather smile and seeing Anna laugh. I remember watching those two little girls go out front to the tree house in front of the cabin and talk and talk and talk. Everything seemed so wonderful and everything seemed so great. It was as if we had never even found out that our daughter was going blind. But . . . she was going blind and a new key had been added to the key chain. The key of acceptance. As I sat staring out that window and then back at my beautiful wife, I allowed the door of reality to open and fully understood that it was time to take off my tool belt. I was officially walking through a door of feelings that I, for the first time in my life, as a father may not be able to fix.

I struggled for the next few days at that cabin. But I had some alone time to think, ponder, and pray. On our last night at the cabin, as we sat around the bonfire as a family, I had been prompted while praying in the woods to hold a special family meeting. In that meeting, I gave the opportunity to each family member to share their feelings about our family and more importantly Kennedy's new situation. I was so worried about the many things we may have to eventually give up. Boating, hunting, skiing, the cabin, and so on as a family. But, to my surprise, the meeting was incredible. At such a young age, I witnessed little Kennedy and Anna both propose to sell our boat and to give up some other things we typically do. They both felt that it would be too hard and costly to keep up with some of the hobbies we may not be able to do anymore with the loss of Kennedy's sight. They both agreed that simple hikes or playing in a tree house was more important than the RVs, boats, and other items we had acquired. We outlined our time together and the hobbies of each child, and we decided as a family how we were going to move forward in helping Kennedy see everything she could with her eyes as long as she could. The proposal was to sell off some things and take a vacation together to Mexico. Proposals were made to do more things together locally and to see more things. And proposals were made to just be happier.

As we sat around that fire, little Kennedy could not hold back. She stood to her feet and bore a strong testimony to the fact that it was ok and that we need not worry. And once again, she testified and bore record to us that in her heart SHE KNEW that Heavenly Father and Jesus would heal her eyes one day . . . in heaven. As she said this, I could feel that key of reality be completely added to the key chain. Although this gave us peace, it also gave us that door of reality that something else was going on. The tool belt was removed in order to not fix, but now find the problem.

CHAPTER 16

The Zip Line

"She's stuck, Jason, she's stuck!" screamed out Heather. Sitting hundreds of feet above the rain forest of Mexico, Kennedy sat stuck on a zip line. We had moved forward as planned and sold our boat and RV and were on a dreamlike family vacation in Puerto Vallarta, Mexico. On this day, we were on an adventurous excursion of zip lining through the jungles of Mexico. But, things suddenly got serious because Kennedy did not make it all the way to the other side. With her sweet little hesitant personality, the only thing that we could think of is that, amidst her fears, she had braked too much on the brake line that controlled the speed of travel down the zip line.

This was the longest zip line on our adventure tour, spanning over 1600 feet and sitting over 500 feet above the jungle floor. Kennedy could still see at this point and she instantly began to call out for help. Heather became increasingly nervous as she grabbed onto my arm and began to ask what we should do. The guide came over and assured us that everything would be ok. On both ends of the line, there were platforms. And on each platform sat a different guide, helping to accommodate tourists with their equipment, belts, and rides in this jungle. Both guides immediately began to call out to Kennedy. They instructed her how to pull herself along the zip line. Neither guide was very good at speaking English, so the instructions were, to say the least, confusing. As they both yelled to Kennedy across this vast jungle canyon, I knew in my heart she was struggling. That her little emotions were beyond fear and that she was beginning to panic. The guides anxiously kept telling her to pull herself along the line. Kennedy tried—she tried so hard. She was pulling but not moving. She was struggling and sat dead center in the middle of this line. All she could see was thin air and a small river below her. There was no net to catch her, no platform to stand on, and no one around her to give her comfort and aid. After what was probably five minutes, but seemed like an eternity, she had maybe moved a total of five feet. She could not do it any longer. She had tried so hard and she had not given up, but she ultimately began to scream, "Help, help, help!"

At this point, Heather began to panic a bit. I called out, "Hold on, Ken. Help is coming. Everything is going to be ok." She began to cry. Her little whimpers echoed in the canyon and you could hear them bouncing back to us. The guide on the starting end of the platform attached himself to the zip line and assured us that she would be ok. "I go get her," he said. He set out on the line, weighing it down quite heavily with the two of them on it. Kennedy began crying even harder. "Help, help, help!" she screamed. "I am scared. Help!" Heather and I felt helpless. We continued to yell out to her that help was on the way and that she would be ok. We tried to assure her as best as we could. Seeing her sitting there and hearing her little cries was starting to tear at my heartstrings. I began to feel protective and worried. I also began to tell the guide, "Hurry, man, hurry. She is really, really scared!" At this point, we could only trust two things: #1 time, and #2 the guide. Slowly and surely we watched as the guide arrived to Kennedy. We could hear them talking, but we could not fully make out what was being said. The guide connected himself to Kennedy and also wrapped his body around hers. Slowly and surely he pulled the two of them the remaining 800 plus feet to safety.

Everyone cheered. Heather and I felt relief and Kennedy was safe. We could not get across that line quick enough and we could not arrive soon enough to hug her. As we did, we told her how proud we were of her bravery and her patience. We also assured her that she was ok. We still had a long, long way to go to complete this adventure and it took a bit of coercion, but ultimately Kennedy continued on. Zipping from tree to tree, down line to line. By the end, she was screaming with excitement like Jane in *Tarzan*. She was laughing, yelling, and having the time of her life. The toll of the zip line she got stuck on had now become the icon to her bravery for the rest of the day. Yet, why could I not stop staring at her? Why was my heart so intent on feeling grateful that she was ok? Why was I so deepened with emotion on this day? And why was my mind reflecting on two things: time and the guide?

As we arrived back to the resort where we were staying, it seemed my mind would not stop on this racetrack of emotions. I kept seeing her on that zip line, stuck in the middle of this canyon. So helpless, so alone, and so in need. I could not thank my Father in Heaven enough for keeping her safe, alive, and well. My heart was bursting and I just needed her for a moment. "Kennedy, let's go on a walk," I said.

We walked hand in hand from our room down to a beach. I felt electricity between our hands. I felt it in the air and I felt in our hearts. We talked about her bravery and we talked about life and all that was going on. Her little heart was just bursting with love and I could feel it. We walked down to the beach where Kennedy stared out deep into the ocean and at the sunset beyond us. She suddenly squealed out, "Look, Daddy! A pirate ship, a pirate ship!" Away in the distance, a pirate ship turned into a party ship for tourists and was sailing away into the sunset from us. In my estimation, I figured that it was probably a good mile away from us and Kennedy could see it just fine. She began to say "Look at the sun, look at the parasailer, look at the sand! Oh Daddy, I love it here! I just love it here!" She then turned to me and said, "Look at me, Daddy." I looked at her and her beautiful face, her deep brown eyes, and her braided hair. Her little glasses were shaded black from the sunlight. She had began to wear special lenses that would darken with any sign of bright lights and she looked so cute, so amazing, so right. I peered into her soul and she peered into mine. "Do you know how much I love you, Daddy? Do you know that I am your princess always and forever, Daddy?"

Tears welled up. I had to pick her up, and I had to hold her. I did not know that I would be losing her at this point in my life, yet my soul did. But what I did know is that I was feeling something deep, very deep, and it was simply our spirits communicating to one another. I picked her up and hugged her. "Why are you crying, Daddy? Are you sad?" she asked. "No, no little angel. I am not sad at all. I am so, so happy. You make me so, so happy and I want you to never forget all of this. Look around you and enjoy it. Kennedy, it is so hard for your daddy to tell you this, but this may be the last trip and time that you will be able to see so many wonderful things with your physical eyes. Please look hard. Please, please, please. And remember, remember all of it. Never forget this trip or this moment!" I set her down and she stood in front of me. I placed my hands around her little arms and just stared out to the ocean with her. We had our moment and we felt it. We were, in a sense, stuck on the zip line of our lives together. Stuck right in the middle and although we wanted to move forward, we really did not want to move. Suddenly we heard the flash of a camera and turned to see Heather taking pictures of us. "Mommy, Mommy!" Kennedy screamed. She ran to her, hugged her, and began telling her all about everything that we had seen. Quickly the sun went down and the darkness came. The three of us sat on the beach as Anna came to join us. Suddenly, Kennedy squealed out, "Bright lights in the water. Look, look!" Sure enough, plankton had appeared. They radiated. "The stars! Look, Anna, look, Mom, look, Daddy, the stars!" A setting of beautiful stars and plankton beamed around us. The feeling was amazing and the setting was almost perfect. And Kennedy was soaking it in. For you see, she knew. She knew the whole time in her heart that the zip line in her life would catch her in the middle. And although she would get stuck and eventually would not be able to pull out physically, she was doing everything in her power spiritually to pull herself to the end. Yet, we learned that day that those two things were so important: the time we had together and the guide in our lives, both of which we learned to enjoy, trust, and savor.

http://goo.gl/REBSOQ

Scan to view post

CHAPTER 17

Worse than Death

The key chain was getting full, yet the gap in the middle was ever so apparent. We needed to have more children! And now with the devastating news of Kennedy's childhood blindness, we felt we needed to act quickly. It seemed that our entire lives began to be consumed with this. Yet, nothing seemed to be coming together. Our hearts were broken, yet our hearts were full as we were being assured by Kennedy that her going blind was ok. But to us this was anything but ok. We began worrying about her social life, her schooling, and her future dating and marriage and children. We also worried about what she would not be able to see versus what she could see. The pressures seemed insurmountable in our minds and hearts.

We had been investigating adoption through our church's adoption agency and after much prayer, thought, and attending classes, we decided to go that route.

For over a year, this preparation continued and Kennedy was becoming impatient with the wait. We had not been selected and she began to ask why. We kept telling her that it would happen when it was supposed to. But, in her mind, she was losing precious time. Her sight was not getting any better and she began to decline in her learning. In our mind and the school's mind where she attended, this was nothing more than the effects of Stargardt disease and losing her sight. But, in her mind, she knew better. She began to incessantly talk about heaven and earth and how she needed to get her brother here. She began to tell us that she knew he had been chosen to be with us, but we just had to pray harder to get him. Her prayers changed. They became very serious and very to the point. She would tell Heavenly Father that she needed to have a baby brother now so that she could see him and so that she could take care of him and help raise him while she could still see. And then it happened. The phone rang. On the other end of the line, the agency told us that a mother had selected our profile! We were jumping up and down. Kennedy was screaming, "My brother, my brother!" Anna was yelling, "Yippee, yippee!"

We jumped in the car and raced to the agency's location. When we arrived at the agency, we were sat down in a different room from the mother and child. After waiting for a bit, one of the counselors came in and told us all about the mother and the baby. There was a bit of a confused look on Kennedy's face when we were told that this boy was fourteen months old. I worried a bit about this, until just moments later as the mother and baby entered the room. Without even having a chance to soak in the moment, Kennedy instantly stood up and put her arms out. We were all in shock! She was always a bit shy, so this was a bit of a surprise. Before any of us could even have a chance to even know his name, he reached out and went to her! They instantly bonded and she began to baby him. The birth mother saw this and immediately was in tears. A half day meeting ensued where the birth mom had the opportunity to get to know our family and to make her decision of placement. We were sold. This was our boy. The boy that we had prayed for for so long. After an emotional meeting and details provided from the agency, the decision was made. We officially were being placed with a son in our family and he would be going home with us that day! As we drove home that night, Kennedy could not keep her eyes or hands off of her new brother. Anna was so excited and was trying to sing songs to him. We felt satisfied and more than anything, we felt like we were a now complete family.

That little boy and the next four weeks of our lives were darn near next to perfect. He had not had stability and normalcy. He fell in love with us and we fell in love with him. Because he fit in so perfectly and because life felt so good, none of us, and I mean none of us, worried at all about this not going through. But, like most things we have encountered in our life, there was a different plan. One that would require the faith of ALL of the keys on our key chain.

The phone rang and on the other end of the line was a distraught and shaky voice. It was one of the directors of the agency. He simply told us that he did not know how to tell us this, but that our adopted son's birth mom had found a loophole in the law and wanted him back. We once again found ourselves on our knees in our room, pleading, crying, and pouring our hearts out to our Father in Heaven. "Please, please, please change her mind," we cried. "Please!" By law we had to immediately take him to the agency. We traveled to the school and pulled the girls out for the day. We sat them down and with all the tenderness of our hearts we told them the news. Anna instantly began to cry, scream, and fall to the floor. She was distraught and so upset. She began to say how unfair this was and this was not the right thing. Kennedy sat there. She did not move, and she did not budge from her blank stare. Suddenly, she stood up and walked over to her brother who sat in her mom's lap. She picked him up and just hugged him. She held him and loved him. As we loaded him up and drove away from the house, I will never forget little Kennedy at ten years old on the front porch with Anna's arm around her. They stood on the front porch and waved. The last wave that this little boy would ever see from such angels in his lifetime and the last wave they would give him in theirs.

The meeting with the birth mom was anything but pleasant. She described to us that she knew that he was happier and better off with our family, but that she needed him in order to survive. As we gave him back, he clung to Heather and screamed, "No, Mama, no! No! No!" He did not want to go. He did not want to leave. Heather literally had to pry his little fingers off of her shoulders and hands and give him back. He screamed as they walked away and he was loaded into a car. Heather broke and fell to her knees. She sobbed. She wept. Her heart was crushed and bleeding a thousand cries of sorrow. Her boy, her other baby she had waited for so long, was now gone.

* * *

"Mama, Mama, you have to get up! You have to get out of bed! I need your help, Mama! I need you!" Kennedy exclaimed. It had been three days and Heather had not gotten out of bed.

I knew what to do. I walked out and went to Kennedy's room. I found her and then found Anna. "We need to pray for Mama, girls, and we need to pray now." I asked Kennedy to say the prayer. But what I expected her to say and what she did say were completely different things. Kennedy knelt and prayed so honestly. "Heavenly Father, please help us. We are not mad at you. We just need a new little brother and we bless our other brother to be safe with his mom. But, right now please bless our mama Heather's heart to be fixed. Please help her and love her and let her know that it will be all right." I brought the girls into their mom's room and had them lay in her bed. They hugged her and they stroked her head. They rubbed her back and kissed her. They just lay there with her. We prayed together and we prayed hard. We did not pray that we would get our son back. We just prayed that he would be ok and that whatever Heavenly Father wanted would happen. The medicine had been administered and it was Kennedy. Her little smile with her crooked teeth, her laugh, and of course those Hugs! Yes, those Hugs! She never quit on her mom. She just kept hugging and hugging and hugging, until Heather finally got up. She got up and she accepted that feeling that is worse than death. We had been through a very tough, tough thing. The needles of pain were poking, prodding, and being struck so deep.

We stood strong and we moved forward. We did not show anger toward God. We began to show gratitude for the little piece of heaven we had for those four weeks. We did not know all of the reasons, yet we would. For that worse than death feeling and the loss we were experiencing were all preparing us for what was to come. For without having that loss, how could we have ever known the happiness that would be coming our way shortly? And that happiness was made whole through another miracle. The miracle of our little Beau. Because one month after that tragedy, we were selected once again and blessed to have our hearts and minds healed through the adoption of our final piece of our family: Beau Hansen. His addition helped heal the wounds of our family. And without his addition and the loss of our other boy, there is no way that we could have endured and been prepared for the great journey we would experience as a family in losing Kennedy.

CHAPTER 18

What's Wrong?

Retarded?" I asked.

"Yes, retarded," the school counselor explained. Kennedy's core test scores were on the same level as a child who is mentally retarded.

"Look, our daughter is not retarded. She is in dance, she plays with her sister and her dog and cat. She runs, has perfect grades, and ties her shoes. She has an eyesight disease, not retardation. That is offensive," I said. We had been contacted by the school for an evaluation on Kennedy. It seemed that everything had been going so right and now we felt the anxieties again of wrong.

We had adopted Beau without a single legal hiccup just weeks after meeting him. Kennedy and Anna of course were spoiling him. His room was the party central of the house. Each of them would fight to see who could wake him up, tuck him in bed at night, or change his diaper. They both felt secure and our family was finally complete. It felt complete. It felt right and we had gone through hell to reach this heaven. And now we were sitting in the school's conference room with teachers, counselors, and the principal trying to figure out what on earth was going on with Kennedy.

Her digression was so rapid that the school did not know how to respond. They had never seen anything like this. We had seen some digression, but it was the tests—those core tests that at the time I hated and now I love. They were the only indicator to let us know that Kennedy had more going on than her eyesight. But to be told that she was on a retarded-type level just seemed, well, wrong. But, little did all of us know how RIGHT that assessment was.

In the meantime, Kennedy was in her prime. She had friends all over the neighborhood and she was a daddy's little girl. We were hunting a bunch and fishing, hiking, camping, and riding four-wheelers. We were snow skiing. And Kennedy was doing it all. On top of this, she had started softball. No one could think, in any shape or form, that she was on the same level as a retarded child. But, then . . . then something happened. Then something changed. I was working on a math problem with Kennedy. We were doing homework and it was simple math. We had printed the numbers much bigger so that she could see them. She was a straight A student and I was committed to keeping it that way. No one was going to tell us that our daughter could not do something. But, that night, those problems, those equations, became so, so hard. "I'm trying Dad, I'm trying!" she screamed.

"Kennedy, this is easy. What is 5 plus 5?" She paused and looked endlessly into space. I had never seen her look like that.

"I don't know. I can't do this, Dad. . . . I can't." I became agitated. I became upset. Her best subject was math.

"What's wrong?" I asked. "What's wrong?" We were stuck on the same group of problems for almost an hour. We had not moved. We had not progressed. Kennedy was done and I was done. I could not figure out what was going on. Only that she was not right. She was not Kennedy, and we definitely were frustrated. She began to cry, and I raised my voice out of frustration. "Kennedy, you are not trying. You are not trying!" My emotions got the best of me. Heather walked through the door, just bringing Anna and Beau home. Kennedy instantly jumped out of her chair and ran to her mom. She looked up at Heather and said, "What's wrong, Mom. What's wrong?"

That night, it hit me. I knew that things were different. I also wanted to know the answer to the "what's wrong" question. I lay in bed and stared at the dark ceiling. I prayed silently in my mind to my God. I prayed that nothing seriously was wrong with Kennedy. I crawled out of bed and fell to my knees. "Heavenly Father, isn't going blind enough for a ten-year-old? Please, Heavenly Father, please do not let this be anything serious. Kennedy will have enough to go through. Please, Heavenly Father, please. Help us figure out what's wrong."

The next morning, I apologized to my angel. I drove her to school in my truck. I vowed to never, ever be impatient like that with her again. It was just her sight, I kept telling myself, just her sight. I hugged her and hugged her a little tighter that morning. And all Kennedy could do was look at me and say, "What's wrong? Daddy, what's wrong with me?" I told her nothing was wrong. That it was my fault the night before and that everything was just fine. She hugged me again and said, "Remember, Daddy, that Heavenly Father and Jesus will heal my eyes when I get to heaven. Do not forget that! Ever!" When I drove to work that day, I cried. Not out of frustration, but out of happiness. How was I so lucky to have a little girl who could be so humble to understand such a concept at such a young age? I was happy and smiled. But then it hit me. Heaven? She said heaven and had been saying that every time. Kennedy never said, "Heal my eyes on earth." She always would refer to "heal my eyes when I go to heaven." My heart raced, because my soul was trying to tell me. But I was not ready yet. I was not prepared. I questioned this, and I thought about this. But the only thing currently on my mind was the question "what's wrong?" And as her dad, I was going to fix it.

CHAPTER 19

Walk, Don't Run!

Everyone close to Kennedy knew that her sight was failing. So it was easy to just blame everything on her sight. However, there were those close to her in school that began to notice other changes. Socially, Kennedy became quite introverted. She began to close down and withdraw somewhat from her peers. While many of the girls, including her sister Anna, were gravitating toward boys, clothes, parties, school dances, cell phones, and many of the worldly changes at hand, Kennedy seemed content to stay at home and play with Barbies and dolls with many of the younger neighborhood girls whom she loved and adored.

She was in the 6th grade and was probably one of the tallest if not the tallest kid in her elementary school. She decided to quit playing soccer because the foot to eye coordination was too difficult for her to handle. She absolutely loved dance and was in full swing with her dance classes and local studio that she attended. As she began to shut down with many of her peers, she began to turn inward toward her brother, Beau, her sister, Anna, and her mom and dad. She longed for family get-togethers with her cousins where she could be herself and feel normal. She truly was so sweet, so genuine, and so, so innocent. Yet she was not excelling.

And it was at this time that we really began to see and hear dramatic differences in her speech. She began to rush sentences and pause on words. She was difficult to understand and she knew it. She would put her hands on her face and shake her head with frustration. Even she knew that she was losing the ability to communicate and this was very, very hard for her to accept and handle.

It was early on in the school year, but the school was already recognizing it and when we found ourselves in the school's conference room again, we were all heavily armed with concerns of her rapid digression in not just her sight now, but her cognitive areas. It was recommended to place her into heavy resource interaction and to also have her begin attending the Utah School for the Blind as part of each of her weeks in order to learn blind life skills. At first Kennedy could not stand this. She absolutely hated the idea of using a cane. "A cane?" she said to us. "A cane? I am not old." She did not like the fact that she was beginning to learn how to read with her fingers. This was A LOT to take in and on top of it all, she was in special classes at school in order to help her progress and learn.

But, one thing was for sure, Kennedy never complained. She moved forward with a smile and began to touch the hearts of her new teachers, blind liaisons from the Utah School for the Blind, and counselors from the school. She never expressed complaints. She just adjusted and moved forward. But, for a little eleven-year-old and for her parents, we knew better and we knew her heart. And more than anything, we were concerned. And that same feeling kept coming strongly into our hearts. *"You always listen to the Spirit, which is a higher power, and if you do, you will know exactly what to do."* We were feeling a higher power directing us to begin extra testing for Kennedy. We prayed fervently about where to go and how to have her tested. We ended up having her see many doctors, who ultimately told us that a psychological evaluation was necessary. Little Kennedy went through a week-long evaluation where a professional handed over a binder the size of Texas with the results of the tests. Ultimately, the bottom line diagnosis was a severe learning disorder with digression similar to that of a mentally retarded child.

Our concern deepened and our hearts ached. What was wrong with our daughter? Why was she digressing so much? And what could we do about it? As usual, we found ourselves on our knees, pleading to the God we believe in. We asked him for help, direction, and guidance for ourselves and our little girl. The feelings we received were quite strong. Along the way, Anna was feeling like she could not move forward with her own life and her own social circle. She was feeling stuck at Kennedy's side and wanted to not have to bring Kennedy to every activity, party, or friend's house. We recognized this and felt that it was very important for Kennedy to spend more time with us as parents, one-on-one, and to let Anna move forward as a normal 6th grader.

So, we began to spend more one-on-one time with Kennedy. We took her on special dates and did special things. She was always a daddy's girl, so spending more time with Daddy was not a problem with her at all. She loved to hike and hunt with me during the fall. So I began to spend more time with her doing this. Anna was so involved in sports, school, and dance that she really did not have time to do this. I took Kennedy scouting with me for deer and elk. She hiked hard and she worked hard. I never had to worry about her keeping up. She had always been a hard worker and she was willing to work as hard as I asked her. But, on one particular beautiful fall day, that all came to an end. We had been watching some elk, deer, and moose in one particular area that was quite hard to get to. There was a very large and steep rocky trail that rose to the top of a ridge at quite a slope for about ¾ of a mile. We would always bust up that hill with fury knowing that once we reached the top, the rest of the hike was fairly reasonable and easy. We also were always excited, because at the top of that ridge we knew we would see animals. As we began the climb that day, for whatever reason, I began to feel a bit odd. I was not quite sure what I was feeling, other than I knew that the Spirit was telling me to watch Kennedy carefully. So I did. She plowed up that mountain that day. It seemed as if she was on a mission to get it done and impress me. We made it to the top and hiked a few more miles to our spot where we watched many deer, elk, and moose for the morning. I had purchased a spotting scope to zoom in on the animals and field judge them better. But that scope was a godsend for Kennedy because it allowed her to see the animals up close and personal. "Daddy, he, hhhe is hhhuge!" she screamed. We were looking at a beautiful mule deer buck and Kennedy was on cloud nine. She was jumping up and down and screaming.

"Shhhh, shhhh, look Kennedy, look!" I said. I pointed not but fifty yards from us at a beautiful bull moose that had been spooked by her excitement and was running up the ravine next to us. "Ddddadddy, wow, wow! He is beautiful!" she said. She sat between my legs and peered through the scope. We ate jerky and fruit snacks. Our two most favorites, next to Coke, of course. My emotions were so sticky that you could almost feel them sticking to my heart. We were so connected, so happy, and so bonded. It was a morning that I will never forget for the rest of my life.

As the morning rolled on and the sunrise turned to day, we packed up and headed out. For whatever reason, we were in a bit of a hurry. I cannot remember exactly why, only that we needed to get back a bit quicker. As we hiked, little Kennedy kept right up. I was actually quite shocked, yet so pleased that she was able to see all of the wildlife and enjoy this beauty still with her sight going so quickly. As we came to the big hill that we now had to hike down, Kennedy knew we were in a hurry and she knew that we needed to bust it. I was moving very quickly and in order to keep up, she began to run. Instantly, I had the feeling come over me that I had felt earlier that morning. The Spirit instantly filled my mouth and I yelled out, "Walk, don't run!" Kennedy came to a halt, being the obedient little bugger that she always was and said, "Ok, ok." She began to take the steep incline walking and was getting to the most rugged part. It was very steep and had many, many rocks. I felt a bit worried and wanted to make sure she was ok. I sped up to catch up to her, when suddenly she walked completely off of the trail. She was heading for a little edge that would take her into dangerous territory. There was nothing I could do but watch as she lost her footing and tumbled head over heels down the mountain. Over and over and down the rocks she went, banging and hitting and letting out painful sounds as she went. I instantly ran as fast as I could and bolted down the mountain, jumping in front of her and diving to her side almost on top of her to stop her from continuing. She shook her little head. Her glasses were scratched. Her arms were cut up and she had dirt in her hair and all over her face. She looked at me and was breathing heavy in shock. I looked down the hill and we were inches from a small drop off that could have made things really ugly. She began to cry. "Dddaddy, I am ssssorry. I am ssssso, ssso ssssoorry. Dddaddy, I am so sorry for mmmmmakkking us late!" she cried out. *Are you kidding me?* I thought. I wrapped my arms around her and just hugged her.

"It's ok, Dee. Dee, it's ok." I said. "I'm here, I'm here." She looked up at me and kept telling me she was sorry.

She then told me, "DDaddy, I can't do this anymore. . . . I just can't see!" She proceeded to tell me that although she could see the animals, during the last several trips we had made, she had not been able to fully see the trail. She told me that she felt so bad, because it would ruin my hunt if she did not go, so she did not want to say anything. But she told me that she had remembered and memorized the trail in her mind, so she thought she could just do it. As she cried, I cried. We just sat there in the middle of that rocky patch on the mountain with dirt all over us and cried. Ultimately we got up and of course I held her hand all the way down that mountain to the four-wheeler. We made it to the truck and drove to first gas station we could find and you got it, we bought Cokes. And those Cokes seemed to make it all feel better.

I arrived home later that day and had the opportunity to tell Heather about what happened. I knew that a new key had been added to our key chain. The key of caution. The impression to tell Kennedy "walk, don't run!" was one that, in my mind, saved her from ultimate disaster and serious injury. Had she been running, she would have definitely been catapulted over the top of the rocky ridge and seriously hurt. That night, I had to ponder. I had to think. How was I going to hunt without my little buddy? How was I going to not have her by my side and with me? My emotions were stirring and I prayed. In that prayer, I thanked Heavenly Father for saving her. But I also asked if Ken was done. Did I need to back off and not push her at all to do the things that we loved? Was it time to truly give in to her disability of blindness? As I arose from my prayer, the answer was clear. I could see her in my mind, telling me sorry and I could hear my voice screaming, "Walk, don't run." The indication was clear. That would be the last official big game hike that we would go on. It was now time to walk, not run and sadly, oh ever so sadly, I knew it and so did our little Ken.

CHAPTER 20

ALL ALONE

Our home was and is much too big for our family. But we knew that we were supposed to be in it. So any church event, neighborhood event, or friend event that happened, we would offer or open up our home. It seemed that the one person, the one angel who always loved this was Kennedy. Whether it was a family reunion, a work party, or simply neighbors visiting, Kennedy was the ultimate door greeter, butler, cook, game host, and of course, hugger! Many times, she would not say too much when people arrived that she did not know. But by the end of the day or evening, rest assured that you would feel love from her through a hug and her mere presence.

By 7th grade, Kennedy had shot up like a sunflower. Her beauty seemed beyond her years as we would hear comment after comment and receive praise after praise about how gorgeous she was. But her inner beauty was suffering. Kennedy had begun to become socially awkward and self-questioning. It seemed that all of her peers were moving on from the Barbies, dolls, outside games, and cartoons. But to Kennedy, little Kennedy, life was still the same and simple as ever. All of those simple things still existed all the way up until the day she passed away. And for the world, that was a blessing. That was a hallmark piece of not just how Batten disease affected her, but how she affected us. Kennedy wanted to be with her family. She wanted to still play house and tag and Friday night Kick the Can. She still wanted to watch her favorite kid cartoons, movies, and television shows. She wanted to kiss her daddy's cheek and tell him she loved him. She wanted to hug her mom and do whatever was asked of her.

She was so different, so much alive, yet failing physically before our eyes.

Due to her learning decline, we opted to continue to have Kennedy in resource. This was hard for us, because Kennedy was like most kids. You want your kids to be normal, yet you also want what is best for them. So, against every fiber of our social beings and with every fiber of our loving beings, we enrolled her in the resource program at her junior high. As this happened, something changed in Kennedy. She began to recover versus decline. She seemed happier, and she seemed more at peace. She seemed to be the Kennedy we had not seen in a long time. She became more social, more talkative, and more full of life than ever before. And the best part was that she wanted to go everywhere and do everything with her family. We took advantage of this. It seemed everywhere we went, she went. However, her peers were moving forward and they even seemed to try to include her in all that they did, but she just could not fit in.

Meanwhile, her sister, Anna, was really getting involved. Playing sports and getting into the school band, choir, and plays. Anna had so many friends and was hanging out with boys. Anna tried so hard to bring Kennedy, to include Kennedy, and to always be by her side. But eventually this became harder and harder and harder for Anna. Being enrolled in the Utah School for the Blind, losing her sight, and wearing special transition lenses that would turn dark when put into bright lights made Kennedy different. We were told to cover her eyes as much as we could from the sunlight and to make sure that she wore these glasses at all times. Kennedy began wearing hats everywhere. We bought her the cutest hats and she was fine with it. If you saw Kennedy outside, it seemed she always had a hat on. And her glasses would always go dark whenever bright lights hit them. Sometimes those glasses intimidated people, especially her peers. They would make her look a bit nerdy and very different. But Kennedy did not care. She simply tried to be herself and do the best with what she had. With her declination in sight came her cane. She was learning how to use the cane at the Utah School for the Blind and she would go on outings with her liaison. She wanted to feel normal and like any other kid. But for Anna it seemed even harder. Where was her normal best friend? Why was this happening? Why couldn't Kennedy just like the things that everyone else was liking, doing, and saying? Meanwhile, the cane would have limited use and it seemed we would have to highly encourage Kennedy to use it. What was going on? Why was Kennedy losing her cognitive, speech, sight, and social abilities all at once? We all had these questions and none of us had answers. I remember specifically sitting down with Anna and having a very long talk. Anna wanted to just be normal and she felt like she had to take Kennedy everywhere with her. It was taxing on some of her relationships, because her time would be limited in order to spend time with others. I simply felt so inspired to tell her that one day, one short day in the future, it would all make sense. I reminded her about another little girl, so awkward, yet so cute who came into Kennedy's life not so long ago. I reminded her how Kennedy also put her arms around this girl. She watched her, she babysat her, and she included her with everything! With everything and everyone. I also let Anna know that it was ok to treat Kennedy normal in order for her to feel normal, but that Anna needed to also create her own circle of friends, influence, and associations. This was a lot for a twelve-year-old girl to accept. But she did. Anna did her best with Kennedy. Did she get frustrated? Yes. Was it hard? Absolutely. But the one thing that Anna never did was leave Kennedy's side. Anna was her other half as Kennedy was all alone. As their 7th grade year moved on and Anna moved forward and Kennedy moved back, the two of them seemed to find their middle ground. Instead of hiding her interest in boys, Anna began sharing her feelings about boys with Kennedy. We would catch them laughing and giggling and talking about Anna's crushes. Anna found that this made Kennedy feel normal instead of excluded. They would write little notes and they began calling boys on the phone. Now, I do not know how I felt about that, but I let it slide. Anna began to move into the teenage shows, clothing, and teenage slang. She helped Kennedy understand this part and we would catch her teaching Kennedy many of the words, sayings, and things that were popular. Although all alone, Kennedy still had her other half. Anna was a sister who had been loved and now was giving love right back. The tables had turned, and the roles had reversed. For the next four years, Anna would have to do hard things. Things that no teenage girl should have to, would want to, or would ever sign up for. These things would prove how defined the relationship was and is between Kennedy and Anna. A relationship where they literally were each other's other half and will be for the rest of eternity.

http://goo.gl/7FCSO7

Scan to view post

CHAPTER 21

The Changing Day

Things were not right and we all knew it. Kennedy began to severely decline in her speech and she even began to walk a bit pigeon-toed. Her ability to run and jump seemed to change. Every day, every morning—in fact every minute—it seemed that I could not get her out of my heart and mind. She was withering, but with what? It was the middle of the night when an almost deathly scream wailed out from her room. "Mom, Mom, Mommmy, help, help me!" she screamed. "Heeeellllllpppppp!" We immediately woke up and ran as fast as we could to Kennedy's room. She was sitting on the edge of her bed and just screaming. We did not know what had happened. We did not know why she was screaming. And this scream was not just a little helpless middle of the night nightmare. This was a serious, serious scream. She proceeded to tell us that she had had a nightmare and that she was so, so scared. From that night on, I do not believe that we experienced one night for the next four years of her life where Kennedy did not wake up multiple times screaming, agitated, or in pain. And later on, we would come to find out that these night terrors were accompanied by seizures that were waking her up and then were followed by terror in her mind due to dementia. This was more than her sight. This was much more. We had seen doctors, received an analysis from a noted psychologist, and had attended the best eye doctors in the country. What was our next step? What were we to do? And how were we to do it? We felt lost. We felt alone. We felt so responsible for our daughter, yet irresponsible for not knowing what she truly had wrong with her.

It was at this time that Kennedy really, really began to gravitate to us as her parents. She was a very tall girl and so muscular. She was around 5 foot 6 inches and easily 125 pounds. It was difficult for me as her dad to have her come and want to snuggle. "Snnnnugggle, me, Daddy, sn, sn, snnnuggle," she would say. I truly struggled with this. Probably what made it even harder was the fact that Anna was driving her little life in a completely opposite direction. She was beginning to be too cool to hug Mom and Dad or even to hang out. The polar opposites seemed to drive us to the North Pole on one day and the Sahara Desert on the next. Hot and cold feelings so real that you could have placed a thermometer on our feelings and it never would consistently register. I began to feel bad. I began to find myself almost avoiding little Kennedy. Not because I did not absolutely love her, but because I did not know how to act around her. Why was she acting like a six-year-old, when she was thirteen years old? That was the one question that truly burned within me. I turned to my wife and more than anything I turned to my Heavenly Father. I wanted her to play dolls, I wanted her to snuggle and kiss and sing pre-school songs. But I wanted her to be normal! I wanted her to be the cheerleader she had always talked about, to cheer at the football and basketball games. To go to the school dances and to hang out with boys. I wanted this because Heather and I had experienced that joy ourselves. But what I wanted and what was happening were all too different. And unfortunately, NOTHING I could, or did do, could change the disease that none of us knew she had. And day by day, hour by hour, it was slowly killing our beautiful daughter and none of us had any idea, until the changing day arrived.

We began to attend the noted Primary Children's Hospital and were assigned to the wonderful neurological department. The hospital and this department truly were that—wonderful! Visits to the hospital became almost a biweekly if not weekly affair as test after test, analysis after analysis, and doctor after doctor tried to figure out what was happening with Kennedy. These visits began to wear on us a bit and it seemed that we just wanted an answer. Something, some closure to be able to know what was slowly shutting Kennedy down.

One particular day seemed usual and our family went through our typical morning. We arose, had scripture study, prayer, and breakfast. We sent the kids off to school, and Heather got dressed to go to the gym. I remember her leaving a bit earlier than usual that day for some reason. So the house was completely empty and it felt empty. Was I supposed to be alone for some reason? Out of habit and necessity, and as I do daily,

I knelt by the side of my bed to say my morning prayer. I was struck immediately! There was no hesitation, there was no waiting, and there was no question. As I began my prayer, "Dear Heavenly Father, thank you for . . ." BAM! My entire body quivered and was overcome with a warm yet comforting and very serious spirit. To this day, I do not know if I heard the voice just in my mind, or if it was out loud. But I was immediately told, "I need her home, my son. I need her home." I had to stop. I opened my eyes and looked around the room. Was this happening? Was this really happening? I closed my eyes and again began to pray, "Heavenly Fath . . . ," and again came the confirmation, "I need her home, my son. I need her home." This time it was even more powerful than the first. It was as if the room was now engulfed in a bubble and I was not allowed to move, potentially causing it to burst. I did not move from where I knelt on my knees. I trembled and tears began to flow. "Father . . . I, I, I . . . ," again a third time it came: "I need her home, my son. I need her home." This time there was no questioning. The feeling, the voice, whether in my head or out loud, was so real, so powerful, and so firm. Physically I was shaking. The tears were now rolling and spiritually I was overwhelmed. How was I supposed to respond? What was I supposed to do? I felt crushed. I felt confused and I felt grateful all wrapped within this bubble that so consumed me. I rose to my feet and immediately went to the shower.

Now, keep in mind, I am not a long shower type of guy. Like most guys, I am in and out quickly. But on this day and at that moment, all I could do was turn on the hot water, sit down like a little boy, and cry. I think I sat in that shower and cried for almost two hours. To this day, it was the longest shower that I have ever taken in my entire life. As I sat and cried, I had a recollection of Kennedy's entire life. OUR LIFE! Our time together. Heather, Kennedy, Anna, and Beau. It replayed through my mind like a movie, one that I could not shut off. I remember thinking, *Why, why now? Why today? What is the significance of today?* And suddenly it hit me again, like it had so many times before. *"You always listen to the Spirit, which is a higher power, and if you do, you will know exactly what to do."* This was it! This was my answer. Why on this day? Why at that moment? Well, because we had been praying, searching, and showing forth as much faith, care, and commitment as we knew how. And now, He knew. Heavenly Father knew. He knew that it was time to reveal to us that her time had come and was coming near. And coming quickly. I sat in that shower and talked out loud to him. "Ok, Father,

Ok, I will do it. I will accept it. You can have her home. But, please let me go and just see her in person and have it FULLY CONFIRMED. You gave her to us for a time and now we will prepare her to go home." I left the shower and got ready for the day. My heart was torn, yet my heart was full. I finally had an answer. And although I did not know exactly what Kennedy had disease-wise, I knew this. She would be going home and going home soon. She would be taken from us and there was little time to do what we could to make her journey, preparation, and life the very best we could.

I drove to Kennedy's junior high, which was just minutes from our home. By this time, it was lunchtime and I hoped to find Kennedy in the lunch room. I just wanted to see her. I just wanted to touch her face, feel her hair, and hug her. I also wanted to receive a FULL CONFIRMATION with her before me. That was the only way that I could or would fully accept this. I entered the lunchroom and by complete luck, there she was, sitting all alone at a table eating her lunch. She was probably twenty yards from me initially. There were a few other kids who were sitting at the other end of the table. Kennedy and the resource kids were always brought to the lunchroom earlier than the other kids. So, without really knowing what I would find, the timing needed to be and was perfect. As I entered that cafeteria and saw her sitting there, it was as if an aura surrounded her. She looked perfect! This was my daughter. My first born! My little angel, my little Dee Dee, my princess, and my perfect little girl. I moved a bit closer and next to a wall. I became so emotional as I just stared at her that I had to lean against that wall. As I sat and stared at her, it was confirmed. "I need her home, my son. I need her home." I shook my head in agreement and said out loud, "Ok, you can have her. I am fine with this, but I am going to need all of the help I can get."

"Excuse me, excuse me, sir? Sir?" a voice muttered. I looked up to see a police officer looking at me. I was in a trance it seemed and he knew it. "Are you all right, sir? Can I help you, sir?" he asked.

"No, no, no," I said. "I am sorry. See that beautiful girl over there, sitting all alone? Well . . . that is my daughter Kennedy and I am just here admiring her. Just if you would let me look at her for a bit and I will then go and talk to her." He could tell I was emotional and he could tell that something was definitely going on. "You bet, sir," he said. I slowly made my way toward Kennedy where I sat down directly across the table from her. She immediately perked up and looked right at me. But, due to her blindness, she had no idea that it was me. She tried to look, but she just kind of stared toward me. She leaned forward and then sat back down. She continued to eat and all I could do was sit and look at her. This was real. This was really happening. As I sat there, I let it sink in that in the last three hours I had been told and had confirmed, and I was agreeing to let her go. I could not take it anymore, I leaned forward and put my hands on hers and said, "Kennedy, it's Dad." She stopped eating. She paused. Immediately a smile beamed across her face. "Dddadddy, wwhaat are you doing here? Ddddadddy, Ddddadddy!" All I could do was sit there and, with tears strolling down my cheeks, tell her how much I loved her. "I love you so much, Kennedy. I love you so, so much. You are so beautiful and you are my most favorite person in the whole world and my best buddy and friend. I just really needed to see you today." "Oh . . . Ddddadddy, th th thaaat is ssooo sweet. Come and eaaat l, l, l, llunch with me!" I gave in and against all of my dietary standards, sat next to her and ate a junior high lunch. We laughed and laughed and just had fun. It was a moment that was so hard, yet so wonderful. I sat there knowing that I would be losing her. I did not know when. I did not know how. And I did not know to what. All I knew is that it was confirmed.

That was the changing day. That day officially changed me forever. Because, from that moment on, no Barbie was too much money. No snuggling was off limits. No watching *High School Musical* again was too much and no hugging was too overwhelming. From that day on, I had been given a great burden and a great blessing. The blessing to act as the patriarch of my little family and to lead them through this journey. To prepare my daughter and family as best as I could for her great celebration of going home. And it was also the great burden of wondering how I could be worthy to be the one called to help prepare her. I think I gave her one of the biggest hugs I have ever given in my life that day. As I hugged her and left, I realized that I had a great job and great challenge ahead of me. I now had the challenge of telling my beautiful wife, Heather, the news. We never and have never held anything from one another. This would be a conversation I never wanted to have. It would be a moment that I never planned on experiencing and an answer that was given to me with great responsibility.

I did not work that day. I could not. I had to think. I had to ponder. I had to pray. How was I going to do this? What was I going to do? And how was I going to lead? I once again felt so alone and so helpless. I could not and would not tell anyone about this until I told Heather. And that was the next step. I found myself on my knees again pleading for direction. And the same answer came that always came, to follow the spirit. This was the changing day. This was the day that from here moving forward added a multifaceted key to our key chain that now would open up not tens, not hundreds, not thousands but millions of doors and hearts to a story about a little girl who simply wanted to and did Hug the world!

CHAPTER 22

You Have to Accept This

The key chain was getting full and now the main key was added. The key of knowing that we would be losing our daughter. For many, many days, I struggled. Each time I would try to approach Heather, my own emotions and inner demons would shut me down. How could I tell her about my confirmation? How could this even be good news? How could we come together and make this a good thing for us, for Kennedy, and for our family?

After about three days, I could not handle it anymore. I sat Heather down next to me and became more serious than I ever had in our entire marriage. I conveyed to her what had happened and been confirmed to me. She looked horrified. She looked devastated. "No, no. That I will not accept! There are a lot of things I can accept. But, not that. I have already lost my mom and I cannot and will not lose Kennedy." I took her hand in mine. I consoled her and hugged her.

I told her, "I am so, so sorry. I know you think I am crazy, but you have to get ready, Heather. This is more serious than any answer I have ever received and I know that this is true. You have to get ready. You have to pray about this and get your own confirmation. I know you think I am crazy. But, this is not from me, this is from our Heavenly Father. I am so, so sorry. I am so, so sorry."

Time began to pass and with each passing day, the feelings of losing Kennedy became stronger, more apparent, and very real within me. I would find myself just staring at her and not wanting to look away. I began to tuck her in almost every night and began to really, really try harder to understand what she was saying and take advantage of any little moment that she would give to me. She was digressing mentally and socially at such a fast rate it seemed. The school, her doctors, and other experts basically told us that she had declined and was sitting at about a 1st to 2nd grade level at this point. But within her father a deep well of emotions was being pulled to the surface. Hand over hand and rope after rope. My bucket of emotions was full and was being poured all over Kennedy and my little family. It HAD BEEN CONFIRMED and I could not deny it. We would be losing Kennedy and she would be going home to her Heavenly Father. And there was no way of me ignoring or changing this fact.

From that day on and for not days but years to come, something happened every night with Heather and me. As a couple, we have always made it a habit and practice to kneel down by our bedside at night and to pray to Heavenly Father. But, at that time in our life, the prayers really began to revolve around Kennedy. There was so much concern, so much anguish, fear, pain, and unknown. And although an answer had been given concerning her future, the details were still not there. But, every night as we would have prayer and kneel across from one another, I would remain on my knees and then look over at Heather after our prayer was finished. She would look at me and I would gently say the same thing every night. "You have to get ready, hon. You have to get ready."

"I don't want to talk about it. I do not want to think about it. This . . . Jay, I will not accept. I am not ready nor am I going to lose her," Heather would say. I would leave it at that and we would go to sleep. There were many nights where I would stare into the blackness of the night along with Heather and it was all I could do to bite my tongue and just let it go. But without hesitation the very next night after prayer, I would kneel down again and would stare into the heart-stricken worrying eyes of Kennedy's amazing mother and say, "Babe, you have to get ready, you have to accept this." And again, her gentle voice would tell me, "I can't, I just can't."

Some people may find it odd that I kept this conversation up every night from that point moving forward for almost three years until we received Kennedy's diagnosis. But, for us, it had to happen that way. Especially because Batten disease is one of the hardest disease's in the world to detect. But each night, each conversation, and each moment that we shared discussing this brought us closer together. And amazingly, we never, ever had any contention when it came to Kennedy throughout her entire journey and illness. Never once did we argue, disagree, or have a fight when it came to little Kennedy. And every night, the church bell seemed to ring as the same conversation occurred over and over again. And what some may not understand is that I was simply trying to prepare her, to help her, and to gently allow her to accept what was to come.

Later that year, Kennedy had an event to raise money for a blind foundation in Utah. She invited everyone. The event was a gala held to raise money for kids who are blind or were going blind. As we prepared for this gala, we asked that each set of our parents and siblings who lived close to us would meet at our home for a short meeting before attending the event. Most of them were wondering why we wanted to meet with them. The event was in Salt Lake City, which is a good thirty-five minutes from our home. So they were curious as to why we were meeting at our home first.

By this time, we had pretty much exhausted most options and resources for testing little Kennedy. We had been furiously meeting with the pediatric neurology department at Primary Children's and still could not figure any type of diagnosis out. But, one thing was for sure, I still knew and it was still was being confirmed daily that Kennedy had something much more serious than any of us could imagine, and that we would be losing her.

That day we gathered our family members who could be there together I will never forget the looks on those faces who were there as I relayed to them my experience of being told that we would be losing Kennedy. Some were in shock, others were in tears, others looked at me as if I was crazy. I shared with them that we would need their support, love, and advice. I also asked that they keep this private, within reason, and that I did not expect them to accept this or even believe it. But, I explained that I KNEW and would not and could not deny what had happened or was happening. I told them that we loved them all. As you can imagine, the room went silent. Many did not know what to do or how to handle or accept this. They were only there for a support dinner for Kennedy and now were being told by her father that she would be passing away and soon. I can only imagine how they felt or what they thought. I also told them that I felt strongly, very strongly, that this party and night would be the last true night that Kennedy would be able to see them and enjoy them with her physical eyes and that they needed to take full advantage of this. The room went silent and I even took Heather by surprise. She was looking at me with a look that I could fully read her mind with. Her look was like, "Really, Jay, really? On this night? On Kennedy's night and you are telling everyone this?" I felt relieved, yet I felt hopeless. I finally got a great burden off of my shoulders and back that I had been carrying for a while. The secret was out and whether my family believed it or not, at least they now knew where I was at.

That night went as expected. Perfect. Kennedy was on cloud nine. The event had auctions, recognitions, a great meal, and of course dancing. Kennedy seemed to look around and as I had expected, she could see everyone. She was laughing, dancing, and just being herself. Many, many pictures were taken and everyone seemed to have a great time. It was February, so many of our family and friends were there celebrating Valentine's and supporting Kennedy at the same time. She was so happy, so relieved it seemed. *Relieved?* I thought. *Why?* But as I watched her and cried that night, I knew why. It was because she was able to have everyone there whom she loved. And she was able to see their faces and feel of their spirits. She hugged them all and spoke to them. She danced with them and ate treats. And she of course thanked all of them. And this was the last night that she was able to physically see all of her close family with her physical eyes. That night as I tucked her in, she looked at me and she said, "Daddy, I saw everyone tonight! I was able to see everyone!" "I know, Kennedy. I know." I told her. She reached up and gently placed her hand on my cheek. "You, yyyyour eyes are brown like mine! I, I, I, IIII ccccan see you. I rrreaaallly lllovved tttonigth, Dddddaddy, and IIII llooove you!"

I remember going to bed that night fulfilled, happy, and not scared. For I learned something that night. I learned that Kennedy and I were on the same wavelength. We both knew. We both were feeling what was going on and coming up. And, we both were slowly accepting that it was ok.

The next day, my father called me on the phone. He said, "We need to talk." He of course thanked me for a great night at the event. And then he began to gently tell me that he was very concerned and others were as well. He told me he loved me and would always support us, but he then asked, "Don't you think you may be overreacting a little bit to Kennedy's eye disease and situation? Some of your family are concerned and worried about you and what you conveyed yesterday." I had to think for a minute and I had to gain my composure. I literally pulled my car over to the side of the freeway and stopped. I simply said this.

"Dad, I want you to think back to when I was thirteen years old. Imagine, if I was going blind, declining, and having the same issues as Kennedy. And I want you to ask yourself this question. If Heavenly Father told you that you needed to prepare to lose me at that point as your son, what would you have done and how would have you reacted?" There was no hesitation, there was only instant reaction.

"Son, I am in. I get it. I believe you and I will be right by your side throughout this whole thing. I love you," he said.

My eyes were swollen with tears. My heart was full, yet my mind was racing. I had literally sat down our closest of family and told them basically, "You have to accept this." And that conversation was just as hard for them as it was for me. But, something happened that night, that weekend, and that day. I learned that, starting with my own father and now rolling all the way down to strangers in different countries, many, even eventually millions of people, would ACCEPT this and would support us. That day was paramount. It was needed and it was a day that will never be forgotten. For the worst was coming and I now knew that aside from my wife, little family, and Heavenly Father my earthly father had my back. He had always taken care of me, supported me, and loved me. But, more than ever, I would now need him and all of those closest to us and around us. For a storm was on the horizon and the first drops of rain had begun to fall.

CHAPTER 23

You Can't Have Her Yet

Everything seemed normal that night as we went to bed. I tucked Beau, Anna, and Kennedy in. Heather came to bed and we fell asleep. One thing that we were used to was Kennedy waking up in the middle of the night with night terrors. These were becoming all too frequent and it seemed that every night one would occur. We would get up and go to her room and let her know that it was ok. We would calm her down and then help her get back to sleep. They were different than typical nightmares. They seemed so horrific, long, and painful to her. It was as if she was in a different world, a different paradigm, and could not break out of it. She would call out every night for one of us. Over time, I began to just get upset at her. I would tell her that this needed to stop and that she was old enough now to not have nightmares. Unfortunately, I thought that this was just a fabric of her own imagination. But, boy was I wrong.

That night as the house was so peaceful and everyone slept so soundly, we heard Kennedy scream out again. But, this time the scream was accompanied by a loud bang and a crash. It sounded as if a bomb had gone off in her room. Heather and I ran into her room as fast as we could. As we turned on her light, the scene was horrific. Kennedy was on the ground in a full blown seizure. She was convulsing so violently that she had flipped her bed onto the ground and had snapped her mattress frame in the process. We did not know what was going on, other than she was having a seizure. Heather screamed, "Kennedy, Kennedy, Kennedy!" I told her to just move away and let her finish. She was having a seizure. I had witnessed seizures before from a childhood friend, so I knew somewhat what to expect. I cleared things out of the way as best as I could and Heather dove to her side. I really do not know how long that seizure lasted, but it seemed like forever. Finally, she quit convulsing and then began to twitch. Heather put her hand under her head and tried to communicate with Kennedy. She was trying to get Kennedy to respond. I turned her head to the side to make sure her airway was open. But instead things got worse. Kennedy was trying to breathe, but could not. She twitched every 5–10 seconds and she was turning white. As we tried to get her to respond, we realized that her jaw was locked. She was not breathing. Heather began to scream at me, "Do something, Jay, do something!" I tried to open her mouth, but it would not open. I could not get it open. Kennedy began to make a gurgling sound and we could tell she was choking on her own saliva and tongue. She was literally drowning and not able to breathe. I again tried to pry her mouth open. I pulled and pried with all of my strength and could not get it open. In the commotion, Anna woke up and came running in. She looked horrified. She began to cry. I turned to her and said, "Call 911." She called them as I began to lift, turn, and try to position Kennedy into a place where she could breathe. She was slowly going, slowly leaving us. By this point, she looked greenish white. 911 answered and Anna put the phone on speaker. We quickly updated them and they began to tell us what to do. We tried everything. Everything! Kennedy lay lifeless and there was no breath, no sign of life, and no fight from her to breathe. 911 was instructing us to start CPR. We could not, since we could not get her jaw open. As we sat there helpless, watching Kennedy fade, that same feeling hit me as it always did. *"You always listen to the Spirit, which is a higher power, and if you do, you will know exactly what to do."* In our religion and faith, we believe in the power of prayer and in the laying of hands to give a blessing by one with the proper authority. I had been ordained and given the priesthood and serve as an elder in our church. I had the authority. I had the priesthood. All I could do was lay my hands on Kennedy's head and command her to breathe. The instant as I did this, she suddenly relaxed and I grabbed her little jaw and it opened right then!

We were so blessed to have a fire station less than one mile from our home. We heard the sirens and instantly Anna ran to the front door. The EMTs showed up and ran to the room. They immediately began to revive Kennedy. Beau woke up and Anna had him in her arms. He was crying and Heather was crying. I began to cry too and was overcome with emotion. *Not yet*, I thought. *Not yet! He cannot have her yet. Not yet! She cannot go yet!* As I watched them work on her, she suddenly gasped and took a small breath. "Yes, Kennedy, yes! Breathe! Breathe!" we all screamed. She barely began to get a pulse and they quickly loaded her onto a gurney to transport her. They were breathing for her and had started an IV. One of our neighbors happened to be working that night at the fire department and was there on the call. The EMTs were rushing Kennedy out toward the ambulance and asked that one of us go with them. Of course, I told Heather to go. As this neighbor came out and looked at me, I grabbed his arm. "Tell me, tell me, is she going to be ok? Is she ok?" He looked down and bit his lip. He did not want to answer. "Tell me, for heavens sake. Tell me!" He looked back up and said, "you need to pray as hard as you can and get to the hospital quickly. To be honest, I do not know if she will be alive by the time you get there. I am so sorry, Jason. She has gone a long time without breathing and we are having a hard time getting her stable." They rushed out the front door and Heather jumped in the ambulance with them. One of our neighbors had woken from the sirens and offered to take Beau and Anna. I ran to my car and my hand was shaking. *Not yet*, I thought. *Not yet! It is not her time. We are not ready yet.* I had to calm down to even start the car. I said a prayer in my mind and then began driving. Suddenly, I was overcome with more sadness, more despair, and more anxiety than any I had ever experienced in my life. I was speeding to get to the hospital and yet was so overcome with tears, emotion, and the rawness of this. I was worried about Heather and if she was ok. And I was in shock when suddenly I yelled out, "Heavenly Father, YOU CAN'T HAVE HER YET! YOU CAN'T HAVE HER YET!" I began to literally yell out loud at him.

I ran into the hospital and to the emergency room. No one really could tell me where Kennedy was. I began to freak out and to panic a bit. I was pacing and I was crying. A minute later, one of the doctors came out and I recognized him. Another blessing—it was a friend of mine from high school and ironically enough, this friend was the brother of my childhood friend whom I had watched have many seizures. So his compassion was more than just being a doctor; it was a blessing to have him there. "Jason, what are you doing here?" I told him what had happened. He said, " Well, you are in luck. I am the doctor overseeing her. Let's go!" He took me back to Kennedy's room where they had tubes, IVs, and monitors on her. He explained that her seizure had been severe and that she now was in a coma. He said it was typical for this to happen for a short time after a seizure and that she was somewhat stable. But what they could not figure out was why she was not coming out of it. I asked him if she would live. He told me that he thought she would become stable, but that we just needed to wait it out. As time went by, she became more stable, but the doctors were concerned. Kennedy had remained in a post coma for eight hours. This was very atypical and concerning to them. They felt that she should have already come out of this and should have already been coherent. We sat by her bedside and held her hand and rubbed her little head for those eight hours. We knelt and prayed together. We pled for Heavenly Father to save her. And Heather and I consoled one another. As I was able to talk with some of the doctors and other EMT staff, many said that Kennedy was lucky. With the amount of time she quit breathing and with no CPR, they did not know how she came back. But we knew. We had been through enough and experienced enough to know that it was the power of our Heavenly Father through a blessing that brought her back and kept her alive. She was commanded to breathe, and she did. We knew this and that gave us peace. As I sat there staring at her, I silently thanked my Heavenly Father. "Thank you! Thank you for not taking her yet." And as I thanked him, I was overcome with a spiritual sensation that gently whispered to me that she was going to be ok for now. But this experience was just a taste for us of what it would truly feel like to lose her.

As we sat there staring at our daughter, she suddenly opened her eyes and looked around. She woke up and was so confused. She tried to talk, but could not. We explained to her where she was at and that she was ok. She looked around and began to cry. It crushed us. She was just so confused and had no idea what had happened. After an hour or so, she was able to begin to talk. When we asked her if we could get her anything, her response was, "Can I, I hhhave aa Coke?" We laughed and knew that our little Kennedy was back with us. We spent all night and the majority of the next day in the hospital. The doctors were still puzzled. What had caused the seizure? And why was she so comatose afterwards?

We loaded up Kennedy later that day and took her home. She was exhausted. It took her three days to recover from that event. She was completely physically drained and worn out. As we had time to think on this event, another key was added to our key chain. The key of medical doctors and the medical field. This incident opened up the door to eventually finding out that Kennedy had Terminal Juvenile Batten disease. It was this incident that referred us to neurologists, geneticists and MDs of all kinds. It was the key given to us to open up the great door of knowledge, searching, and testing. All of which were needed to find out what was wrong.

Our extended family was wonderful and our friends were all so supportive. Quick word spread about what had happened to Kennedy and immediately we felt all of the support. But, one thing was for sure. There was no question, no hesitation, and nothing that could have confirmed more to me as her dad that she would surely be going home. And we needed to enjoy every moment, every breath, and every day that we would have left with her. For the day would come where my cry would be heard, "YOU CAN'T HAVE HER YET," but it would be returned with an answer of, "I need her, my son. It is her time to come home." And that day was not far away.

CHAPTER 24

SHE KNEW

When Kennedy was really little, she would sit on my lap and yell at the TV. Yes, yell at the TV. And there was good reason, at least in my estimation. Because that was when we had a team. And a dang good team at that. The Utah Jazz.

As she got old enough, we made it a tradition and did everything possible to go to one Jazz game together per year. The fact that we only were able to afford to go to one game together per year made these games very special to us.

And this year was different. Unfortunately, I had already written off going to a game with her. Her sight had really gotten bad and it was getting hard for her to navigate public places. So I did not think anything about going. It seemed that many things were becoming a fabric of my imagination with incredible memories woven into a tapestry of moments that had been quilted within our lives. Going to a Jazz game seemed almost impossible to make happen for Kennedy, and I thought, quite frankly, that she had forgotten.

Boy was I wrong! That year the season started and you would have thought that a bomb had gone off. She immediately began to beg, "Ggggaaaame, Dddddad, gggaamme! Wh, wh, when are weeee gggoing to a Jazz game?" I felt so hesitant because of her disability and digression. I wondered if it would be worth it and how to make it a great experience for her.

In the meantime, we were still aggressively pursuing avenues for more testing, doctors, and experts to address Kennedy's symptoms. By this point, we were talking with anyone who might have any experience with neurological type diseases and symptoms. We were exhausting most of our alepathic efforts and began to investigate all homeopathic efforts as well. As this was going on, my best friend referred me to a very good friend of his whose daughter had been diagnosed with a neurological disease as a little girl. This disease seemed so similar to what Kennedy had been experiencing and exemplifying in her digression. My friend set up a time for this gentleman and me to meet. In the meantime, I arranged 12th row tickets to a Jazz game for Kennedy and me. She had known about this for about a week and just could not get it out of her mind or her mouth. The whole week was Jazz, Jazz, Jazz. And she began to ask if she could meet the Jazz Bear mascot and some of the players. She told me that she wanted a Deron Williams jersey, since he was now her favorite player on the Jazz, and she wanted it in pink. She was so excited and of course was already talking about the Coke and popcorn. Ironically, the meeting I had with this gentleman fell on the same day as this game. We went to lunch together and he was able to listen intently as I told him all about Kennedy. By the end of the conversation, he was able to direct me to a contact of his at the University of Utah genetics department. Due to his daughter's situation, he was well ahead of us medically speaking and able to direct us to this contact. He also wanted to know all about Kennedy's interests, hobbies, and so on. He was so helpful to get us steered in a direction that we had pursued but were waiting on. We were on a list for the genetics department and, with his help, we were accelerated on that list. The meeting and conversation were inspired.

As I arrived home that night, Kennedy was all ready to go—her hair curled, her favorite pants on, and her very favorite shirt. She was dolled up and ready to go on her date with her daddy. We of course drove the truck that night. We cranked our famous Toby Keith songs and, by tradition, we had to stop at a gas station and get a Coke. We sipped on that Coke the whole way down to the game. When we got there, we immediately went to the gift shop where we bought Kennedy a pink Deron Williams jersey. She could not really see it, but she put that thing on in about ten seconds after buying it. We found our seats and of course had our popcorn and Coke in hand. We cheered like crazy and the Jazz were on fire that night. As halftime neared, my phone beeped indicating I'd received a text. I did not recognize the number. The text began to ask me what seats I was sitting in at the Jazz game and section. I was a bit nervous, so I inquired who it was and found out it was the gentleman I had met with earlier that day. He began to tell me not to move from our seats because a surprise was coming. We sat still and then looked down in time to see the Utah Jazz Bear coming up the railing and aisle toward us. Where we were seated was above one of the tunnels, so we were kind of far from an aisle. It did not matter. The Bear climbed up over the railing by the tunnel and came right toward us. He kept coming and coming, and he had a little basket full of Jazz items. Usually he sprays people with party spray or water, but not this time. He walked right up to Kennedy and knelt down right in front of her. The big screen zoomed in on us and her. She could not see him and I had to tell her what was going on. She began to scream and reached out and hugged him. She just kept saying, "Thank you, thank you, thank you!" She said it over and over and over again. "Thank you for coming! I knew you wwwwould ccccome!" She then reached out and did something that only one could experience themselves if in the moment. She pulled the Bear in and gave him a Kennedy's Hug. The kind where she would pull you in and squeeze you so tight and then just kind of shake you. And pull you in again and squeeze you even tighter. She just kept hugging him and would not let go. She told him that she loved him and then the Bear talked to her. Now, rumor has it that he has never spoken to a fan. If that is true, I do not know, but he did to Kennedy. He simply stopped and sat there with his hands at his sides. He looked touched, even with a mask on, and he reached out and said. "Are you Kennedy?" Kennedy said, "Yes." He said, "Thank you, Kennedy, for making my night. All of this stuff is yours. Never forget this night. Never, ever forget it." And with that, he stood up and began to spray people with party spray again. It really was as if the night had stopped.

By the 3rd quarter, Kennedy had to go to the bathroom, so I took her up the long stairs. It was quite a distance and very hard for her. I could tell that she was having not just a hard time seeing, but the start of her walking decline was already affecting her. As we got to the rotunda to go to the restroom, she immediately reminded me that she wanted to meet a player. How in the world was that ever going to happen? Just as I said this, a Utah Jazz Hall of Fame legend literally walked right into us. It was Thurl Bailey. He and Kennedy bumped into each other since she could not see. We apologized and he seemed in a hurry. But then something happened. Kennedy lit up as though she knew what was going on and she reached out and embraced him with a Kennedy's Hug! It melted him and I had to ask for a quick picture. He of course stood for one and then he began to ask all about her. He was supposed to be analyzing the game, but he took the time to talk with her. Once again Kennedy's wish and dream came true!

The Jazz lost that night, but the mood in the air was still radiant. As we left the stadium and stepped outside, it was as if time stopped once more. The feeling in the air was one that I do not know if I will ever experience again. I literally was stopped in my mind and forced to look around and be reminded to feel this moment and never forget it, for much would change in the near future. And then it happened, suddenly that feeling that I had felt so many times began to overwhelm me. I had a strong feeling to stop and pay attention to Kennedy as we walked back to the truck. And as I did, a miracle occurred. When I arrived home, I immediately recorded it in my journal that night. Here is an excerpt from February 9, 2011:

> Heather and I have felt strongly as of late that she [Kennedy] is too strong for this life and that our time with her is growing short. Tonight, we were able to go to go to a Jazz game together. The night was just wonderful being able to spend time with my little angel. As we left the game, Kennedy and I were walking outside together toward the truck. She is so hard to understand right now with her slurred speech. But she took my arm she was holding onto and kind of pulled me in and perfectly and eloquently told me the following: "Dad, there is something that I want to talk to you about. I am going to miss you so much when I die. But, I want you to know that if you go to the Temple and if our whole family goes to the Temple, Mom, Anna, Beau and you and if you go inside of it and go outside of it and go to church and do what's right and choose the right and make right choices and be modest, then we will all be together forever. Dad, that is what you have to do so that we are all together." Her speech was so perfect and the look in her eye was so steady. She has not spoken or looked at me like that ever, if not maybe in years. She was very serious and literally stopped and then held my hand and leaned her head against my chest and said, "Dad, I want you to know that I LOVE YOU SO MUCH. My heart Dad LOVES you so much!" It was a priceless moment and was angelic. It was my true Kennedy speaking to me as she really should be. She then asked where the Temple (Salt Lake) was. I pointed amongst the tall buildings of Salt Lake with all of the bright lights and construction and said, "you can just see the top of it Kennedy." She looked and said, "Oh, there it is. Yep, I can see it! That is where you need to go Dad!" It was a miracle that a girl who could not even see the basketball court from the 12th row, could

> see the Temple. What an experience and what a wonderful Young Woman. I am going to miss her so much!

That night was monumental. As an LDS family, we hold our values very close and dear. And in our religion, we believe that families are sealed together forever through sacred covenants in temples that our church organization has throughout the world. So, for Kennedy to see the temple and to convey that to me was so, so important.

That night was irreplaceable and it officially broke the lock off of our key chain that was holding Heather back from opening up the unfortunate door to the rest of Kennedy's short life with the key from the changing day. As I sat on our bedside and poured my heart out to Heather that night, I completely sobbed. "She knew," I said. "She knew. Her little spirit knows and was opened up to mine tonight. She knows that she is going home, Heather. He needs her home and this is the one thing that I cannot fix as your husband and her dad." That night, although so perfect, was so, so hard. I watched and consoled my wife as I saw a part of her die that night. She still would not accept this and told me that, but she had finally at least let the key open up the door to the next glistening room of rainbows. Full of so many colors, experiences, and moments that no sky on earth could hold them all. And the crazy thing was . . . she knew. It was just so, so hard to accept.

CHAPTER 25

THE BATTLEFIELD

Everything was gathered. All of the pieces to the puzzle were there. Yet they were gathered all over the place. The battlefield of Kennedy's mortal life and our life to lead and guide her to the end had officially begun. We were the generals with the large key chain around our necks that now possessed so many different keys to so many different doors of experiences and life lessons. And the battlefield spread out before us with an unseen army. We could feel the pieces to the puzzle there and we now knew that the biggest battle was coming. Yet we did not want to face this enemy. Because the enemy waiting upon that field was Terminal Juvenile Batten disease. And in a short time, we would meet it face-to-face. We would piece the puzzle together and slowly complete the fate of its outcome while at the same time produce the beauty of this puzzle so jumbled, yet so beautiful once complete. It was now Kennedy's turn to begin to touch the world in ways that she never had done before. The battlefield would become the breeding ground of picking up the wounded in heart, the lost in spirit, and the many wandering souls who would be touched individually to watch a great battle turn into a beautiful victory. One where no one would want to raise the flag of victory and eventually bury the casualty of such a war. The casualty would be the death of Kennedy Ann Hansen who would lead us all through this battlefield as our captain with such grace, such dignity, and such humility. The battlefield, in the end, would be covered with a field of roses that had produced many painful thorns along the way. Yes, the battlefield was upon us, but we were armed and ready to go.

Kennedy was relentless with her love. But the battlefield had its piercing arrows as well. Kennedy's eyesight was deteriorating at a speed that made any race car seem slow. She was showing the true signs of being completely blind and there was no shield that could stop such a penetrating blow. Her need to read books, see pictures, and participate in activities with major physical assistance was now upon us. Yet her smile broadened, her hugs expanded, and her love deepened. Why was she not getting frustrated? Why was she not giving up, crying, or whining to us about this? It seemed that she was growing internally while dwindling externally. As this slow and cruel physical transformation occurred, all we could really do was watch, love, help, and support her.

Each and every year, a massive dance recital was held by the company where she and Anna were enrolled in dance. This recital was one that the whole family looked forward to. It was their mom's time to doll them up and curl their hair. A time to make them feel like beauty queens with layers of makeup and incredible costumes. It was always a big day and a big deal around our house. As this day came in Kennedy's 9th grade year, we were all curious. How was this going to turn out? What was going to happen? They were questions that burned within all of us and concerned us greatly. Heather had already had many discussions with her studio and dance instructors. And it was clear that Kennedy needed and was receiving extra help from those instructors beyond the norm. But they were so patient, so loving, and so kind. They could only help Kennedy as they felt the love and help back to them.

As the big night arrived, Kennedy was ready to perform. She had enrolled in cheer at the dance studio that year and she believed that she was the greatest cheerleader on earth. As we attended the recital, we held our breath as Kennedy walked out with the other girls. She was assisted into her spot on the stage and the performance began. From the start, she was completely off sync with the other girls. They would jump and she would jump a second later, they would cheer and raise their pom-poms and she would a couple seconds later. As this went on, one thing was for sure. Her voice and the cheers themselves were dead on from her! You could hear her belting them throughout the entire auditorium! And as the group continued, one parent behind us commented, "What is that girl doing? She is completely off from the rest of the group." As hard as it was, I sat and listened as this innocent bystander, who knew nothing about Kennedy, continued to speak out loud and question the situation. I was filming Kennedy and Heather was at my side. Without question, our hearts were full and our tears were streaming. What was

Kennedy doing? What was happening? She was doing her best! Without complaint. Without hesitation and without help. She was smiling, she was beaming, and she was, in her mind, the very best cheerleader on that stage. As the comments continued behind me and the performance came to an end, I put the camera down and slowly turned around to this stranger. I simply said, "That girl on that stage who you were asking about, well, that is our daughter Kennedy. And what she was doing up there was her best. That is what she was doing. See, she is blind and is currently losing all of her motor skills. And for her, what she was doing up there was nothing less than her very best and I am so, so, so proud of her." Silence entered that row and this poor woman apologized to me. Yet, I was fine. I was not offended, nor was I upset. Because the battlefield was not one that any of us had wanted, asked for, or even created. The battlefield was there because of a genetic disease that, at the time, none of us even knew she had. And the comments, the stares, the ignorant scoffs, judgments, and moments were all done in innocence. For no one really knew, could know, or could react to a disease and situation such as this one at that moment in time.

CHAPTER 26

THE TIDE

Everything changed and would continue to change quickly. We had been running our own business for many, many years and it was growing like mad. But as we continued down the path of testing for Kennedy, things were becoming real. Our health insurance premium cost was skyrocketing. The insurance we did have was good, but not great. We had begun Kennedy on medication for her seizures and it was not cheap to do so. We were feeling a bit hopeless, because by this point the visits to her specialists were so frequent that we felt like timeshare owners of the hospital where we took Kennedy. As this went on, inner feelings began to pull and tug within us and that same feeling that had overtaken us so many times before hit us very, very hard. *"You always listen to the Spirit, which is a higher power, and if you do, you will know exactly what to do."* We were being told to find full-time employment and to get on a solid medical plan with a solid health savings account to pay for Kennedy's medication. In reviewing the costs of our insurance, the costs of her medication, and the costs of her tests and medical search, yes, we were scared. Yes, we were nervous. We were spending almost as much on those bills as on our house payment, if not more some months. With the referral to the genetics department at the University of Utah hospital, we were well on our way to testing for Kennedy in a whole different way. Unfortunately, not all the tests that we were about to embark on were covered by insurance. Each test would be costly and each test would be different. The tests would help unravel the genetic DNA of Kennedy to find out what was and had been going on from a genetic standpoint within her.

Heather and I were prepared for anything and everything to help assist Kennedy through this process. As we moved forward with faith, we prayed. Oh, how we prayed. And as we did, that higher power whispered to us to go and get full-time employment with a solid company. I had not worked for someone directly for over five years. So this would be a major adjustment. As the search began and as we met with and investigated several companies, we were given several offers. Ultimately, we took an offer from a company that was over an hour and a half away from our home. We had other offers just as good and some that were even better than this company from a financial standpoint. The benefits were very good and we were open with the company about Kennedy's situation. At this point we still did not know exactly what she had, so it was all an open scenario. But this much we did know: we had been listening. We had been praying, and we had been living as best as we knew how. And because of that, we were told to take this position and job.

As we did, we slowly transitioned out of the old insurance, allowing it to cover the end of Kennedy's testing. Ultimately, the transition went smoothly and everything landed how it was supposed to. And now looking back, without that coverage and insurance, our path and our situation could have and would have resulted much differently than it did.

But, the tide of life most definitely changed. As Kennedy's father, I was going to do everything that I could to make sure that she was taken care of and that she was comfortable. My life dramatically changed since I was used to calling all of the shots of our business and driving to an office a short five minutes away. My new life consisted of rising at 4:30 a.m., maintaining and checking on my business and preparing for my day. The commute to work was a nintey-minute drive, but at times it could be up to three hours depending on weather and traffic. The new job most definitely fit my background in sales and executive management. I was hired as a senior VP of sales and was placed within a brilliant circle of some incredibly talented and intelligent people. Being new required massive learning and adjustment. And on top of it, I was feeling the unending pressure of spending time with Kennedy and our family. I knew she was leaving us, I just did not know when or how. As the days turned into weeks and the weeks into months, I could only work harder. I did not sleep much at first. It seemed that the goal was to make this job happen and still keep our company running. That was a tall order. I had to step away from our company and its day-to-day operations. I had to rely on our employees and their talents and abilities. And for my personality, this was tough to do.

But, the tide was pulling and I felt alone at times on an empty shore just trying to get all I could done before the oceans of life would fill back up my bay. And at the top of my list and beyond any other priority was Kennedy. She was my number one priority. To find out what was going on with her and to get her the very best medical help, advice, and treatment possible for her condition that was still unknown.

By January 2013, we were well on our way with the genetic testing. Kennedy had experienced many, many grand mal seizures and we were meeting with so many neurologists, pediatric neurologists, and specialists for her. After being introduced to the genetics department, one of our neurologists simply told us that there was nothing else that they could do. Sometimes children have diseases unknown and their lives are cut short without ever knowing what they really had.

This did not upset us; this did not hurt us. This simply drove us even more into finding out what was going on with Kennedy. We were persistent and oh how Kennedy's mother, Heather, was persistent. She would document everything! Every seizure, every medication, every appointment, and every digression and progression of Kennedy. She was a full-time caregiver, secretary, mother, and best friend to Kennedy. Her energy was relentless and unparalleled. Her love was unending and her faith seemed unbreakable. She was going to find out what her little girl had and was never, ever going to give up.

I believe that without Heather we never would have found out what Kennedy had. You see, it was confirmed to me. I already knew that she was going home and would be leaving us. And I felt that every single day of my life. I would look at her and feel the tide of emotions pulling so hard at me that I wanted to cry, throw up, and smile all at the same time. For me, I wanted to know, yet I did not. I had received the news from the most important doctor of all. The one who created, loved, and sent us here to experience all of this. Our Heavenly Father.

So for me, yes, I was tired, getting worn, and feeling the physical wear of it all. The double duty of work, combined with family, church responsibilities, and other social aspects was beginning to take its toll. But as the tide pulled at me, I found that I began to be more efficient. I would look out across the vast bay of our lives as it would empty out in the morning and realize that I must accomplish everything I could within a day before the water would fill back up. And I learned a valuable lesson from my father. He told me simply at this time in my life, "Do not take one day at a time. Take one breath at a time. Just breathe and take it one breath, one second, one minute at a time." So I did that. I began to look at my time differently. If I saw a minute that was important, then everything else would become unimportant. And I began to apply this to our little family as I knew that every second counted for our time with our dear little Kennedy.

As for Heather and I, we were becoming stronger. We were communicating much more and, more than anything, we were a better team. Kennedy's night terrors were increasingly horrific. She experienced dementia, pain, and seizures at night. She continued to scream every night, multiple times a night, and Heather would be right there by her side. I do not believe Heather slept much during this time of our lives. It seemed like she was always up and down, up and down, constantly running to the screams and aid of Kennedy. Kennedy needed her not just physically, but emotionally as well. Kennedy would scream out for her and no one else. The two of them earned a distinct respect for one another. A bond that in time would completely and physically wipe Heather out, yet she would miss it so badly after Kennedy was gone. And for me . . . well, for me the nights became lonely.

I would reach over to feel the warmth of my beautiful wife, only to feel the cold emptiness of her spot beneath my hands. I was beginning to miss her, even though she was a short twenty feet away down the hallway in Kennedy's room. This became the routine: get ready for bed, pray together, and then talk until fairly late hours of the night. Those talks now are priceless to us because we would discuss so many concerns and things on our minds. Most important, we would discuss Kennedy's future and the futures of Anna and Beau. Our children by far were and are our largest and most sacred blessing of our lives. After these discussions, we would fall asleep only to be awoken a short time later as I would watch my beautiful wife leave me for the night. I was used to this. It had been going on for years. But now it was bad. Really bad. Because Kennedy needed her all night. I would toss and turn and look at the clock each night. I knew that 4:30 a.m. would come very soon and I was not looking forward to the battle of the next day.

On one night, I was feeling a little alone, a little frustrated, and quite a bit lost. For years, I had knelt across the bed from my wife and each night told her that she needed to get ready. To get ready to lose Kennedy and to prepare to send her home. But, she could not, would not, and was not accepting this part of the journey. And I could not argue with her, or change her position. I did not blame her for how she felt. Her hope was that we could and would find out what disease Kennedy had and would be able to treat, fight, and address the disease, saving Kennedy in the end. But on this night, I really felt at the end of my rope. I just could not carry this burden alone any longer. I was beginning to think that I was going crazy. I mean, we had experienced years of testing, years of digression, and too many doctor and hospital visits to count. We had exhausted so many resources and now our last resource was genetic testing. For the first time in this journey and my life, the tide was pulling so heavily at me that it was pulling me out to the vast ocean of no return. I did not know if I could carry this any longer alone.

As I fell asleep that night, I drifted into a very, very deep sleep. I did not even hear Kennedy's screams or Heather get up that night to go and help her. At around 2 a.m., I woke up and looked over to the sight of Heather sitting in a chair with a light on. She was just sitting, looking down with tears streaming down her face. I looked at her and it was one of the most serious and caring looks I had ever seen before on her face. I quickly got out of bed and went and knelt down by her side. "What is it? Heather, what is wrong?" I said. At this point, I knew that she was most definitely experiencing a lot of emotion. We sat there together for probably a good minute before she finally told me. She said, "You were right. This whole time, you were right!" She looked at me and began to cry harder. "Heavenly Father woke me up tonight. Not Kennedy. I was awoken out of my sleep and was specifically told that he needs her home. I was told that you were right and that she will be going home soon. I was told that we need to be together on this and that we need to get ready and that we will have answers soon as to what she has disease-wise. Jason, I am so sorry that I ignored you. I feel horrible and you probably are so upset with me. For the last several years, you have carried this alone. Alone! And I was too selfish, too in denial and too absorbed in my own selfish feelings and desires to accept this."

I sat back on my knees. My head dropped down to my chest and I began to cry. I cried and cried and cried until I raised my head and had a smile on my face. Yes, a smile. "Heather, I love you, and I would never, ever and have never been upset with you. I am so happy now that I am not alone on this! Finally, I will have someone by my side that understands. In my mind, this is a huge relief and a huge blessing. I love you so much and am so thankful to you for being open, righteous, and available to the Spirit of Heavenly Father." She leaned forward and I sat up. We embraced and we wept. We probably sat there for another five minutes, just crying. The tide was officially pulling at us, but we were not going to let it win. We would let it pull and tug the water from the bay, but we would not allow it to destroy us or Kennedy's journey. I was so relieved and so grateful to have her in. Fully in! As we sat hugging, suddenly the scream, "Mom, Mom, MOMMMMMY!!!!" rang out from Kennedy's room. Only this time, we did not run. This time we did not scurry or rush to her aide. This time it was different. For now, we knew. We knew that there would be no rush, no prescription, no test, no medical treatment, and no turning back physically for Kennedy. We both now knew and we both were now sewn together even tighter. Weaved together as a fabric so tight that literally nothing could pull us apart.

As we walked down the hallway and into Kennedy's room, we both felt it. The key of acceptance had now been placed around Heather's neck and she was ready. She now felt the burden and the great responsibility that I had been feeling for years. But now, in a way, we could breathe a little easier. We sat down on Kennedy's bed together and we calmed her down. We all sat there that night and just held each other. Kennedy was in seventh heaven having us both there with her. She could literally feel our love and she knew that something was different. "Dddaddy? Dad? Why y, y, you here?" she asked. She was so used to just having Heather by her side and just having her to help her. But on that night, we all were together and we all felt a new bond and a new beginning. The tide that had been pulling so hard at us would continue to pull, but we now were all on the shore together and we were not going to be dragged out to the endless depths of the oceans of despair. And that night, unlike other nights, was the first night that Heather woke up before Kennedy. It was the first night that together we faced the tide—completely together, the three of us joined in a little cocoon, a cocoon wrapped in love that would pull us in so tight until the one day that Kennedy would receive her wings and fly away.

CHAPTER 27

Tickle Me, Daddy, Tickle Me

Kennedy screamed out from her bed, "Tickle me, Ddddaddy, tttickle me! Mmmmonster game, monster!" Things had changed since Heather received her answer from Heavenly Father about Kennedy going home. It seemed that from that moment on that Kennedy's decline became even more severe. So, in my mind, I had to spend more time with her. Knowing what she had was important, but not as important to me as the time that we had left with her. I would work so hard all day and then come home at night to be with her and the family. And every night we would play the tickle game. I would lay down by her and roar like a monster. All the while, I would tickle her until she would scream so loud that at times she would spit while trying to control her emotions. This became a daily ritual for us and I loved every minute of it.

Meanwhile, Heather was taking a different angle. Now that she really knew we would be losing her, Heather was even more aggressive with getting Kennedy the tests and the doctor's appointments needed to find out what she had. Heather's world was completely different than any of ours. Heather had to know what she had because it would make the caring of Kennedy easier to understand and more comfortable. Heather is so smart when it comes to Kennedy and to the other children. She became relentless in following up with the doctors and the tests that were occurring. She wanted to know, she needed to know, and she was going to find out what Kennedy truly had.

We completed the first round of genetic tests on Kennedy. The tests were administered and then we would wait 4–6 weeks for the results.

After waiting on the first round of tests, we were anxious, scared, and ready to hear the results from the attending doctor assigned to Kennedy. We met with the doctor at the hospital who was one of the most loving and caring doctors ever assigned to Kennedy through her journey. This doctor sat us down and first spent some time with Kennedy. She talked with her, and she asked her about her interests, her life, and her family. She truly tried to gain a relationship with her, which she would continue to do for the rest of her involvement with Kennedy. She then asked to meet with us without Kennedy in the room.

She proceeded to tell us that the first round of genetic tests came back negative and showed normal. What this meant was that nothing abnormal was discovered with Kennedy. We were a bit frustrated and we looked at each other and took each other's hand. We told the doctor that it was ok and we were ready for the next step. The doctor suddenly became extremely emotional. She began to cry. She trembled and her hands were shaking. She reached over and she handed us a paper. On the paper was the acronym JNCL and the words Juvenile Neuronal Ceroid Lipfuscinosis. We had no idea what this meant. This was a very big and long medical term.

We looked at her with a look of question on our faces and a look for some direction and help. She was so nervous and she was so caring, yet so uneasy. She then proceeded to tell us that when she was in medical school, she had done a thesis on a disease called Batten disease. She told us that its official name was NCL and that in teenagers it is referred to as JNCL. She continued on to tell us that the disease is fatal with no cure and no history of any survivors. She then became even more emotional and shared with us that she truly felt that this was the disease that Kennedy had. She also said that she was frustrated because she had been watching Kennedy and our family and she truly wanted a different diagnosis and answers as well. But as she had been assigned to, watched, tested, and worked with Kennedy and our family, Kennedy had shown textbook signs and symptoms of this disease. And she continued over and over to state that she hoped and prayed with everything in her heart that Kennedy did not have this disease, because she felt it was the nastiest disease she had ever encountered.

As we sat there, that same feeling came over me that I always would feel. At that very moment and that very time, I had to excuse myself from that little hospital room. I asked Heather to go and get Kennedy and said I just had to excuse myself. She asked, "Where are you going? What are you doing?" I just had to leave. I had to get up and leave. So I did. I walked outside of the office and gave Kennedy an enormous hug and I proceeded to walk furiously down the hospital hallway.

I looked around and being in a children's hospital, I began to really take notice of all that was around me. I noticed the families, parents and siblings. I really, for the first time, began noticing the many sick children, most of them terminally sick, sitting in hospital beds or doctors' waiting areas or being wheeled down the hallway on a gurney. And I noticed the many paintings, toys, visitors, clowns, and people who were there to brighten these children's day and make them feel some hope. I felt like I was in a whirlwind and I could not breathe. I had to get outside. I had to get fresh air. I had to just walk. I ultimately made it to the outside door where I walked outside and immediately bent over and placed my hands on my knees. I was having a hard time breathing and was having an even harder time controlling my emotions. As that doctor told and explained to us about Batten disease, it was confirmed to me that this was the disease Kennedy had. I felt overwhelmed, yet I felt relief. I still did not have 100 percent confirmation on paper from a doctor. I only had a guessed opinion. But I had been here so many times before. I had experienced being told spiritually that something was what it was. And every time I was told, it always came to pass. But I had waited so long. We had searched so hard and prayed and prayed and prayed. And I had been told specifically that we would be losing her. Now, finally, we were at the edge of the iceberg and it was melting fast. We were so close and now I knew. It was confirmed. This was the disease. This was the piercing javelin that would ultimately break our worldly hearts. I gathered my breath and turned back and traveled as fast into the hospital as I had out of it. I felt bad that I had left. I felt bad that I had just got up and bailed at such a critical moment in conversation. But, truly for the first time ever in my life, I felt extreme anxiety. I felt the weight that many had spoken of and it now was real. I entered the doctor's office and sat back down. "Are you ok?" Heather asked.

"I am fine." I said. "I just do not feel that well and had to get some fresh air." As I sat there in despair, shock, and pain, Kennedy slowly moved toward me and put her arm around me. "It's ok, Daddy, it's ok," she said. She slowly began to rub my back as we sat and completed some paperwork and scheduled the next test. Kennedy had a smile from ear to ear and she just kept rubbing my back. She had no fear, no anxiety, and no knowledge of what was to come.

The conversation that the doctor had with us revealed the harshness, cruelty, and damaging effects of this disease. It literally was the most cruel and nasty disease that we had ever heard of. We left that office and went and got a sandwich and a treat in one of the hospital cafes. We sat there and somehow, someway, we began laughing. Laughing and laughing and laughing. It was as if we were just having one of the best days of our life. How was this possible? How was this happening when we had basically been notified that we were finally close to the devastating, yet realistic news that we had been searching for for so, so long? I remember seeing those big brown eyes that could not see us gleaming. Food exploded from the mouth that contained the cutest and most chubby cheeks you have ever seen. Kennedy was so happy and her spirit was radiating. The key chain now officially had another key. The key of radiating peace. A peace that would be upon us very shortly and very soon. This key would be felt, needed, and experienced many, many times in the next fifteen months of our lives and of Kennedy's life.

That night, Kennedy screamed out again, "Tickle me, Daddy, tickle me!" But now it was different. Now it was special. It was no longer the game that the two of us had played for so long together and for so many years. For as I tickled her that night and as I heard her laugh, I began to have an ever stronger knowledge that it was close, very close. I stayed up the entire night that night and read about Juvenile Batten disease. The next morning when the sun rose, I was discouraged, and I was a bit hurt. For I had known for over three years that we would be losing her, yet I did not know to what. After reading about this disease, all I could do was recognize that Kennedy was built for it. That she was one of the few angels on earth who had been, could be, and would be able to endure such a rare and devastating disease with so many terrible effects.

I felt a nudge within me to go and wake up Kennedy and tickle her. But I did not have to wake her up. It was around 5:30 a.m. and she was already up as usual. She was walking around the house and in the kitchen. I went up behind her and scared her. She laughed and screamed out, "Tickle me, Daddy, tickle me. . . . Pppplease tickle me." I tickled her that morning until I could not any longer. It was a tickle torture session that basically ended with hugs and her telling me, "I, I, I, llllove y, you, Daddy! I, l, l, l, love you!" And then it was done. My little girl and our time together would be short-lived and end shortly. Those sessions would soon be gone, her laugh would disappear, and the sounds of her telling me she loved me would slip away physically, but would be with us spiritually forever.

CHAPTER 28

June 5, 2013

Another genetic test was administered and another negative and perfect result came back to us. This time we were baffled, as were the doctors involved. We really thought that this test would give us the definitive direction, diagnosis, and news that we did and did not want. The doctor told us that we had one test left and if that test did not bring back any positive results or a diagnosis, we would probably never ever know what disease Kennedy had.

The final test was administered and our hopes were high. We had to wait for the results for a few months like we did before and we really did not know when the results would come. The typical pattern was the results would come in and would be followed up by a phone call for a face-to-face appointment and a letter in the mail.

We were up to our eyeballs busy with our business, employment, church callings, and kids' activities. Of course we had not forgotten, but we also did not have a day circled on the calendar with hopes of an answer. So, school was let out and Kennedy and Anna were stoked for the summer. Beau was following Kennedy around everywhere, and we had purchased a brand new puppy we named Aggie. Kennedy was taking this puppy everywhere with her like a little baby. She draped Aggie over her shoulder and would sneak her into her room, against her mother's will, and snuggle with her in her bed. She would feel her ears and stroke her little nose. Aggie is a Drahthaar, which is a breed of a German wirehaired pointer, so she has a beard and long hair. Kennedy would feel her little beard and pull on her long hair. Kennedy was so happy to have her at home and to have her for the summer!

As school let out, I immediately left for a high adventure camp in Moab with a group of Varsity Scouts. I had been a Varsity Scout leader and church leader to these boys for many years and we had planned an amazing adventure that would begin on June 5, 2013.

As June 5, 2013 came, we loaded up the boys and left for Moab. It is about a four-hour journey from where we live. As we drove, something inside told me that all was not well at home. I could feel it and knew once again through that same feeling I had felt so many, many times in my life. *"You always listen to the Spirit, which is a higher power, and if you do, you will know exactly what to do."* I tried to call Heather, but I did not have phone service for a good portion of the drive since the camp is in a remote area. As we drove, I had a feeling of peace overcome me that was different. Something was different and something had changed. As we arrived in Moab and set up camp, my phone service came back. There was a message from Heather. She was crying on the message and said, "Please, please call me as soon as you can. It is about Kennedy. She is ok, but you need to call me." I immediately dialed her number. She said, " Jason, you need to go on a walk and go away from the boys and the other leaders for a moment where you can talk alone with just me and you."

I walked far away from our camp and questioned, "What is wrong Heather? What is going on?"

Through tears, sobs, and muffles, she said, "The doctor called and said it was urgent that we meet with her today. I told her that you were gone and she said that it was an emergency to meet and she could not give information from the final test without your presence or you being on the phone. We tried calling you and could not get a hold of you. I told her, 'Just tell me. Please, Doctor, just tell me.' She began to cry on the phone, Jason, and told me that it has been confirmed. Kennedy has been diagnosed with Terminal Juvenile Batten disease. Jay, we were right. You were right. It is terminal. She is going to die and we do not have that much time. What are we going to do? What are we going to do? There is no cure, very little treatment, and most kids have never lived past their early twenties with this disease."

I believe that, at that very moment, my spirit left my body and traveled back to my little home and family in West Haven, Utah. For instantly, I felt different. I felt a different presence. I felt a burden so large taken from me and a new one even heavier placed upon me. "Jay, are you there? Jay, what are we going to do?" My heart stopped and exploded a new heartbeat that was different and to this day is forever different. "We,

Heather, are going to prepare her to go home. That is what we are going to do." There was pure silence on both ends of the phone, followed by tears. We both just cried. I could feel her with me as she could feel me with her. We were bound together for time and all eternity and we had already been through so, so much.

"Heather, we know! We finally know. We have waited for so long for this news. And this is not the news that either one of us wanted to receive ever in our lives. Have you told Kennedy? Does she know?" Heather responded, "Of course not, I would never do that without you here."

"I will pack up and come home. You need me and the family needs me. I will be home in five hours. I love you and we will get through this. I will do EVERYTHING in my power as her father, your husband, provider, and patriarch of our family to make her life the very best it can be for what we have left. I promise you that! I promise!"

There was another silence on the phone. "No, Jay, no. You need to stay with those boys. They need you. You have everything planned and coming home will not change this diagnosis. She has time. Little time, but time. Coming home is not going to heal her or change that."

"Did the doctor tell you how much time we have?" I asked.

"No," Heather said. "She wants to meet with us face-to-face when you get back and as soon as possible."

I just wanted to pack up my truck and go home! I wanted to hold my wife first and then my little family in my arms. All of them, not just Kennedy! I wanted to envelope them in my arms, my love, and my life at that instant. I wanted them to know that it was all going to be ok. But I sat 270 miles away in a scout campground with a bunch of boys and Scout leaders. Instantly, the thought came to me to have a prayer with Heather. As weird as this sounds, we said a prayer over the phone and I told her how much I loved her. I also told her that I was going to go and find the bishop from our church group who was on the trip with us and speak with him. I was very intent on just packing up and going home. My heart was broken, my heart was full, and my mind was intensely heavy. I just wanted to fix it all, but I had already crossed that bridge and knew I could not.

I hung up the phone and slowly found my way back to the Scout camp. We had brought RVs for the leaders and cooking needs. Our bishop was inside of his RV reading when I opened the door. This man most definitely was and is a man of God and was called of God in my belief. He was our neighbor and had known Kennedy since she was six years old. As I opened the door and he looked at me, he immediately could tell that something was wrong. I looked at him and sat down. My breathing quickened, but my voice was calm. I looked at my good friend, spiritual leader, and bishop and proceeded to tell him about my phone call with Heather.

Fortunately for us, he was completely aware of the situation with Kennedy and also aware of many of the experiences that we had endured. He was also aware of and believed in my feelings and experience being told we would lose Kennedy. I looked at him and said, "I think I should go home. But Heather really feels I should stay here. I just want to be there for my little family. But I also know that Kennedy would want me to stay with these boys and complete the high adventure that we have planned." You see, Kennedy only wanted what was always best for everyone else and not herself. She truly only wanted others to be happy and others to experience all that life has in it that is good. We had planned this trip for over one year and we were ready for an amazing adventure. The other part of the story was that there were three of these boys that I had been their scout leader and church leader since they were twelve and this was our last trip together. So there still was a lot of emotion on the other end of the weighted balance to consider. My bishop sat and looked at me, and he had tears well up in his eyes. He walked over and he put his arm around me. He told me that he loved me and that first and foremost he wanted me to know that all would be ok. He then asked if I could leave for a few minutes so that he could pray and think about what he felt would be the right thing to do.

I saw him turn around and begin to walk toward a room at the back of his RV. I stood up and opened the trailer door to leave. As I did, I looked over at him only to see him stop dead in his tracks, turn around, and say this. "Kennedy's calling and election are made sure. Your place is here." It caught us both by surprise. It was as if it was someone else who was saying those words. It was as if the voice of both comfort, answers, and clarity came clearly and smoothly from my bishop's mouth.

But I believed him. I believed and still to this day believe that he is a man of God. I shook my head up and down and said, "Ok, ok. I get it. Let me go and call Heather and a few other people and I will plan on staying." I went on a short walk alone in the middle of the desert sand in Moab, Utah. It was hot. It was evening and it was quiet. I found a place where I could sit alone for a minute and just think. I began to think and then I began to pray to my Heavenly Father. This had been such a journey to get to this point. So much had happened! So much had occurred and so much was occurring! I sat there pondering and praying out loud to him in a whisper. This was real and this was really happening! As I sat there, if you can believe, I thanked Him! I thanked Him for allowing me to know before the tempest of the storm hit. For allowing me to prepare myself, my wife, and those around us for the inevitable. I also pled with Him. I pleaded now for His support. I pleaded for his direction and his love. I pleaded for assistance and angels to be with me throughout this journey. And more than anything I pleaded for Kennedy, Anna, Beau, and Heather. I pleaded that His comfort would instantly be upon them.

I asked that they would be ok without me. As I sat there in the middle of nowhere with no one around but my Heavenly Father and me, something happened. Something that to this day will forevermore sit with me as a miracle. I recognized that our Heavenly Father had blessed us in not having any more biological children for all of those years. Because the one thing I had learned about Batten disease was that it is a genetic disorder that most likely all of our children would have been born with. To say I was thankful would be an understatement. I WAS STRENGTHENED! I felt a new energy. A different kind of energy and feeling that hit the walls within my soul with such fury and such explosion. I felt it and I knew that I would need it. It was as if my soul and my physical nature was doubled in comparison to what I was before.

Looking back, I did not really understand what was happening, but I do now. For from that day moving forward and for one year exactly to the day, I would need that energy. I would need that additional support from on high. In exactly one year from that day, on June 5, 2014, I would lay our daughter and angel Kennedy Ann Hansen to rest. And as I would, I would look back and fully know that I had given and gave her everything—EVERYTHING that I had as her father. But more important than that, I would also look back and shake my head at how we lived, survived, and traveled through that last year of Kennedy's life without breaking, without complaining, and without giving up. The true measure of my manhood, fatherhood, husband-hood, and friend-hood would be tested beyond human limits for the next twelve months of our lives to the literal second. And those words that this bishop uttered, "Kennedy's calling and election are made sure," would prove themselves to all who came in contact with Kennedy and her story. For those words would assure all of us as we knew that a place was reserved for her in heaven as she left us all behind with a lifetime full of memories and a year full of miracles.

As I sat in that desert and listened to the crickets chirping and the birds singing, I looked up at the star-blanketed sky. One thing was for sure. June 5th for the rest of my life would become a hallowed day. A day that would soon become more than a birthday, more than a holiday, and more than an anniversary. June 5th for the rest of our lives would become a celebration day.

CHAPTER 29

DADDY, YOU'RE HOME!

It seemed that those days in Moab were some of the longest and shortest days of my life. The leaders were told of my situation, but we kept it from the boys. The high adventure camp was a riot and the boys had a blast. Looking back, I now know that I was experiencing grief. Great grief and great emotion, along with great happiness. The reality was finally here and I do believe it was a blessing to be away from our home and have some time to process all that was just revealed to us. I would look at these boys, who many were the same age as Kennedy, and I would just think, *Is this really happening*?

What was I going to do without her? What was her sister, Anna, and her brother, Beau, going to do without her? And most importantly, the lifeline, the caregiver, the eyes, and the constant companion to Kennedy, her mother—what was she going to do without Kennedy? How was she going to cope? How was I going to console when I needed consoling? What was going to happen? How fast were things going to go? What were the drastic effects of this monster called Batten?

All of these emotions clung close to my heart as we gathered for a meeting the last night on a moonlit evening in Moab on the edge of a cliff. The stars dazzled us with brightness and the moon was so bright that no flashlights were necessary. I sat and listened to these young men as they each shared emotions through personal testimony about their values, families, friends, and lives. Many of them thanked me that night for the trip and how they had learned lifelong lessons. As I sat and listened, tears slowly ran down my cheeks. My heart was so full and yet so empty. I felt on that rock the sweetness of Kennedy. She wanted me there and it was the right choice. She needed me to be there and not at home. These boys who were turning into men needed me there as well and it would only be a few days in the distant future that they would greatly return the favor with a gift to Kennedy that will forever be embedded in their minds and hearts.

As I arrived home, I will never forget the hug that followed my entry into our home. There was a different feeling in our home that day, and the hug that followed my entry was from a sobbing wife who needed me back that day. She was at odds with all of this and more than anything was ready for some answers from our doctor and the hospital. She knew her role as Kennedy's mother and caretaker, and she had been through this before. She knew the vast desert that lay before her that would somehow have to produce flowers from growing cactuses. She knew that Kennedy was going home and the reality was now the hardest part.

I took her to our room, where we had a very short discussion. After hugging her, I selfishly just wanted to find my little Kennedy and hug her with all my might. Before leaving our room, we did kneel down together and pray. We prayed for strength that day and we prayed for direction. We prayed to know how to lead our family through this desert and how to provide water to the thorny and painful cactuses that somehow would produce blossoms. We truly felt that way and it was emotional. Very emotional.

I stood up from the side of our bed and I traveled down the hallway to Kennedy's room. I could see her from a distance. Her long beautiful brown hair hung all the way to her waist. She was kneeling on the ground and playing with Monster High dolls on her floor. She was facing away from me and I could not see her face. I slowly entered her room and then stopped. All I could do was stare at her profile as she turned sideways and paused, knowing someone was there. "Dddad, Daddy, is that you?" Immediately the tears came and I said, "Yes, Dee Dee, yes, it is me."

She jumped to her feet and reached out toward me with a small little leap. "Daddy, you're home!" I can remember the feeling of her breathing on my shoulder and neck and her warm embrace. I can remember seeing the smile on her face and the sound of her squealing. She was now screaming and jumping up and down as she hugged me. "Ddddadddy, yyyou're home! You're home! You're home! I, I, I, I mmmmissed you so much! I missed you!" She could not see me. She did not know. She had no idea what was going on.

I just sat and held her for a very long moment that day. I hugged her as I wept quietly. I did not want to let go. I never, ever wanted to let go. As she hugged me and I hugged her, I turned slowly to see my beautiful wife with her hand covering her mouth staring at us from the hallway. She was crying and she was struggling. Together we held in this moment with Kennedy not knowing and not caring or even understanding. Kennedy had her daddy home and that was all that mattered. "Play, Daddy, play!" she screamed. I immediately knelt down by her and began to play. I cannot even tell you to this day what we played. I do not even quite remember. But, I can remember how I felt. I NEVER and I repeat NEVER wanted to leave that room. There was an angelic feeling there. I turned my phone off and shut out the world that day. I ignored everything but her and my family.

As I went to bed that night, the words could not leave my mind as they echoed loudly in my ears! "Daddy, you're home! Daddy, you're home!" That night I went to bed with a smile, knowing that very soon those same sentiments would be coming to Kennedy as she would embrace her Father in Heaven and He would say, "Kennedy, you're home. Kennedy, you're home." And that feeling, that knowledge, and that peace would resonate, carry, and provide happiness for the months that were now to come.

CHAPTER 30

THE PROMISE

The key chain around our necks now felt heavy. We had just added another key. The key of a terminal diagnosis. That group of words was so hard to accept, yet so necessary to move forward. Our key chain had begun to feel heavy, but now felt like a gauntlet around our necks. We had two choices. Choice #1 was to allow the heaviness of this key chain and all that was on it to drag us down to the deepest depths of our life's sea. Choice #2 was to move forward with faith, happiness, hope, and love. To become a lighthouse on top of the hill above our life's sea. To be that beacon to all who would become involved in Kennedy's journey and to shine out to the darkest parts of that sea. And as the troubled waters came, and come they would, our light could be the guide for all who felt hopeless, sadness, and peril to come ashore and have arms wrapped around them, telling them that it would be ok.

I will admit that those few days following my return home and being with Heather and the family were agonizing and rewarding. There was a lot of tossing and turning in bed and late night discussions. There was hours of research online about Batten disease and what we were about to endure and take head on. And then there was Kennedy. Her choice had already been made. She, of course, had already chosen to take Choice #2. She had been moving forward with faith, happiness, hope, and love for years. To her, faith was exactly what its definition is: "To hope for things that one cannot see." How long had Kennedy not been able to see? Yet how long had she shown forth hope each and every day? Those days were heavy. We only lasted the first night before Heather and I called a family meeting in our home with Anna, Beau, and Kennedy.

In that meeting, we explained that Kennedy was special. Very special. As her parents, we explained that she was so special that she had been given a very unique disease called Batten. We were very cautious with how we approached this meeting. We felt strongly that Anna needed to know the devastating outcome of this disease. But, we also felt strongly that we needed to be extremely cautious explaining only the effects of the disease to Beau and Kennedy. Before the official sit down, we met privately with Anna and we told her the reality of the news. We explained to her that this disease was terminal and that there was not much time left for Kennedy according to doctors.

Most of the signs and effects had obviously already started and were taking effect. So, we made the meeting a positive one and explained how special Kennedy was in order to be literally a drop in the bucket. One of millions and millions and millions to be chosen to have Batten disease. Many questions were asked. "What does this mean, Dad? What is it? What does it do? And how long will she have it?"

This is where the conversation became incredibly difficult. We had chosen to not let our key chain drown us. So there was no holding back. "Kennedy will eventually be in a wheelchair and we need to get her ready for this. She will have a harder time talking and will also have a harder time moving around. She will not be able to talk as well and she will need a lot more help from our family." For a moment there was silence in our home as Kennedy, Anna, and Beau all processed this thought. This was now as real as it had ever become and the future was most certainly unknown. After an extremely long thirty-second span, Anna leaned over and hugged Kennedy. They sat and hugged. Tears rolled down Anna's face and a slight look of confusion was on Kennedy's. There was so much to take in, so much to experience. Nothing was said and nothing was done, other than a hug. After this hug, little Beau traveled over to Kennedy, where he hugged her and hugged her and hugged her. He told her that it would be all right and that he would still play with her even if she was in a wheelchair. Heather sat next to Kennedy and embraced her in tears. She hugged her and held her and was the lifeline that Kennedy needed and would need. Heather also comforted Beau and Anna and gently placed her arms and love around them as well, letting them know that all would be ok.

We watched a short video on Batten disease. The mood in the room changed. Although there was sadness, there was also a peace never before felt. That peace was one that would be with our little family until the end of Kennedy's life. And then I made Kennedy the promise. I promised her as her father that I would do everything in my power to make her life and her journey with Batten disease a miracle journey. I promised to do everything in my power to make sure that she was financially, physically, emotionally, and spiritually ok. And that together we were going to make this journey something that our family would and could look back on as the most beautiful experience of our lives. I promised to be there for her as her dad and that I would spend every waking moment that I had for the rest of my life with her supporting her down that journey. And I promised her that no matter what, we would stick by her side and never, ever not make it fun!

Now this may sound weird to many. Yes, fun! You see, fun is what Kennedy thrived on and lived for. It was one of the few things left in her life that she still understood: the word *fun*. As we discussed this, the mood in the room seemed to change. But what had really changed was the situation. It was all too real now. It felt real and it felt scary, tough, and beautiful all wrapped into one bowl of ingredients. My only hope was that the recipe would end up producing a beautiful cake. And with the promise, we now knew that it was time to take our cake and eat it too. Our time was now short. Very short.

http://goo.gl/bkUpgK

Scan to view post

http://goo.gl/dxGEz3

Scan to view post

CHAPTER 31

The Violin

The next several days were anything but normal. Our emotions were like an old violin. It seemed that so many beautiful songs had been played on our violin. Many strings had been broken on this violin. Our violin had scratches, dents, and marks from the many journeys that it had seen along the way. This violin was us, our emotions, our family, and Kennedy. As we moved through these emotions and began to rebuild our violin, I found myself on my knees more than standing up. I was trying to wade through the realities of all of the responsibilities that I now had as Kennedy's father. Her disease was unlike others. It would not put her in the hospital for long periods of time. There were no treatments or cures. There were and are different tools available to help keep juveniles with Batten disease comfortable. But, the reality was that Kennedy was going to need many adaptive tools: beds, a different bathroom, vehicle changes, lifts for our home, mattresses, medications, and so forth.

I began to make lists and plan. I began to truly stress knowing that the amount of tools necessary far outweighed the amount of funds that we had available. I truly wanted to play this violin and just produce beautiful music. But I knew that I had to fix some strings and I knew that I had to make it smooth in rough places and produce a new and everlasting shine.

So, I did what I had done on everything up to that point in my life. I asked my God in heaven for help. As usual, that same feeling came over me that I always felt. *"You always listen to the Spirit, which is a higher power, and if you do, you will know exactly what to do."*

As I listened to that Spirit of the higher power that we believe in, I was directed. I was told to simply reach out to my network and let them know how I felt. Many meetings on the phone were held. My father, father-in-law, and my siblings all reached out. Our best friends, business associates, and acquaintances all called. And many people, whom we did not even know, reached out who knew about Batten disease in order to lend a hand of support and a voice of love. Ultimately, I felt strongly to reach out publicly on Facebook in order to let our family and friends know of these emotions. And through this sharing of emotions, the violin began to play.

These emotions ultimately created Kennedy's Hugs: a Facebook page for Kennedy, designed to tell her story and the story of our family with her journey. And on June 25, 2013, the first chord of this beautiful song was played as Kennedy realized that she was going home. We had attended a family meeting with Kennedy at her grandpa and grandma Hansen's home where many of her aunts and uncles and cousins came. In that meeting, the announcement of her disease and a video explaining its effects was shown. As this video played, it finally hit Kennedy. And although her spirit knew, now her mind knew. She now felt and was feeling the mortal reality of this. And this created our first Kennedy's Hugs Facebook post, with a picture of us embracing as she cried and cried and cried.

After this family event, the violin began to play furiously. There was so much being done to fix the violin, yet so little time for it to play. And as it played, many listened and many paid attention. For the music it was producing was so inspiring, so beautiful, and so different that many could not ignore it. The violin strings were now screaming with fury, "I love you. I am going to touch you, and I am going to share with you Kennedy's Hugs." This is the song Kennedy was playing to the world.

http://goo.gl/SntuQE

Scan to view post

CHAPTER 32

The Dance

Oh the feeling in our home back at that time. I wish I could turn back the pages and crawl physically back into those chapters. You would walk into our home and you could just feel the presence of greatness. This greatness, of course, was Kennedy's spirit! It was crying out to share and live and be bold with all whom it would come in contact with.

Kennedy had become shy by nature due to her disease. She had slid into her cocoon and had been hibernating for years. But her wings were built. She was ready to fly and she was ready to soar! There was no fear at all within her when it came to going home to her Heavenly Father. It was not something that we spoke of openly around her until the end. But it was definitely something that she spoke of. And she spoke of it often. She began to talk about heaven, and she began to talk about home. Yes, going home.

But, with all of that talk, she also realized that her key chain was now full. The keys on our key chain as a family now needed to open up all of the doors that they would open. And unknown to us, and unknown to the world, was the story that would be taking place over the next year. Our violin of emotions was playing rapidly and its music was reaching those who would need it the most.

As the news of Kennedy's terminal illness spread, it seemed that many of the right people began reaching out. As mentioned, we belong to The Church of Jesus Christ of Latter-day Saints. Most people call us Mormons. And in our church, the youth group programs, especially the Young Women program, are a big, big thing. Each summer there are great programs for these youth to go to and experience. And this summer was no different. Our church takes areas demographically and splits them into what are called wards that are headed up by a local bishop. Those wards combine together to form what is called a stake. Each stake, depending on the state and geographic location, can be comprised of between 5–10 wards. Within those stakes there are A LOT of youth. And those youth need good influences, guidance, and experiences. The world is full of too many bad influences, so as a church we try to influence these youth with good!

That summer a youth conference had been planned within our stake. There were so many fun activities they planned, including a ropes course, a water fight, some barbecues, some service projects, and, of course, a dance. Heather and I were lucky enough to have an assignment within our stake to be in charge of all of the food for these events. We enjoyed this because it gave us an opportunity to be able to be with Anna and Kennedy at these events.

Upon arriving to this great conference, there were some who were hesitant to speak to us or Kennedy. I mean, what do you really say to a sweet girl who has just been diagnosed with a terminal illness and had been told by doctors she had less than eighteen months to live? In our minds, this was perfectly normal. We understood and so did Kennedy. As each event took place, either myself, Heather, or one of the other adult leaders would be by Kennedy's side. We would help guide her and talk to her. We helped her to each activity and she began to laugh and scream. She was having so much fun.

While at the ropes course, I was concerned. We all knew that she would not be able to participate in this event. She sat at the edge of the course in a chair on the grass. While sitting there, she looked concerned. I walked over to her and asked what was wrong. "Want to, want to!" she said. She wanted to participate so badly. She could hear the screams and the laughs, the echoes of fun belting out into the summer air. As this happened, I had to explain to her that it was too difficult for her to participate in. This was so hard for her to accept and she began to cry. She cried hard and was very upset. As her crying continued, suddenly it seemed that most things stopped. Kids began to gather around and kids began to talk to her. They began to ask her what was wrong and what she would like to do. They took a sincere interest in her and wanted to get to know her. As they did this, they began to play dolls with her that she had brought with her. They laughed and she laughed. The crying stopped and the sweet spirit of love entered. A smile appeared and beamed on Kennedy's face. She felt loved. She felt accepted. She felt appreciated. Eventually, the group finished the ropes course and came into a bowery we had set up for lunch. Everyone it seemed turned their attentions to Kennedy. She felt it too.

And after lunch, the youth participated in games and skits that they had Kennedy be a part of. As Heather and I watched from a distance, our eyes filled with tears. Our hearts were touched. No one made her disease a subject. Instead they made Kennedy a subject. They turned their attentions to her and helped her feel included. Kennedy was having so much fun. Yet, you could also tell that she still withheld from FULLY being herself. And as her dad, I sat waiting. I was waiting to see the true her burst from within. I knew it was inside of her, but the right combination of nutrients needed to hit the dirt for her to blossom.

Later in the conference, the kids had a dance. Of course, this was the highlight for them. Loud music, dancing, and picking out that special someone to dance with. We completed dinner and all of the kids moved into a church gymnasium. The music began and kids started to dance, showing off their moves, joking, laughing, and eyeing down another cute boy or girl. The dance had just started and I left the gym to find Kennedy sitting inside the kitchen with Heather. I tried to get her to come and dance. She just shook her head and said, "Can't, can't! Don't know how and n, n, nno boys wwwant to dance with me." I tried and tried and tried. But, nothing seemed to work.

You see, Kennedy had never gone to a dance. She had been in dance, but she had never attended a school dance or church dance of any kind. She always felt that her blindness and her disabilities would hold her back. Many times Anna would invite her, but Kennedy never would go. This pained me as her father greatly. I wanted her to feel. I wanted her to experience. I wanted her to know how beautiful she was inside and out. And each and every time as these dances would occur, Kennedy would wait at home patiently for Anna.

Right by the door in fact. She would jump up and down and want to know who it was that Anna had danced with and who everyone else had danced with. She always wanted to hear every detail and would listen with great intensity. But, if you ever asked her to go to a dance, well, there was no way that was ever going to happen.

As I looked at her, I could see her little foot tapping to the tunes.

Kennedy knew every word to almost every popular song out there and you could see her little mouth almost perfectly singing those words. Suddenly I felt that feeling come over me, *"You always listen to the Spirit, which is a higher power, and if you do, you will know exactly what to do."* I left the kitchen and found myself in the gymnasium watching a couple hundred teenage kids having the time of their lives. I leaned up against the wall by the stage and folded my arms where I silently said a prayer. The Spirit was telling me to pray to my Father above. I simply prayed that somehow, someway Kennedy would be allowed and want to come into that gym and into that dance.

I knew in my heart that her time was so precious. Each and every day, each and every hour, and each and every minute. And I wanted her to feel the mortal feelings of what all of the other kids were feeling. As I did this, I suddenly looked up to see one of Kennedy's Young Women leaders leading her by the hands into the gym. As she did, time stopped before me. I testify and will never deny that I saw a glow around my daughter brighter than ever before. This great leader took her by the hands and began to dance with her. She encouraged her and she helped her. She communicated to Kennedy what to do and Kennedy did it! Kennedy began to dance! She began to really move. She began to sing the words and began to laugh. She was moving side to side, and she was moving her arms back and forth. A prayer had been answered and I was witnessing it before my eyes.

As this went on, I suddenly felt a nudge and looked over to see my bishop by my side. He put his arm around me as tears rolled down my cheeks. No words were said as we both wept. And then it happened. The gymnasium full of kids seemed to come to a screeching halt as all of the kids saw Kennedy. They rushed to the front of the gym and formed a circle around her. They began to chant her name, "Kennedy, Kennedy, Kennedy!" She could not hold back. She transformed before my eyes into that girl that I so badly wanted to see. That daughter that I knew was inside blossomed! She blossomed right before my eyes that night.

And in that group of kids were three boys who were probably some of the most popular boys at the local high school, Fremont High. All three had just graduated and all three I had served and been assigned to as a Scout leader for multiple years. Suddenly, the music changed and a new song came on. As it did, one of these three boys stepped forward and asked Kennedy's leader for permission for her to dance. Kennedy could not believe it! She screamed his name out. He took her by the hands and danced with her.

He danced with her and made her feel loved and then suddenly the next boy and the next boy and the next boy came. One by one each and every boy in that circle danced with Kennedy. You really had to be there to feel of it and know the feeling. It was incredible. It was indescribable. And to see this new flower blossom right before my eyes was the most rewarding thing I had experienced yet as a father. Someone had gotten Heather from the kitchen, and the whole gym was now watching. And then it was my turn. I slowly walked out to that floor, where I took my angel's hands and said, "It's Dad. Will you dance with me?"

"Yay, Daddy, yay!" she screamed. I took her hands and we danced. She could not see me, she could not see all of the faces seeing her or the tears that ran down those faces. This would be a monumental moment in time that I will forever cherish, forever adore, and forever hold dear. I placed her head on my shoulder and I told her, "Kennedy, I love you so much and I will love you forever."

She said, "Daddy, I love you to! But . . . wwwwherer are the boys?" I knew my time was up, I knew I had to let her go. So, again more boys came, more danced, and more showed her the greatest evening yet of her life.

The next day in church, the following experience happened. I will quote it from my journal:

> I was in charge of the lesson for the boys. As I went about preparation for the lesson, the spirit indicated to me to invite Kennedy to come and bear her testimony to the Young Men. She also wanted to thank them for dancing with her.
>
> As Kennedy entered that room, The room went quiet and the Spirit entered entirely. Kennedy bore her testimony. She said she believes in Heavenly Father and this church. She then started to cry. I have never seen her cry in a testimony or spiritual setting before. The spirit was so strong. Top ten in my life!! She then wanted to thank the boys for dancing with her, but she could not speak it. So, I helped her and told her it did not matter, because the boys were all ugly anyways and she adamantly said, "NNO, NO, DAD, NO!" She was so cute. I then had one of the boys take Kennedy back to her class.
>
> The room was already flowing with tears. After she left I bore testimony of the strength of those boys and how they carried me on our High Adventure camp after I found out about Kennedy's diagnosis. The spirit was strong as I told them that Kennedy would be going home. After my testimony, I asked them to bear their testimonies.

> Each of them did extraordinary as they challenged the other boys to go on missions for our church. One of the leaders referenced a scripture talking about "The worth of bringing save one soul unto our Father." He bore testimony of how it was not by coincidence that the lesson was on this subject this day. He then said something that I will never forget. He said that Kennedy is a single soul who had influenced these boys to all serve missions and that this "one soul" had influenced them to now serve, which would bring millions in the future unto the Gospel. Not one boy wanted to leave, they all sat just relishing in the spirit. Then the bishop closed with a prayer and invoked a blessing on our family and also thanked Heavenly Father for allowing the veil to be a glimpse to us . . . Wow!!

The boys all cried and no one wanted to leave. The feeling in that room was unbelievably strong. As they finally left, their parents were astonished that they stayed late and that they showed tears. And waiting right outside that door was Kennedy who embraced and hugged each and every one of them. And from that day forward her glow followed her. Church would follow each Sunday with constant Hugs and long talks and walks and no one, I mean no one who was present, could ever, or would ever forget THE DANCE and the testimony that followed of what happened that night.

CHAPTER 33

Any Wish in the World

The awakening of who Kennedy really was seemed to bring her to life—to come alive. She was different after the dance that night. Her true beam of sunshine really began to fully shine forth and burst its rays all over everything in its path. We began to calculate our life in moments. As each moment occurred, we would quickly take a picture or sit down and soak in that moment, knowing that very soon it would leave us and we would never have it back again in our lives.

Heather and I felt a strong urge to ask Kennedy about what she wanted. We knew that we needed to make this all about her, yet we also did not know exactly what that meant. We truly wanted her to have the memories and experiences that she wanted with the short time left. So we sat her down one day and asked her if she could have any wish in the world, what wish would be her dream wish and what might be her dream trip or item that she could have?

At this point, we had not thought of the Make a Wish foundation, nor did we know that much about it. We were only thinking of our daughter and what we could do in order to make her journey perfect. As we asked Kennedy about this wish, we thought that her immediate answer would be a trip to the Barbie factory, American Girl factory, or Disneyland. We were confident that this would be a wish for a trip and that she would select one of those things. We also told her that we wanted her to really think about it and make sure that her wish was what she really wanted. As we had this conversation, we tried to explain to her as lovingly, cautiously, and openly as we could about her time left on earth. We wanted her to know that this wish was that special and that she needed to have this wish be something for her to enjoy. To our surprise, there was no hesitation, no stop for deep thinking or for questions or pondering. Kennedy quickly blurted out, "C,c,cousins, d,d,ddolphins, Hawaii, Hawaii!" She kept screaming out the words, "Hhhhawaaiii, Hhhawaiii!"

Now for many this may seem like the easy typical answer that you hear from many families who have a child or family member with an illness, right? We all see the pictures of the dream trips that are taken. Hawaii, Disneyland, Florida, or a cruise to Mexico. But, for us, this actually touched us deeply. Kennedy instantly told us, as she always did, what she was thinking and feeling with her heart. She did not care about herself; she did not care about her own wants and desires. Kennedy was caring about everyone else. For Kennedy, it was not about the snorkeling, the swimming, the sunsets, or the dolphins. It would be about her spending time with loved ones who lived very far away and with whom she was not able to spend time.

It was rare to see her aunt and uncle and cousins who live in Hawaii. And in her heart and in her soul, she knew that they needed this time with her worse than she needed it with them. She began to scream, "Sssurf! Uncle Dane! S,sssea shells! Aunt Keri!" Her instant smile and sweet demeanor brought us so much joy. My instant thought turned to a feeling of "How in the world am I going to pay for such a trip? How am I going to take the time off? And how are we going to travel clear across the globe with Kennedy being blind and becoming more and more incapacitated?"

All of these questions came to a halt as Kennedy slowly reached out and we hugged. She wrapped her arms around Heather and me both. We all sat for a minute and hugged. Heather and I both drew tears and Kennedy drew nothing but smiles. I remember that moment as if it were yesterday. We made the phone call to her aunt and uncle. She screamed out the news to them over the phone. She tried to tell them about all of the things that she wanted to do and that they were going to go and do together.

There was a pause on the other end of the phone and a slight gasping. You could then hear the crying voice of her Aunt Keri (who is my sister) as she told Kennedy how honored she felt that her wish would be to come to Hawaii to see them. Keri and Kennedy began to talk often and somehow, someway, Kennedy had this magic ability to be able to dial people from her phone even being blind. The phone calls and plans began and the trip was a go.

On our end, we were struggling to look at the expenses of the trip and the time we would need to take for such an adventure. As this was all taking place, a very good friend reached out to us and asked us if we had met with the Make a Wish Foundation. We told them no. This person became our sponsor and contacted them. Instantly we were contacted and discussions began surrounding Kennedy's wish. As I reviewed this in my own mind and in our financial situation, I began to fear this would not happen. I again found myself on my knees and asking Heavenly Father for help. I suddenly felt that same feeling again, *"You always listen to the Spirit, which is a higher power, and if you do, you will know exactly what to do."* I prayed about what to do with this trip. It seemed that there was just not enough time to put the trip together for the available time that we had. And in our hearts we also knew that Kennedy did not have a lot of time.

But this higher power that I spoke of whispered for me to call and speak to my best friend about our situation. As I explained my dilemma, he suddenly said, "Guess what? One of the executives of our company is the chairman of the board for Make a Wish Utah. Let me give him a call and tell him what is going on. I promise we will make this happen." I hung up the phone and felt a feeling of peace. It was officially out of my control. This was out of my hands and now in the hands of others. And this man, this chairman whom my friend spoke of, did exactly that. He called me and assured me that this trip would happen for Kennedy. He then proceeded to share with me that many years prior in his life his teenage daughter had contracted a terminal illness and had passed away. His emotions overtook himself, as did mine, as he proceeded to share with me that it was not by chance that my friend connected us. While on a business trip, I was alerted that all of the pieces were in place and I needed to get home a bit sooner in order to meet with Make a Wish and grant Kennedy's Wish. I flew home a day earlier than expected and found an amazing group of people called wish grantors sitting in our home. They were amazing as they listened to Kennedy extend her wish and they granted it to her that night. I had to stand up and walk into the other room. I was simply feeling sad, upset, and happy all at once. I reentered the room and these amazing people began to ask Kennedy specifically what she would like to do while on her trip to Hawaii. Of course, her reply again was, "Cousins, Dane, Keri!!" But it was followed by conversations about dolphins, snorkeling, and surfing. Details were made and we visited the Make a Wish Foundation of Utah. They granted Kennedy's Wish in their wish center and presented us with all of our trip details.

And in Kennedy's world, her dream of going to see her cousins, aunt, uncle, and Hawaii was about to come true. A wish that could have only happened with her faith, diligence, and great understanding of simply believing in things that we cannot see.

http://goo.gl/lhy9PR

Scan to view post

CHAPTER 34

SHE COULD ONLY SMILE

The trip to Hawaii literally came together in less than ten days. The blessing of it all was that Kennedy's Aunt KeriLyn and her family were already in Hawaii and our accommodations were all set. The only expectation for them was to show up. A magnificent bubble seemed to surround Kennedy at this time. Ever since the dance, Kennedy was different. Many may not believe this, but we witnessed it. A bright aura surrounded Kennedy that would follow her. Her true self was now being exemplified. The dance woke up the real Kennedy and allowed her to be shared with the world. So it seemed that everywhere we went and everything we did was open to the world. People did not just notice Kennedy's cane, but they noticed her spirit and it was beaming!

We left on this trip and boarded the plane. It was the beginning of July, so it was hot! It seemed that we sat a very, very long time on that grounded plane, and there was no air conditioning available on that plane. Ultimately, we were told that the plane had mechanical problems and that we would have an even longer wait. But they kept us on the plane. We were seated in different places. I was at the front with Beau and Anna, while Heather and Kennedy were several rows behind me. I traveled back to speak with them and the crowd was getting pretty upset with the planes staff. It had been hours and it was getting hotter and hotter. Many wanted to leave the plane, but the airline had us stay on board. I asked the stewardess for an update and none of them seemed to know. As I traveled back to Heather and Kennedy, I was worried that Kennedy would not be doing well. While sitting there, I turned to see a big man traveling down the aisle. I noticed that it was the captain of the aircraft. He proceeded to walk by us and to the back of the plane. On his way back, he stopped and put his arm on my shoulder. He looked down at Kennedy and then back at me. He simply said, "Is that your daughter?"

"Yes," I said.

"Come with me."

"What? Why?" I asked.

He just said again, "Come with me and bring her with you."

Heather gave me a bewildered look but said, "Go ahead and take her." So, Kennedy and I went to the front of the plane with the captain. When we got to the front of the plane, the captain turned to me and said, "Tell me about your daughter." I began to tell these pilots about Kennedy and her disease. I told them about this trip and how it was her dream. The one pilot looked at the other and instantly you could see emotions rise. The pilot began to tell me that he could feel and felt something special as he walked past Kennedy that day. It was so interesting. He also told me that he wanted to bring her into the cockpit where it was cool. The air conditioning was somehow working in the cockpit. Since we sat there for some time, you could tell that the pilots were frustrated. Apparently a part on the plane had been replaced, but it was faulty. So, we were waiting for it to be flown in from another city. As we felt this frustration, what did Kennedy do? She hugged these pilots and told them thank you and it would be ok. I turned to see the entire staff at the door of the cockpit. One by one, the staff came in and met Kennedy. There was no prior phone call. There was no alert, and there was no personal connection. The only thing that existed was Kennedy's Hugs. She hugged each one of these people, one by one. I noticed as she did this that each one of them became emotional. The staff ended up bringing Beau (age five at the time) up to the cockpit and he was able to look at all of the controls and feel like a pilot. I traveled back and brought Heather to the front to meet the staff and the pilots. As this all happened, Kennedy just sat back and smiled. But, her smile was not a giant one with laughter. It was a peaceful smile that just seemed to provide peace and a calmness to all of us who were there.

CHAPTER 35

Sand and the Trust of an Uncle's Hand

The birds sang loudly, the rain had stopped, and the dripping of water echoed through the beautiful jungle where my sister's home resided. I looked around and thought, *This is it. This is the last trip that my little family will ever have together. This is going to be the most magnificent trip that Kennedy will ever have.* We had arrived in the middle of the night, but I could not sleep. I was still on Utah time and I also had to continue to work my new job and run our business. There was no time for me to rest or to sleep. I sat for a moment and soaked in the environment. I let the rainwater drip on my face from the edge of the trees and I let the humidity wet my nose.

I thought I was all alone, but I turned around to see Kennedy at the screen door that led from inside the house to the porch where I sat. She was trying to open it up and was saying, "Dddad, Dad, help me Dad, help!" I jumped up from where I sat and ran to the door. She was giggling and she began saying, "Hawaii, Hawaii, Hawaii!" She was ecstatic. She was on cloud nine! She was somehow and in someway already soaking in the feeling of Hawaii without even being able to see it. I quickly put my arm around her and led her outside where we sat together and just soaked in all of the sounds.

That first day was remarkable. Not far from my sister's home is a beautiful little private beach. We traveled to the beach, where we all watched in awe as Kennedy felt the sand with her feet and splashed in the ocean. She took a walk with her mother and built sand castles with her cousins. She could not stop laughing and even got sand in her mouth. As I sat and watched her and took pictures of her, the tears began to come. Tears that for the next year would seem to be unending. Simply flowing from within me and from parts of me that I never knew even existed.

I cried as I watched Kennedy appreciate, ten times greater than all of us, these simple things. The view was spectacular and the ocean was as pretty as a painting in a collector's art gallery. But I could not get over how happy Kennedy was. We walked hand in hand down that beach. I asked her what she liked and what she did not like. She of course told me she loved boys and she loved her dolls and Twilight. But, as we walked back, she told me that more than anything she loved me. "Yyyou, Dddad, you. I, I, I, I, llllove yyyou!" She pointed with her other hand toward me and poked it in my chest.

I had to stop. The wind left my sails and I sat idle where we stood. I simply reached my arms around my precious daughter and pulled her into my chest. I then told her, "And I love you, Kennedy. I love you, so, so much. You have no idea how much I love you." As I held her, I looked up to see my beautiful wife taking pictures of Kennedy and me together. The moment was one that I will never forget, because as we sat there holding one another, she suddenly said, "I'm ggggoint to miss you, Ddddad. Ggggonnna mmmiisss you."

That moment truly set the tone for the rest of the week as a family. It seemed that my sister and her family were just enthralled, amazed, and stunned by Kennedy. They just wanted to watch, stare, and spend every minute with her. We took their boat out to a secret snorkeling spot that was special to their family. As we anchored the boat, we began to put on our snorkeling gear. We knew that Kennedy would not be able to snorkel, so we gave her a treat and had her sit on one of the large seats in the boat. As we were all getting ready to jump in, her uncle jumped in first. He was laughing and screaming about how great the water was. We were all paying attention to him when suddenly we heard a splash! We turned around to see Kennedy gone. We panicked. And then we looked into the water, where she sat treading and laughing.

"Fun, fun, fun!" She had jumped overboard into the water, without any hesitation, without any prodding, and without any invitation. She wanted to do everything that we did and more than anything she did not want to spoil the fun. Her uncle quickly swam to her side. She had so much faith, so much trust, and so much spunk to just jump into the water without any direction. She sat in that water with a massive grin on her face and could not stop laughing. Her uncle was right by her side and helped her swim in that beautiful ocean. He helped put goggles on her face and a snorkel in her mouth and he made her feel normal. And . . . she snorkeled!

Later that night, Kennedy lay asleep, exhausted from the day. Her American Girl doll lay tucked under her arm and her beautiful hair was draped over her pillow. She looked like our little girl, yet she also looked older. She looked more mature and more seasoned. In one day, her first day in Hawaii, it seemed that her spirit was resonating through her body that she was maturing. She was growing and she was somehow shouting out, "This is me, this is the real me. This is Kennedy Ann Hansen."

CHAPTER 36

SURFING AND THE TRUE FIREWORK

As our Hawaii trip rolled on, it seemed that everything that Kennedy should not have been able to do, she did! She insisted on surfing and was adamant about this. With it being summer, the waves were small and this actually made it perfect for a trip to the beach with her and her uncle. His idea would be to simply have her hold onto the board as he would act like she was surfing. But, Kennedy was much too smart for that. She could hear the waves, the screams, and feel the current. She wanted to surf, she screamed to surf. "Surf, surf, suuuuurff!" she screamed out to her uncle.

So, with strength like an ancient Hawaiian warrior, but with the heart of an ever loving uncle, he paddled Kennedy out to the line where the surf was making its best waves. We were all very worried that she would not be able to kneel on the surfboard. Her body's flexibility had become more rigid and parts of her ability to understand were gone as well. But, earlier in the day, we had taken paddleboards and paddled up the Waimea river. Kennedy was able to kneel down easily on the paddleboard and to hold onto its sides. As she did this, she was able to enjoy different things. At one point, she pointed and said, "Look. Turtles!" We looked ahead and saw some giant sea turtles that lived in this part of the river. We all were astonished that she saw them. She pointed them out and she just smiled. She would comment on the breeze and the smell of the flowers and greenery on the bank. She even would reach down and splash water on her cousins and on the rest of us as we would get close to her and the board she knelt on. And she insisted that the board she was on be that of her Aunt Keri.

So, as the time came to surf, her Uncle Dane was already halfway there with explaining to her that she needed to kneel on the board. She gladly did, with one of the biggest smiles you have ever seen. We worried a bit as he paddled her out quite far from the shore to catch the waves. Upon arriving at the waves, we could not hear what was being said. But a little discussion of "trust me and hold on" was being explained. Our breaths were held and our hearts were pounding as we suddenly saw the line of waves coming. Dane paddled as hard as he could. His monstrous quads and calves could be seen through the water as he kicked with all of his might. And like a perfectly threaded needle, he gently yet firmly pushed and released Kennedy into the wave. She screamed, "Yay! Surf, surf, surfing!" Her board glided perfectly through the water and toward the shore, where her Aunt KeriLyn was there to catch the board before a full landing on the shore. The ride was perfect. Her form perfect. She surfed, she actually surfed!

And although this was on her knees, it still counted. Kennedy had finally done what she had always dreamed of. She had ridden a wave. And like so many before her and so many to come after, this wave was one that brought so much happiness and so much joy. Her uncle quickly swam back to shore and congratulated her. She was so proud and could not stop laughing. We sat on that beach and we watched our daughter feel normal. We watched her feel happy. The humidity was present, the sun was shining, and the gentle breeze was pushing water in the air and down our bodies. As I sat there and watched, I could not help but notice the simple tears that were coming from the eyes of all who watched. These tears were now normal. They were daily, sometimes even hourly. And without any warning, they would just come.

After surfing, Kennedy and I were able to play on the beach and go into the water and swim together. She let me hold her in the water and the buoyancy made her feel so light. She swam around to my back and told me to swim like a whale. We had done this when she was little, but she wanted to do it now. I quickly gave in and we swam around in that bay. We laughed so hard and we swallowed a lot of water. She would swim up to me and hug me so tight and laugh and laugh and laugh. Was this paradise? Yes, yes it was. What more of a paradise could we ask for then the simplicity of family together in such an environment? A little piece of heaven on a sandy beach earth.

That night we traveled over to Turtle Bay, where we were spoiled with good food and a massive fireworks show. It was July 4th and the celebration was huge! As I sat on our blanket looking up at the massive sky lit with God's tapestry of stars, I looked around and that feeling came over me as it always seemed to in our life, *"You always listen to the Spirit, which is a higher power, and if you do, you will know exactly what to do."* I immediately was impressed to just stare at Kennedy. I turned and just stared at her. As I did this, an instant glow protruded around her. She was beaming! At first, I thought it was just me, that maybe I was adjusting my eyes to a different shadow, scene, or light. But, I was not. I was seeing the glow of an angel.

She beamed, she glowed, and she sat peacefully. I could see her entire body, her whole face and the concern on her face. I quickly slid next to her and asked if she was ok. "No, see fireworks, Ddddaddy. Ssssorry, sorry." She said. She was so worried about seeing the fireworks and concerned that this would affect all of us. I quickly put my arm around her and said, "You know what, Kennedy? You are my favorite firework. You are prettier, bigger, and greater than any other firework on earth. I will sit next to you and we can hug each other and talk during these fireworks." The two of us sat, eating chicken together and laughing and talking about boys. I do not really remember any of the fireworks that night. I know they were there and I know that this show is one of the greatest on earth since it showers over the waters of Turtle Bay. But, to me, yes, to me the greatest show and the greatest firework was right before my eyes and she was glowing. As I sat with her, a calm, yet reassuring feeling came over me and into my mind. It simply said, "This will be the last 4th of July you will ever have with Kennedy on earth. Enjoy it. Enjoy every single molecule of it, for next year, she will be gone." This feeling, this experience again came from that feeling that I had felt so many, many times. So, I simply just sat and hugged Kennedy. That was all I could do until the show was over and it was time to go. The last 4th of July fireworks show where my arms would embrace the physical angel who was so far ahead of the rest of us. Exploding not just on holidays, but every day. With a tapestry of colors so bright, so powerful, and so amazing that no artist would be able to display her explosion of love. A love that, to this day, we all miss so much.

CHAPTER 37

Who Are Those Men, Daddy, and Goodbye

If I close my eyes and think about this trip to Hawaii, it is not even hard to remember it. I can replay each day, each moment, and each treasure in my mind. The little things, the big things, and even the smells that we experienced are easy to recall. The entire week included magical dreams for Kennedy. She was able to swim with and pet dolphins, ride horses, feel the spray of giant waterfalls, and experience all of the traditions of the cultures while attending the Polynesian Cultural Center. The week was a staged production most definitely rehearsed and played by angels unseen for Kennedy and our family.

On one particular day, we decided to go to the flea markets and then afterward visit Pearl Harbor. On this day, we could tell that Kennedy's physical abilities were breaking down quite a bit. She had pushed very hard throughout the week and, ironically, had slept great. She had not woken up with night terrors or seizures. But her walking and coordination seemed a bit off. So for the first time ever, we resorted to using a rented wheelchair we had brought on the trip with us. At first, the thought of it deeply concerned and depressed Heather and me. *A wheelchair?* we thought. *Are we and is Kennedy really to that point?* I will never forget pulling that wheelchair out of the back of my sister's truck. As I lifted it, it almost seemed as if I had emotions of resentment along with gratitude all wrapped into one swift moment as I swung it out of the back of the truck and unfolded it. I had promised to NEVER become angry during Kennedy's journey. Instead, I found her and told her that her race car was ready to go. She laughed and got situated in the chair. We had a ball! The chair worked so great and she was so comfortable in it. We were able to move around so much easier and travel so much quicker. We popped wheelies in it and made race car sounds. Little Beau and Kennedy's cousins pushed her.

Everyone seemed to make this a fun instead of miserable moment for Kennedy. She was able to be wheeled right up against the items at the flea market and feel them with her hands. She was always a little shopper and little deal maker, so the flea market was most definitely her piece of heaven. We loaded up bags full of souvenirs and all rallied around her. We sang some fun little songs and just soaked in the moment. Not far from this flea market sits Pearl Harbor. We loaded up the cars and drove to this sacred and special place. We toured the majority of the memorial and we took a boat ride out to see the ships still sitting where bubbles and even fuel still spill from their bows. Having Kennedy in this wheelchair made the trip ever so much easier and enjoyable.

As we arrived at the *USS Arizona* wall, Kennedy's face immediately became very serious and almost sober with concern. She asked me to wheel her forward closer and closer to the wall. When we got as close as we were allowed, she asked, "Whwhwho aaare all of those men?"

"What men?" She pointed to the wall. Struck by surprise, I knelt before her and relayed to her what had happened at this place and with these fallen heroes. Her face had so much concern. She asked me to read her every name on that wall. Of course, there were so many that I could not. I again tried to explain to her, as best as I could, what had happened. She asked to let her sit there and think. I was astounded. How did she know there were names of men there? Who was she seeing? The last thing she said was, "Dddied for us, ddddied for us."

"Yes, they did, Kennedy. Yes they did." Her spiritual interactions, feelings, and emotions were always on such a simple yet much more powerful level than the rest of us. For Kennedy's heart was feeling, and she knew things that many of us thought we knew. But compared to her, we were mere spiritual babies. For her level was beyond this world, and she would prove it time and time again.

* * *

Though we all dreaded it, we knew that it was coming. The trip was ending and there was nothing we could do about it. Heather and I would sit back and watch Kennedy with her cousins and with her aunt and uncle. We would think and even say, "This is the last time she will be with them and they do not even realize it." We would kneel down at night in the bungalow where we were staying and we would pray and thank Heavenly Father for such an amazing trip given at the perfect moment for our family and for theirs. We did not feel hopeless, we did not feel guilty, and we did not feel sad. We felt alive and grateful, yet brokenhearted in some ways for the cousins who would soon have to tell Kennedy goodbye.

On our last day of the trip, we took Kennedy back down to the beach. We brought along with us a very large jar of seashells. We sat a boogie board on the ground and then carefully buried the seashells in the sand surrounding Kennedy and this boogie board. We had her sit down and then together we emotionally watched as Kennedy began to dig and find probably over fifty seashells. She was screaming, she was laughing, and she was having the time of her life. Those shells traveled home with us. And on many hard days over the next year, when Kennedy was in pain or was struggling to breathe or think, we would find her in her room with the seashells spilled all over her carpet, combing through them with a smile and remembering the sweet Hawaii air, the softness of the sand, and the greatness of the hearts of her family.

http://goo.gl/aV8TTf

Scan to view post

CHAPTER 38

The Front Page

The days began to feel long, but the weeks began to pass fast. Our summer was anything but stagnant. It seemed that each week, we had some type of church activity, family activity, or work event. One of our responsibilities was that Heather had been given the assignment from our church to be the director of our church's girls camp. This entails finding a camp and planning activities for girls ranging ages 12–18 for almost a week. The camp includes spiritual events along with life learning skills on how to be a better young woman and a better mother and wife for the future. It is a wonderful opportunity that our girls always looked forward to. But to plan and be in charge of the whole thing was most definitely a very large responsibility on top of everything that was going on in our family.

I helped Heather as much as I could, as did Kennedy and Anna, and we sent them on their way to have a great girls camp that summer. After they left, it was then that it felt like the days felt longer and the weeks were moving faster. But I had the company of little Beau, our dog, Aggie, and Kennedy's cat, Mario, for company. It had been a couple of days after they left and things were getting crazy! I was running late one day and having a hard morning with Beau. We were trying to get out the door, change sheets, shower him, make lunch, and get him ready to take to a neighbor's house. My phone was ringing off the hook; I had emails pouring in, an upset customer, and family trying to reach me. I got in the car to find it was out of gas! I left the house and had to turn back around because I forgot to turn off the water in the yard. I got home and accidentally set the house alarm off. . . . GRRRR. It was already turning out to be a crazy day. I was feeling overwhelmed and I pulled into the gas station to fill the car up with gas. I went into the gas station to use the bathroom and as I walked in, I look down and there was Kennedy on the front page of the newspaper.

I had to stop twice and look again. I had no idea that a story was going to post about her that day. I proceeded to use the bathroom, purchase the newspaper, and discover once again that this angel of ours totally tears me up. She humbles me and makes me realize that my life is anything but tough. I could barely read through the article between the sobs that I produced while sitting in my car. I had received a phone call from a reporter, but I had no idea that she was going to produce an article that week. The picture on the front of the article showed Kennedy at girls camp with all of her friends from church helping her walk.

I was surprised, shocked, and literally caught off guard by the front page article about our daughter. And then it hit me. In my mind, a voice simply said, "This is it. This is the start of her touching the world through her story. It is ok. Let it be shared. Let it be told. Let it flood. It is ok." I proceeded to go to work that day with a heart full and a brain revolving with so many thoughts, emotions, and items spinning. The article was needed. The article was the start. The article was inspired to now share Kennedy's Hugs with the world and to understand the great responsibility that we held as her parents to do so.

http://goo.gl/7XsXYL

Scan to view article

CHAPTER 39

The Unspoken Connection

One of the hardest parts of Kennedy's terminal illness and disease was just that—her disease. Batten? What is Batten? Where does it come from and what does it do? How do we treat her? How do we make her comfortable? How do we help her? How do we do all that we can in order to have her life be the best? And if there is a chance of a cure, how do we find that? We would live each magical day as if it were her last. Our feelings had not been wrong yet. As a parent, you seem to always want the best for your children, yet you also instinctively do not want to do anything that would over spoil, favor, or place one child above another within your family unit.

So as our feelings, experiences, and trials became ever so apparent, we more than anything wanted Kennedy to have it all. Not meaning to buy her everything or to give her everything, but to have it all before she would leave this mortal state called life. And when it came to Batten, we wanted to become experts, yet we also did not. We felt that it was more important to focus on what we knew best and let the medical experts focus on what they knew best. And with that focus, of course there came A LOT of questions.

But, our time was so limited and more than anything we wanted our study to be on our beautiful daughter. So we did. We carefully planned each and every day knowing full well that they were our last. In some ways, we felt bad for ourselves, yet in others, we did not. In this way it was easy to share her, share her story, and share her hugs! Yet in our alone and dark moments, we still felt alone. We still felt like there were parts that no one else could understand or believe nor did we even expect them to try to.

To our knowledge, Kennedy was the only living child or person with Batten disease in Utah. But when we had asked the doctors assigned to Kennedy if there were any other children or individuals with the disease, they told us that they could not disclose the name (due to privacy laws), but that there was one other case. Immediately we felt a strong urgency to know who this was and where this person was located. And through a national Batten network we were led and guided to this other family in Utah whose sweet little angel named Charlee had Late Infantile Batten disease. It seemed that we were destined to be connected and were in need of one another as we had the opportunity for the only two living kids with Batten disease in Utah to meet.

We decided to meet this girl. It was a gorgeous day when the knock came at our front door. We opened the door to the heartwarming smiles of Charlee and her family! Charlee at this point was confined to a wheelchair, fully blind, and experienced several seizures each day. Her speech had simply left her and, according to her parents, while she would make different sounds, she had not spoken a word in almost two months. As the door opened and we greeted one another and invited them into our home, a feeling entered that was indescribable. It was as if we had known this family for a very, very long time. There were no handshakes, just hugs, and we were instantly smiling and loving. As we all introduced ourselves to one another, the room went suddenly quiet and you could have heard a pin drop as Kennedy slowly and methodically moved her way toward Charlee. Her face was so serious and her movement was so assertive.

Both she and Charlee were blind but as she moved closer and closer to Charlee, both of them reached out to one another and we witnessed a miracle. Charlee reached out her hand and Kennedy reached out hers, they touched hands together and Charlee said, "Hi." This was and is a modern miracle. As parents, the four of us just stared in awe and soaked in the moment in tears as we witnessed their little GIANT spirits connect. It seemed that time again stopped and the clocks, the stresses, the responsibilities, and the burdens all were set to the side as we simply sat and stared in awe at these two.

These two angels even looked like each other and just sat and held hands. They would not let go of one another and wanted to be by each other's sides. It seemed that so did we as we were educated wonderfully on so many of the things to expect, experience, and understand about Batten disease. A four-hour visit occurred that day and we made friends for eternity. It seemed that Heather and I had a massive burden leave our shoulders as we were able to share feelings, ask questions, and begin to feel as if someone else could understand the great burden that we were experiencing.

As the day wound down, the two girls still did not leave each other's sides. It was interesting that Kennedy being fifteen and Charlee being five were still so connected. Kennedy played dolls with her and put her arm around her. She sang songs to her and stroked her hair. Kennedy and Charlee had an unspoken connection as they were not able to speak physically, but were talking spiritually. As the visit ended and the night came to a close, I found Kennedy alone her room. She was in deep, deep thought. As I entered her room and sat by her side, she said, "Dad, I feel her spirit so strong. Her spirit is so strong. . . . I love her!"

This friendship and this visit would prove to be vital in Kennedy's journey. The unspoken connection between Charlee and Kennedy would prove important as it seemed that Kennedy would follow Charlee's footsteps of this disease in ninety-day increments. Whatever Charlee experienced, Kennedy would experience ninety days later. And the relationship would prove even more valuable when the loss of angels occurred, the loss of life happened, but the friendship forever remained. All because of the unspoken connection between two little Batten angels.

http://goo.gl/TVlNJg

Scan to view post

CHAPTER 40

THE PINKY PROMISE

Kennedy's disease and the summer of 2013 almost felt like an amusement park. Each day we seemed to ride a different ride, with different twists, turns, and outcomes. Sometimes we would laugh, and sometimes we would cry. Sometimes we would leave a ride and want to run back and ride it again. Other times we wanted to find the nearest garbage can and throw up.

We had 24 hours in a day and needed 240! As we battled through each day, moment, and tear, we also had two other very special children to raise, nurture, and teach. Anna was sixteen and fully engaged in the teenage years and Beau was five. It seemed that Anna was handling and taking the pressures and realities of Kennedy's terminal illness like a champ. She stepped up and helped in so many ways. Yet, Beau, little Beau. Our sweet and only little boy seemed to take this much harder. This was his playmate, his best friend, and his sister that was on his same level. She loved to play horses with him, watch kid movies, and jump on the trampoline. And Beau was anything but understanding about losing his Kennedy. He seemed to shut down and close up in some areas. He also began to be more difficult as the attention left him and turned toward Kennedy. It was hard—so, so hard. We were trying our best to give equal attention, but it seemed that we could not.

The nights began to not even be nights any longer. Kennedy's night terrors caused by the disease were creating massive dementia and seizures. It seemed that Heather was up at least half of each night trying to calm her down and remind her of who she was and where she was.

I would run into Kennedy's room, but Kennedy did not want me, she wanted her mom. So, many times I would lay in my bed and not fall back to sleep. Instead I would lay and ponder and wait for her to calm down and go back to sleep. And on many occasions, little Beau would wake up from the screaming, wanting to know what was going on. I would go and take care of him, while Heather attended to Kennedy. It seemed like a nightly ritual as we began to become all too accustomed to this each and every night. Yet there was a pulling from within. A strong yearning for me to try and to be there for Beau in a different way—to try and still have that dad and son bond and to make him feel important.

And since finding out about Kennedy's diagnosis, Beau had been . . . well, anything but himself. As the attention drastically turned from him, being the youngest getting all of the attention, to many events surrounding Kennedy, we did our very best to explain to him why Kennedy was the way she was: why she was blind, couldn't speak well, had seizures, and so on. Since the diagnosis, we had explained to him about Kennedy's grim physical future of being in a wheelchair and losing her physical abilities quickly. We never really said anything to him about death or losing her.

But . . . five-year-olds are smart and Beau is about the most tenacious little guy we know. He would overhear things—he knew, his spirit knew . . . and he was struggling. The day we sat the family down and told them about Kennedy, she was struggling understanding it all. Beau just wrapped his arm around her and told her that he would still have Daddy lift her on the trampoline to play and he would bounce her.

It was these type of moments that melted us as parents. Finally, after a month, Beau opened up and decided to talk to his dad about Kennedy. I took him on a special campout where we rode as far as we could into the mountains so we could just get away. After getting camp set up and lighting a fire, we sat around that fire and began to roast hot dogs. It was at this point that Beau said, "Dad, it was sad when our dog Sunny died, huh?" I said, "Yes, very sad." Beau then said, "Dad, will Kennedy be like Sunny?" I said, "Beau, do you think she is going to die?" Beau quickly changed the subject and went back to the fire. His little mind must have been racing because then he said, "Dad, pinky promise." "Pinky Promise what?" I asked. Beau then spilled his little heart out as best as he could about his care for his sister and what is going on with her.

"Daddy, I know that Kennedy is going to die and go to heaven. I have known this for a while. She and I have talked about it and I told her it's ok. But, Daddy, why? Why does she have to leave me? Why does she have to go to heaven early, Daddy? Why?"

His tears rolled down his face and he looked away and wiped them. He did not want me to see him cry. I could not hold back as I cried and I told him, "Beau, it is ok to cry and it is ok to show our emotions through tears. Tough guys cry, buddy. Tough guys cry. When she dies and goes to heaven, she will be able to be free from all of her pain and her disability and disease. She will be able to fly all over the world and touch everyone in the world."

"Ok, Daddy, ok. I will let her go to heaven. But, will she come and visit me?" I had to stop for a minute and really contain my emotions. I had to sit and think for a minute. "Yes, Beau. Yes, I promise she will come and visit you."

As time moved on, Beau and I held this pinky promise tight to our hearts. At times. we would tie our pinkies together and he would ask me if I remembered the pinky promise.

"Of course I do, son, of course." We held that promise even after Kennedy died. And Beau was the toughest, most loving, most understanding five-year-old that we could have ever asked for that summer. He taught us that taking a back seat is anything but easy, but at times is necessary. And that summer, I learned that a pinky promise is something that you should do with your kids. Promise you will love them, promise you will cherish them, and promise you will honor them. For a pinky promise can go a long, long ways. And in Beau's case, it seemed to carry some feelings that he could only tell his dad around a campfire in the middle of nowhere with only the light of the flames and the stars overhead. And to this day, that promise still holds true in my heart as one of the bonds that held many emotions, secret feelings, and great thoughts that only a little boy could hold dear to his heart about his dying sister.

http://goo.gl/UC4WPb

Scan to view post

CHAPTER 41

THE GATEKEEPER

July 27, 2013 (Recorded from my personal journal):

> My heart is beginning to feel like there are Councils in Heaven meeting and discussing Kennedy's return. Heavenly Father is in control and he knows. Kennedy wrote me a letter yesterday that I could not even fully read! She knows that she is on her way home. I feel that Heather may be the Gatekeeper here on earth with this situation. These feelings just began to hit me strongly as I have been writing this. If that be the case, it is o.k. Kennedy can, will and would do so much good working in Heaven. She is feeling, speaking and working through the spirit! An ambassador for Christ. He will be there undoubtedly to receive her home. For whatever reasons, she is so much a leader in heaven. Why? Why is she so special? I am nothing special. I am just some normal guy. Now, Heather . . . Heather is amazing, outstanding and is very special. I do not know Kennedy's role in Heaven, but I know it will be an important one. Just hoping that I can endure, move forward, be strong and lead. This DAD IS TIRED! Love, JH

No one else saw what I would see and no one else really knew that the GATEKEEPER who held our key chain with Kennedy's giant key was her mother, Heather. Yes, there was so much anxiety, sadness, fear, hopelessness, and loss. Yes, there were moments where we did not know what to do or how to move forward. Yet, this woman, this chosen mother of our daughter Kennedy, was the GATEKEEPER for every molecule of life that was occurring with Kennedy at that time.

Many, many nights, Heather's anxieties would overwhelm her and she would plead on her bedside with God that Kennedy might not suffer greatly and that she might be able to live a beautiful rest of her life without the typical pains of Batten disease and its cruel effects. She would look at me and would tearfully share that she did not know if it all would be ok. How could we get through this and how could Kennedy have a fulfilling remainder of her life?

I had already been given those answers, promptings, and intuitions through so many experiences that it was anything but fantasy. It was reality. I would tell her that Kennedy would have a magical storybook ending and that Heavenly Father had great plans for her to do so. But Heather would be the GATEKEEPER for her and would be instrumental in those plans coming to fruition. "I promise, Heather, I promise that she will have a storybook ending and will go home when she is supposed to. I know this." I would tell her over and over and over each and every day. Yet, how was she supposed to believe?

We realized that Kennedy was in the Lord's hands and not ours. Heather never left her side for hours from that night on and she did not complain—she only loved.

After that night, if the bed squeaked, Heather would run. If Kennedy cried out, Heather would react instantly. Her senses had become Kennedy's senses. Each night, for years, Heather would arise several times and lay by Kennedy's side, comforting her and loving her. This resulted in many sleepless nights for Heather and many nights of comfort for Kennedy.

That summer for some reason, Kennedy did not have as many night terrors or seizures. She was blessed to do well so that she could have the energy she needed to be with those she loved and to touch their lives.

CHAPTER 42

THE RALLY

Without question, Heather and I feel that our circle of friends and family is beyond what we either of us could have handpicked. I cannot thank our Heavenly Father enough for allowing us to have such a great blessing like this as we traveled down the journey with Kennedy. There were some family members who struggled more than others. And in their struggle came our love, our support, and our way of helping to carry them. It was a two-way street where a great parade was going on and we were all involved. The only way that I can describe it is that there was a parade coming from each direction and we were meeting in the middle for a great rally. This rally was for Kennedy. And no one involved was going to let her go unnoticed or uncared for, and no one was going to allow her to become broken from Batten. In fact, we were in a sense celebrating; each of us building, creating, and crafting a beautiful float for this parade. And with each float came the influence of Kennedy. Her beautiful way of impacting each of our minds, thoughts, words, and actions became paramount as we created this parade that would march for a solid year and seemed to be celebrated each and every day.

It was during this time that we sat down and outlined all of the items that would be needed for Kennedy's disease and upcoming care. I was asked to form the list and then send it to some specific family members and friends to help form a game plan. After doing this, we felt a bit overwhelmed and a bit scared. All we knew was that we needed to prepare for the very worst and continue to hope for the best.

It was decided to form a private board for Kennedy and to have her uncle serve as the chairman. This board would be to help raise funds for her through different events, fund-raisers, and donations from specific causes and people. We opted to not start a foundation, but were advised legally to open up a memorial fund. This would enable monies to be donated and used for Kennedy's cause up to and after she passed away. We were beyond humbled as we witnessed family members start up online donation funds and websites, even a donation account. Different levels of donation were offered to different people and the board was anything but timid. They were lovingly aggressive because they wanted to raise enough funds to hit a specific goal in order to make sure that Kennedy would have all of the available and necessary care needed moving forward.

There were many whom we did not even know that heard of Kennedy's story, condition, and illness, and they donated. Stories of little kids' piggy banks and handfuls of change rolled in from all over the country. It seemed that everyone was involved in the rally to make her journey magical. And every day, no one would see the tear stained pillows of mine and Heather's as we would gratefully thank our Father in heaven for all of these outpourings of blessings as we experienced this.

As this was happening, we had another rally going on. The media was exploding Kennedy's story and it had reached some of the highest celebrities. Kennedy's favorite rock band was Imagine Dragons and she was about to attend the rally that they would provide for her. It would forevermore be the first to silence a crowd and the last to make it explode with cheers. For the rally of Kennedy's life was in full swing and nothing could stop such a parade.

CHAPTER 43

THE BUBBLEGUM PINK WHEELCHAIR

It had been only sixty days, yes, sixty days since Kennedy's diagnosis. Yet it felt like sixty years. I hung up the phone at my office and put my head down on my desk. *Hospice?* I thought. *Hospice?* The word *hospice* alone scared the living daylights out of us. Hospice had always meant death, end of life, and simply the end. It was as if we were already being told in a sense that Kennedy was dead while she was still alive. It was decided that hospice would be the best scenario for her since our insurance company, end-of-life care team, doctors, counselors, clergy, family, and therapists all communed together. The amount of upcoming care, expense, and items needed would not fully be covered by hospice, but it would cover considerably more than if we were just on typical insurance.

There was also great concern about Kennedy's rapid digression. As much of an angel as she was and as much of a rock star life as she was living, she still was digressing and dying. Yes, dying right before our eyes. Her changes were no longer subtle, now they were aggressive. Her seizures were worsening and her ability to even walk normally was weakening. With this digression came the pain. It seemed that Kennedy began to complain about different pains, struggles, and areas of hurt within her body. The pain was different. It was not a headache, and it was not a stomachache or a sprained ankle. It was something so deep and dark from within that not even Kennedy could explain it. Kennedy would leave us many times, staring deep off into the distance, while twitching violently and her eyes rolling aggressively around and around and around. This was typical for her since these types of absentee seizures began to occur all too frequently. Her communication was weakening and her ability to run, jump, and play was becoming grim. The all too saddening realization of hospice was now all too necessary.

I walked through the door of our home, and sitting in our living room was the company who would provide Kennedy's wheelchair. There sat Kennedy, Heather, a wheelchair, and this company's wonderful salesman. It was a scene that I wanted to erase but knew I could not. Again, I thought, *Wheelchair? A wheelchair?* Just like with hospice, the questions began to unravel. Yet, the amazing thing was that I felt peace with hospice. And I felt happy about it. And now looking at this wheelchair situation, I was feeling peace and happiness again. Happiness from ordering a wheelchair? Kennedy had an enormous smile on her face and told me to sit down.

As I watched her sitting there and listening to this new friend explain about wheelchairs, I began to see that Kennedy's journey to dealing with Juvenile Batten disease started long ago. And here we were in the last summer of her life with so many meetings, so many doctors, so many people consuming this summer's time for her medical needs. Yet, with Batten disease, there are a lot of equipment needs. Kennedy most of the time would sit patiently in these meetings and listen.

But this was probably one of the hardest meetings for us as we ordered her wheelchair. We never knew HOW MUCH goes into these chairs. It was very complex and so needed, but wow was it an eye-opener. As we met and selected the right chair, had Kennedy fitted, and so on, you could tell that she was concerned. We were so worried that she was just bummed about this next step. We sat next to her and asked her what was wrong. Instead of complaining about her situation and being worried about her condition . . . she simply told us what she just wanted to know. "Ccccan I, I, I g,g,get it in pink, please?"

This little angel was more worried about the color of the chair than the reality of its use. That is Kennedy for you. Our friend slid next to her and said, "Absolutely . . . BUBBLEGUM PINK!" Kennedy's eyes lit up and she gave him a big hug! He felt it, we felt it, and the entire room filled with her love. She then wanted a picture with him and the brochure of her new chair.

Bubblegum pink, that is all she cared about. No concern or complaints for what was happening or coming, no worries about herself, just others. And she wanted to make sure that her new friend got a Kennedy's HUG!

Yes, Kennedy received her wish—a bubblegum pink wheelchair with all the attachments and goodies. As parents, we were asking the tough questions: the mobility, the angles, the height, the cost, and functions. But once again, as an angel, Kennedy taught us all the simple lessons in life and simply asked, "Ccccan I, I, I g,g,get it in pink, please?"

http://goo.gl/oD6WFG

Scan to view post

CHAPTER 44

The First Day, the Last Day

That summer was anything but ordinary. It was extraordinary! It seemed that getting up earlier was not only necessary but easy. And staying up late seemed to be part of the plan. Four thirty to five a.m. would roll around and Heather and I would find ourselves up and going for the day. Kennedy would already be up and playing with dolls or watching a movie. She would still sleep part of the day, so her energy and her need for rest was fine. I would leave for work and begin my day as Heather would provide the much-needed support, love, and transportation to all of the activities that happened that summer.

As the summer was nearing its end, it seemed that Kennedy was ignoring her disease. "Hhhhiiigh sccchool, Hhhigggh schhool!" she would scream. She would watch the High School Musical movies over and over and over in her room. In her mind starting high school was as dreamy as the movie itself. She would tell us that she was going to find her "Troy," the main character from the movie, and that she was going to go to Fremont High and be his girlfriend. She also would talk about being in dance and cheerleading and going to all of the games. In her broken sentences, she explained that she knew she could not be a cheerleader or a dancer, but she wanted to very badly. She also would try to tell us that she was as good as any of the cheerleaders and dancers. She began to make up cheers and would scream, "Wolves, Wolves, Wolves!" Her mind was already at that school and she was already there in spirit. She was not afraid, she was not worried, and she was not shy. She was excited and ready for this new adventure of high school and was ready to take it head on.

Anna was nervous, scared, and doing the typical high school girl things. And as this went on, Anna would tell Kennedy about the different things at the school that were and would be going on. She was so patient, so loving, and so kind to Kennedy when it came to including her in these activities. It was as if her heart continued to melt and was drenching all over Kennedy. And Kennedy would listen intently and want to be involved.

As the weekend before the start of school arrived, we would find Kennedy in her room on the floor with clothes laid on the floor all around her. She would feel them with her hands and pull them right up to her eyes. She still had a tiny pin hole in her right eye that she claimed would allow her to see some things. We really do not know exactly what she could see, but she would try so hard to look. Eventually, as the school year began, she lost that pin hole and could not see anything at all. She would even take her clothes and pull them up to her mouth and her nose. Was she smelling the clothes to try to know what was what? After a few days of this, her mother would tell her to quit taking all of the clothes out of the closet and making such a mess. "Ccccan't, cccan't!" Kennedy would exclaim. "Exxxxcccittted, exxxciiiited!" Her excitement for high school was something we had never seen. We knew she loved school, yet this excitement was new. It seemed that all she could do was smile and tell us about high school. So, of course, we let her just do what she wanted to do.

When the big day came, she insisted on a specific outfit that had already been chosen and was arranged perfectly in her room ready to go. She also loved boots and had a new pair of brown boots that she said everyone would love. She wanted her hair to be perfect and wanted a flower to be put in it. She wanted it curled and said that all of the boys would love it that way. I decided to work from home that morning since I knew that this would be the first day and the last day.

The beginning of school is so emotional for parents. Kennedy always LOVED SCHOOL, so that really was not the issue. With her and Anna both starting high school, it just felt so surreal that our little girls were no longer little.

But, for Kennedy, high school would be different. A special needs bus would pick her up at our front door and bring her right home. This was a first for us and for Kennedy. But Kennedy was ready and waiting right by the front door, early as usual. Anna had already left with some friends, so it was just us and Kennedy that morning. We walked her out to the bus and helped her on. She met the driver, aid, and the bus FULL of other angels with special needs. She was nervous but sooooo excited to wear her new stylish clothes!

As the door closed and we watched the bus drive away, we stood in the walkway to our home and hugged and sobbed. We both knew that this could be the first day . . . but also the last day: the first day of high school, but probably the last first day of school.

When Kennedy arrived home that day, I remember being on the corner waiting for that bus. I was on pins and needles all day as I worked from home. I found myself so many times looking out my office window, wondering, hoping, and praying that her day turned out all right. I was so concerned for her, as was Heather. We just wanted her to feel somewhat normal and to experience the many feelings and opportunities of a normal high school teenager. As the bus pulled up to our driveway and the door opened, I must have jumped on to retrieve my little princess. The bus driver instantly introduced herself, along with the aid, who were so accommodating and beyond good to Kennedy that year. They helped Kennedy stand up and handed her her cane. She had a smile from ear to ear. She looked so happy and was beaming. "Dddadddy, Dddadddy, sccchoool, sccchoool! Fun, Fun!" she screamed. I took her off that bus and walked her into our home. She would not stop talking about the school, the teachers, the new friends, the lunchroom, and of course, the boys. As I watched her interact with her mother, telling her all about her day, it hit me so, so hard. I did not question her leaving us ever. I did not get on my knees and ask God why he wanted her home and would not leave her here with us. I simply questioned why she could not have the normality of the high school scene and the other opportunities that seemed to be given to all of the other kids.

That night my heart hurt so badly for Kennedy. Although so happy, so full of life, and so full of spunk, I knew that she would never get the whole experience. As I went to bed, I found myself again on the side of my bed. I buried my face in our mattress, pleading silently to my Heavenly Father. "Please, please Father in Heaven, somehow, someway give Kennedy the same opportunities this year as the other kids. Please help her to feel normal, to experience activities, to experience social feelings, dances, and even twitterpation and love. Please, Father, I plead with you that she can be granted this. She is so happy, yet I know with her disability that she will not have these same opportunities and these same experiences unless you allow them to happen. I love her so much and am trying so hard to provide everything I can to make her journey and the rest of her life the very best it can be. I am turning this over to you and asking humbly for this blessing for her. Please help me to be open, aware, and understanding to and of the Spirit so that I can help this to happen. Please, Father, please."

As I closed my prayer and climbed back into bed, it seemed as if my world and visions of Kennedy were crashing down and building up all at the same time. For at that moment, a shrill came from her room and Heather jumped up to go to her side as usual. I went to her room and watched Heather consoling Kennedy as Kennedy sat up and screamed, "Mmmonsssters, scccared, scared!" She was sweating and did not know where she was at. Her dementia was worsening and her ability to sleep through a night had entirely faded into the distance. As I looked at this scene, I felt horrified. There was no way that Kennedy would ever have a normal year. There was no way that she would be able to function at any type of high school level to include herself into the normal activities and associations that existed in high school.

I felt alone as I left Heather to lie by her side that night. I wanted so much for her to experience high school, yet felt I was asking for too much. I just wanted some normalcy for Kennedy, for our family, and for myself. I almost felt guilty that night for feeling the way that I was feeling. And as I pondered that night and thought about it all, I suddenly felt that same feeling that I always would and had felt in these critical situations. The Spirit of God came over me, and again, that feeling came to my mind, *"You always listen to the Spirit, which is a higher power, and if you do, you will know exactly what to do."* As this strong feeling came over me again, I seemed to have a little vision open up in my mind. And a voice came into my head that said, "Take her to the football game with you this weekend. Take her and have fun. Be there with her and do not leave her side."

As I drifted off to sleep that night, I had no idea what that meant, what it would mean or would create. I only knew how I felt and what Kennedy wanted. She wanted to share herself with the world. And yet, she was being limited to parts of that happening but being allowed for other parts that were about to happen.

http://goo.gl/ddjdgy

Scan to view post

CHAPTER 45

The Miracle Walk

I followed that prompting and took Kennedy to the football game, not knowing it would be the first of many. That week turned out to be special. It was homecoming week at Fremont High, so the night before the game there was a parade and a huge pep rally. The sound of the band playing, the crowd gathering, the cheerleaders cheering, and announcer screaming all seemed to excite every one of us. But for Kennedy it was more than exciting. It was living! She was in her element and where she belonged. When we arrived at the parade, she sat on the bed of the truck and did not stop cheering or screaming from the minute we arrived until the parade ended.

And as we traveled to the stadium, she even sat with the pep club as they cheered and was screaming so loud and so long that many around us were looking at her. She would listen to the cheers and would try to follow along. Eventually, she memorized most of them and could do them in perfect sequence within just minutes. Heather and I were in shock! Not only could she scream out the cheers, but she screamed them out perfectly. It seemed as if a component of her mind would open up and would have the ability to memorize songs, cheers, lyrics, and quotes from movies.

She had some friends around her and they were cheering with her and helping her. She was a true Fremont Silverwolf and exemplified more spirit in my humble opinion then probably anyone at that rally. Toward the end of the rally, Kennedy asked to go down by the track and field. This request seemed to be awkward and a bit outlandish. “Hear, hhhhear?” she exclaimed. “Hear what?” I asked.

"Go, lllet's go!" she said. She stood up and grabbed her cane and began walking out of the bleachers from where we sat. She was on a mission and no one was going to stop her. I told Heather that I would take her down by the track and on a walk. As we got closer, Kennedy began to walk faster. She shuffled her feet when she walked at that point and walked a bit pigeon-toed as well. But she could hear those cheers. Those sweet cheers. And at that point she knew. But I had no idea. I had no guess nor could I even imagine that those cheers were coming from her twenty-seven other sisters. Sisters whom had been chosen just for her and her for them.

As we got closer, she kept saying, "Lllissten, llllisten!" She could now hear the sound of the pom-poms and voices so strong. She could hear the flyers flying through the air and their cheer skirts whistling as they flew. She walked up to the railing and sat and listened. She had a different smile, a different look on her face. It was one that I had never seen before. It was as if she were coming alive in a different way and in a different physical format.

She probably sat there for a good minute before she said, "Walk, Dad, wwwwalk!" And then she walked. She walked down that track almost perfectly! The bleachers were full and people were staring. People were wondering and people were talking. I have had many, many people tell me their accounts of what they saw on this night as they sat in those bleachers and watched. They were caught by Kennedy and some have said that a glow surrounded me and her as we walked.

We went arm in arm down that track and got closer and closer and closer to these cheerleaders. As we arrived to where they were lined up, Kennedy simply slowed down. She walked slowly and listened to their cheers. She peered her eyes toward them trying to see. She quickly handed me her cane and began to clap her hands and scream out the cheers that they were cheering. She kept walking, and she kept listening. She kept gravitating toward them and moving forward. As this was happening, I pulled her back by my side, not wanting to interrupt them or cause a scene. I only wanted to give Kennedy that small sense of normality and that feeling of being who she wanted to be.

As we kept walking, it would be easy to think that I may have felt embarrassed or overwhelmed by the scene going on. Yet, I felt neither of these things, I felt love, I felt security, and I felt like this is where we belonged. As this was happening, one of the cheerleaders suddenly broke from her cheering and came walking over to Kennedy. "Hi!" she exclaimed. "What is your name?"

"Kkkkenedy," Kennedy said.

"Kennedy? That is a beautiful name! I'm Jordan. Looks like you love cheering!"

Kennedy suddenly began to clap and just scream out "Wolves!" She began to do a cheer and was giving it all she had. The cheerleader she just met had a look of "wow!" on her face. She began to talk to Kennedy a little bit and told her how amazing her cheering was.

Without hesitation, Kennedy reached out and pulled her right into her and hugged her. The cheerleader was a bit shocked but accepted the hug. Kennedy just kept hugging her and hugging her as they stood there together. This created a bit of a scene for the other cheerleaders as some of them made their way over to where Kennedy stood and introduced themselves to her. She just kept cheering and hugging and cheering and hugging. It seemed so right. It felt so right.

As this went on, suddenly it came time for the cheerleaders to hurry and go and make the traditional tunnel that the team would run through. After this was done, a HUGE bonfire was made that the students would all race across the field toward it as it burned in a metal structure shaped like a wolf. Kennedy found herself quickly included by her sister, Anna, and other students as they took her over into the tunnel line. She was laughing and having so much fun.

I held her cane and watched as again tears streamed down my face. Why was I so emotional over such a thing? It seemed that every little thing would set off my emotions, yet it was because these were the first and last things that she would be able to experience here on this earth and in this life. She was home. She was at peace and she was feeling what none of us could feel. Her feet were touching the track, where she had just taken the miracle walk. That walk would open up the door for some of the greatest moments of her life and our lives to take place very shortly. And she was home and she was comfortable.

http://goo.gl/bEmQRD

Scan to view post

CHAPTER 46

Move Over, Cinderella

Ever since the dance that summer at our church's youth conference, Kennedy had let loose with her giant key chain of keys that was now molded into one key. She was unlocking massive doors for herself and the world with her key and it was working! There was no doubt that she was not only unlocking doors of opportunities but also unlocking hearts as well. With homecoming at the school going on, for weeks she would come home and talk about the dance, the activities, and all that she was going to participate in. We worried greatly about all this talk as we discussed her situation and disease and disability. Heather and I were so worried that her heart would be crushed since she probably would not be asked to the dance. Boy were we wrong!

Shortly after school began, a sweet boy who is deaf and has a disability of his own reached out through his mother and friends to ask permission for Kennedy to go to the homecoming dance. Of course, we were honored, surprised, and very agreeable to this. He was so respectful, cute, and excited to ask Kennedy to the dance. After being asked, you would have thought Kennedy was going to the National Presidential Ball. Every day for a solid three weeks, it seemed as if Kennedy, Anna, and Heather were making preparations. The dress had to be just right, and the jewelry perfect. Her shoes, hair, and makeup would need to be stunning. These three were having so much fun and Kennedy was ready. She had quietly seemed to be the Cinderella amongst her friends for years. Not getting much attention and not asking for it either. Quietly serving everyone around her with nothing but a smile on her face and a spring in her step. Because Kennedy knew that her time would be coming and she would have her Cinderella moments.

Anna was next to perfect in the way she assisted Kennedy in her preparations for this dance. All Anna wanted was for her sister to have an amazing time. And I was simply a fly on the wall, wanting to make sure that she had every single thing available at her fingertips. This dance, this moment, and all moments for her needed to be celebrated to the maximum. Kennedy was reaching the peak and pinnacle of her life here on earth and she had not only earned but also deserved to have every second of it.

When the big day came, Kennedy awoke with excitement. This was her day! She could not even contain herself. It meant lots of screams, laughter, and girl time! She was ready.

She waited patiently for her date to pick her up. This dance was very unique. Kennedy was blind and her date was deaf. Want to talk about communication of spirits? I will tell you what, those two are greater than ALL of us put together.

They exchanged flowers and then headed to Kennedy's favorite restaurant: "Texas Roadhouse!" Kennedy's first thing on her list was to order a COKE! They ate dinner and had a ball. A translator accompanied them who translated everything Kennedy said and communicated back to Kennedy what her date said as well. Being excited, happy, nervous, and overwhelmed were all feelings that we had as parents that night. We decided to be flies on the wall and accompany them where they went. We also asked the school if we could be chaperones at the dance. We did not want Kennedy to know we were there, but we wanted to make sure that we were there for her, just in case anything were to go wrong. We sat several rows away and caught wind of lots of laughs! Several times Heather would go to get up to help, because she is SO USED TO HELPING KENNEDY WITH EVERYTHING. I had to hold her back and say, "Just let her experience this. Let her feel normal." After dinner, a limo picked them up. And honest to goodness, they went for the ride of their lives. This limo driver practically flew! We did seventy on a well-known road in Ogden, Utah, Washington Boulevard, and could not catch up to him.

We pulled up to a red light and I asked Heather, "Should I run the light to catch up?" We could see heads and bodies sliding around inside the blue LED lit cab of the limo as they rounded the corner. This guy was crazy! We got to the school and the limo driver had already dropped them off and left. Kennedy could not stop laughing, though her date looked like a deer in the headlights. I asked him if he was ok. He signed,

"That was the craziest ride I have ever been on!" Kennedy could not stop laughing over and over and over. She said, "That wa, wa, waaaas soooooo fun!" Simply put, one wild driver. Very fun times!

We sat back and watched two incredible young kids dance each song together, holding hands and trying so hard to fit in. Kennedy's date could feel the beat of the music and Kennedy knew most of the songs. They danced and laughed and danced. They did not stop. They RADIATED! And that brilliance began to touch so many that night and that coming year. Teenagers and high school kids can be so mean, so cruel, and so ignorant. Yet, there was something different about Fremont High. There seemed to be a different feeling, setting, and group of kids there that year. And on that night as Kennedy and her date danced, you could see it. There was no one making fun, there was no one making comments or laughing. Everyone seemed to accept, love, and understand that what was happening was special. And yet as this brilliance of love occurred, there were not that many who even knew her name yet, or her situation. All they knew was that feeling that most learned to feel as they came to know Kennedy. Because with her, she invited you to feel.

As we sat and watched, several kids stopped to say hi. We sat in the back and watched our Kennedy receive one of her dreams. She got her BALL! She got her Cinderella dress and Cinderella moment. She danced until she was exhausted and done. We shed a few tears, laughed, and simply SOAKED in the moment.

Our hearts were full and to this day are still full of endless thanks to this young man for being a kind, incredible, and respectful; he was a good-looking young man. All this for taking care of Kennedy and asking her to the dance! He opened doors, helped her down stairs, held her arm, and showed great concern. He was a true gentleman, who is growing into a man. We NEED MORE OF THEM!

Her wish was granted and Kennedy's ball was a success! That night she slept like an angel. She was exhausted, fulfilled, and excited. Yet, she was changing and the changes were ever so hard. After such a long day, you could see the wear and tear on her physically. Her eyes glowed almost a deep red and her steps were so out of proportion that you would have thought she was drunk. And it was not just being tired, it was her brain shutting down. It was her brain beginning the process of not being able to tell the rest of her body what to do and how to do it. The blessing that night is that she did sleep like an angel. One of very few nights that year that she slept virtually all the way through. As we went to bed that night, we held each other in our arms with a smile and with slow gentle tears. Tears that were produced not from sadness, but gratitude. For our Cinderella had finally appeared, conquered, and radiated. And for that, we could do nothing else but cry.

http://goo.gl/bfPXZ3

Scan to view post

CHAPTER 47

Cheer On, Kennedy, Cheer On

We had seen so many keys added to our key chain. Monumental moments that, in our minds, could not be surpassed or become any greater. We felt beyond grateful for what had occurred that summer and fall for Kennedy and our family. We were not quite sure what else could top it off. Our goals, minds, and hearts were now set on getting her through the school year and the next phases of her disease. If she were to pass away at that moment, we felt that she had already been blessed with and experienced more then we could have ever asked for. Boy, were we in for a surprise. We had no idea what was coming and about to happen, yet the stars were aligned and still aligning. It seemed that every one of them in the Kennedy galaxy was beginning to shoot to earth to make her life a planet of its own.

The day after homecoming was over, Kennedy could not stop talking about Fremont High: the boys, the cheerleaders, and high school. To her, life had just begun. But to us, her life was ending. It was a battle between two sharp swords that were locked together: so much happiness for her, yet so much reality for us as parents. Kennedy was relentless that Sunday after homecoming to share about it with everyone. She wore her dress to church and looked like a perfect princess. So many complimented her on it and on how beautiful she looked.

She could not wipe the smile off of her face as she described to the other young women her age how happy she was and how fun the dance was. As we witnessed this, the tender mercies rolled in like a wildfire, sweeping up our hearts and making us feel so good. Yet the wildfire of emotions was also slowly burning out, leaving charred pieces of our hearts devastated like ash. We had no idea how we were going to keep this wildfire burning without hurting Kennedy. Yet we did not have to. Because the Fremont High cheerleading coach, on that very day, had her entire world turned upside down for the better as she began her journey with Kennedy. A journey that forever changed the lives of twenty-seven young girls who gave up all to become a sister to Kennedy. And a journey that made a wish and dream come true for Kennedy. The dream of becoming a Fremont high cheerleader.

On that Sunday afternoon the cheer coach received a text from one of her cheerleaders. In that text this cheerleader said that she and her mom had been talking about a girl named Kennedy who had been diagnosed with a disease called Batten and that she had little time left in her life. The cheerleader explained that she had read about Kennedy on Facebook and knew that Kennedy had always dreamed of becoming a cheerleader. She asked the cheer coach if it would be ok if they could have Kennedy come down with them on the track at a game. The cheer coach told her she thought that would be a great idea and that they could talk about it at cheer class. Meanwhile, this cheerleader messaged us on Facebook and shared that she and some of the other cheerleaders had heard and read about Kennedy online. They told us that they were inspired by Kennedy and wanted to know if we would let them include her in a game sometime. Of course we were thrilled and agreed.

The next week at cheer class the cheerleaders gathered around and discussed this girl Kennedy. Many wanted to know who she was. A picture was pulled up of Kennedy and shown to the group. As the cheer coach saw this picture, her heart burst. This was a picture she had seen on her phone randomly the Sunday before as she was looking up a quote online to help her sister. What were the chances? And why would this girl's photo come up randomly? The team discussed what they could do for Kennedy. It was decided that they would have her cheer at a home football game with them. She had to have a uniform and pom-poms for this. But with cheerleading, everything is ordered in May or April so the chances of getting an extra uniform were near impossible. Phone calls were made and miracles occurred. The company that made the cheer uniforms communicated that they had miraculously ordered extra fabric for that uniform order and could have a uniform made to fit Kennedy within one week. This was a miracle. A uniform usually takes 4–6 months to get back.

Heather and I were still soaking in the excitement from Kennedy's

Homecoming experience when the phone rang and the cheer coach wanted to speak with us. She introduced herself to us and asked if we would let Kennedy cheer at the next football game on October 4, 2013. Heather excitedly told her that this night would be perfect for Kennedy! Heather explained that Kennedy's cousin was a cheerleader on the opposing team (Northridge High) who Fremont would be playing. Kennedy had always wanted to cheer with her cousin, but the realities of her disease had squashed the idea of this dream becoming true. This was special.

The cheer coach asked if the cheer team could tell Kennedy themselves about this great upcoming event. We agreed and on September 26, 2013, that amazing group of girls and their angel coach traveled down the hallways of Fremont High where a feeling overcame them that has been described by many of them as "different, magical, special and sacred." The cheerleaders were dressed in their warm-up outfits and were so excited that they practically ran to Kennedy's class. After arriving to the class, Kennedy was told that there were some visitors there who wanted to talk with her. The cheer coach knelt down by Kennedy's desk as the entire team encircled Kennedy. She explained that she was the cheer coach at Fremont High and that she had heard that Kennedy had a talent. Kennedy replied a "Yeah," to her. The coach explained that the team needed another cheerleader and they were wondering if Kennedy would help them out with this. The team set a pair of pom-poms on her desk as Kennedy's face lit up with a look of excitement and surprise. She again responded, "Yeah." The cheer coach told her that they wanted her to be ready for the next home game and that they even had a uniform for her. They then had Kennedy stand up and the entire team embraced her in a hug. Tears were in some eyes as these girls received back their first Kennedy's Hug—one of many to come. Many of them said as she hugged back that they had never felt a hug back like that before or felt the way they felt at that moment. We received a call from the cheer coach after this, telling us all of the details as she cried and we cried. She told us that girls said they felt like their hearts were going to explode and they were skipping back to the gym so positive and so full of love.

Although hesitant in some ways, we were ecstatic in others. Kennedy was going to have her dream fulfilled of being a cheerleader at a football game! That week she jumped right in and began to attend cheer class. She showed up to her first class and did not even hesitate. She began cheering and participating as if she had always just been part of the team.

And she tried, oh how she tried. She wanted to do everything any cheerleader could or would do and she wanted the team to know that she was the best cheerleader in the world.

The anticipation for this game was huge around our house. Kennedy was cheering every day, every minute, preparing and shouting. She would cheer so much that Beau would tell her to, "Stop, stop, stop!" But, they also had fun as he would take his football or basketball and act like he was playing at Fremont High and she would cheer him on.

When that Friday came, so did our new family. This amazing cheer coach and her twenty-seven cheerleaders showed up to our house and delivered an official letter to Kennedy telling her that she was a Fremont High cheerleader. They gathered around Kennedy in our family room where they presented her with an official uniform. As they gave Kennedy these different items, it was very special and the coach awarded her with her warm-up jacket. This sweet and loving coach took Kennedy's hands and held them in her own as she ran Kennedy's fingers over the embroidery and asked her if she knew what the words said. Kennedy did not, so she lovingly told her that she was feeling the words *cheerleader* and *Kennedy*. She then said, "You are a Fremont cheerleader!" The room erupted and the girls cheered. Heather and I were in tears and Kennedy was beaming a smile so big that we all just wanted to run over and hug her.

I will never forget as Heather curled Kennedy's hair and put her makeup on. For you see this was a dream come true for not just Kennedy, but all of us. Together I could hear them laughing and joking as she got ready. I was in my office working when I heard a little shuffle of pom-poms and looked up to see my little girl beaming. She said, "Ddddad, I,IIIII'm aaa ccccheareader!" I could not contain the emotions as I looked at her. Her dream was now a reality. Many thought that Kennedy may only last one quarter of the game that night or at best one half. But that night, oh that night was special. She began cheering that first quarter and just did not stop. It was as if she transformed into someone else and she was cheering at a high school football game! I turned to my wife and said, "He is aware. He is so aware of us."

"Who is aware?" she asked.

"Heavenly Father, Heavenly Father," I whispered. "He answered my prayer." As the tears came, suddenly the track below us filled up with the cheerleaders from Kennedy's cousin's school and with parents, faculty, students, and others. We were asked over the intercom to come down to the track, where we were surprised and awarded with a beautiful tree and thousands of dollars that had been raised as a surprise by both Fremont High and Northridge High School. A giant check was awarded to us from Home Depot and we were told that they would be remodeling Kennedy's bathroom to accommodate her upcoming needs of being in a wheelchair. We were in shock! We were in dismay. This night, this community, these cheerleaders, their cheer coach, and this school—it all felt like a dream, because guess what? It was. It was a dream now becoming reality. And Kennedy, well, Kennedy just kept cheering. She cheered the whole game! And she was not even tired. It was as if she had always just been part of the team.

And so it began, the key around our neck that had opened so many doors now opened another. As parents, we were waiting for someone to pinch us, to wake us up from such a magical dream. In less than one week, we witnessed our terminally ill daughter attend a high school homecoming dance, become a cheerleader, and cheer at a game. We were honored as a community of two schools, businesses, foundations, and people rallied together to support our family for the sole purpose of supporting Kennedy. And although we were living the ending of Kennedy's life, it simply felt like the beginning. There was an excitement in the air that, regardless of the stresses occurring around us, could not be ignored.

Kennedy was more alive now, more than she ever could have been. And from the outside looking in, there were now thousands who were screaming, supporting, and rallying with the saying, "Cheer on, Kennedy. Cheer on." And with that cheering came something that no one could anticipate: the great impact of Kennedy on all those who were cheering. For within her giant spirit and her little world, she had already made great plans. Plans that none of us could or would expect. Plans that would not only change us, but also impact millions across the world.

http://goo.gl/gvBcY8

Scan to view post

http://goo.gl/jm7GkC

Scan to view post

CHAPTER 48

Imagine—Touching the Hearts of Imagine Dragons!

Screams of excitement came from the back of the car. Kennedy had waited so long for this day, this moment, and this night. The song "Radioactive" blasted from the speakers.

The father of one of the band's members had contacted us and said that there might be a chance to meet the band after the concert. But either way Kennedy was just ecstatic to be there. She was wearing the Imagine Dragons T-shirt that had been sent to her by one of the band members and she had completely dolled herself up for the concert.

As we waited and listened to the opening act, Kennedy could not wipe the smile off of her face. We brought her wheelchair with us knowing that she would probably tire out early and need to rest sitting down at times. Upon arriving, we were shocked. Every staff member at the concert was saying, "Hi, Kennedy! Welcome, Kennedy! We love you, Kennedy!" They took us and escorted us to a special area until about ten minutes before the band was to play. It then seemed as if time stopped as we helped Kennedy walk down the loooooong set of stairs at Weber State University Dee Events Center where the concert was held. Her uncle, aunt, and cousins were right by her side. They were the ones who initiated, planned, and made this night happen. Her cousin had introduced Kennedy to the song "Radioactive" earlier in the year and had played it on his guitar for her. She had sung the song many, many times and a Facebook post of this went viral. When the video of Kennedy singing this song had gone viral, we were contacted by a very good friend of one of the band member's family. This friend got in touch with the band and shared

Kennedy's story with them. Through her outreach, the band took notice and was touched to reach out to us.

As we walked down the stairs, people were yelling, "Hi, Kennedy! We love you, Kennedy! Enjoy the concert, Kennedy!" People were coming up and hugging her and shaking her hand. As parents, we were in awe. There was so much support, so much love, and so much awareness of her story surrounding us in our hometown of Ogden, Utah. It was amazing how many people were following, supporting, and surrounding Kennedy and our family with love and support.

Kennedy reached the bottom of the stairs and we all cheered for her. "You made it, Kennedy! You made it!" We had reached the floor area level with the band. Now she was getting excited, really excited. But, that is where it all started. A staff member of the band came up and said, "Kennedy, follow us. We have a surprise for you!" We were escorted to a private room, where in walked, you guessed it—Imagine Dragons! For ten minutes, hugs, laughs, and tears were exchanged and they even signed her shirt. Dan Reynolds whispered in Kennedy's ear, "I love you, Kennedy, and this night is entirely devoted to you!" They were sincere, they were loving, and they were interested. The crowd was antsy, waiting on their toes and cheering. The band was supposed to have started and they sat there with Kennedy. Her dream of meeting this band was fulfilled. But we saw tears, change, and humility as they were given the treat of meeting her. They asked what she wanted and she just said, "Hugs!" She hugged each one of them and then, as best as she could, said, "Wwwwwaiiit!" She then sang "Radioactive" for them.

This was unbelievably emotional for everyone! She did this with no fear but with great love. Her voice rang out in that room and it felt as if we were in heaven together. She tried so, so hard to share with them her singing so that they would know how appreciative and how much she loved not just their music, but them! As we all left that room, I was suddenly stopped in my tracks and peered back into the meeting room where such a sweet moment had just taken place. Something tugged at me and nagged my insides. This room was special. Very special! I did not understand it, nor would I until seven months later when I would stand in that very room and close the casket of our beautiful daughter and tell her goodbye. For that was the room where we would hold her viewing, her life-ending celebration, and our family prayer as we would say goodbye. And at that point, at that moment, I had no idea, nor could

I even fathom that Kennedy's funeral and story would reach a point to be held in a stadium.

The band took the stage and the night was amazing. What a performance, what a crowd. It was sold out! Kennedy left her wheelchair and never looked back at it for a moment. She danced, sang, and laughed for two hours until at the very end.

That is when Dan (the lead singer) thanked Utah for where their band started and for such a great night and concert. And then he did it. He said, "Kennedy, I know you can hear me. I know you are out there and you have touched me. This song is dedicated to you! This one's for you, Kennedy!"

BAAAAAAAAM! The music pounded and the song began. The song, "Radioactive." The crowd went wild. Kennedy was screaming. As parents, we were bawling. She jumped around, she smiled, and she was amazed. She had just single-handedly touched the hearts of the MOST POPULAR ROCK BAND in the world!

This song was her favorite. You could feel the energy, the emotion, and the love from this band as they ended with this song. At the end, Ben, the guitarist, looked down at our family, pointed to Kennedy, touched his heart, and pumped his fist.

What a night and what a journey to get to this concert. Kennedy did not really know her spread of influence. There was a line of hundreds wanting to meet her. We had to have security escort us through a private tunnel to leave the concert. She was upset. She wanted to hug everyone. But they had to get us out of there.

As we were leaving, the general manager of the band came up and said, "Thank you, thank you, thank you. You have inspired us. Kennedy and your family are an inspiration to us and thousands. Her story is spreading and I follow it daily. And believe it or not, it is changing some of our band members. Thank you, thank you, thank you."

No. Thank you. Thank you, Imagine Dragons, for making one of our daughter's earthly dreams come true.

That night I asked myself, "How in the world am I so lucky to have a daughter who is affecting thousands? She does not know who and how she touches. She just does. Whether it is a small girl at the grocery store, a neighbor, or Dan Reynolds from Imagine Dragons . . . Kennedy, yes, is touching people and will for generations to come."

Looking back, I can still see that night in my mind. As her wheelchair sat empty, I was grateful. I was happy, I was overwhelmed, and I was touched. The great dreams of Kennedy were being fulfilled and the aspirations of her heart were not just being considered but granted. To swell so large and so broad that when her heart would finally burst, it would bleed love, love, love forevermore.

http://goo.gl/FB7lY8

Scan to view post

CHAPTER 49

The Start of Something New

There was officially no way of stopping the Kennedy freight train. It was moving ahead at full speed, with full force, and with every bit of steam Kennedy possessed. You see, Kennedy had always been the little cutie. She had always had the beautiful long hair, the batting long lashes, and the engaging smile. From a very young age, she had always had her crushes and her boyfriends. And although she was very shy, she seemed to have a lot confidence in the boy area. Kennedy's days were now full of teenage moments. From sun up until sun down, it seemed that she had an agenda. She had loved going to homecoming and had mentioned a crush on one boy quite a bit. But, these crushes seemed a little elementary and surreal like most.

As parents, Heather and I had accepted the reality years earlier that Kennedy would probably never marry and have kids. Yet, now we did not have any choice but to accept this. This acceptance was pure reality. Our hearts did hurt that we would not be able to see her truly fall in love, to see her experience love, passion, trust, friendship, teamwork, having children, and raising a family. And through it all, we also were crushed that we would never have or see the day of Kennedy giving us grandkids. It was an incessant nagging feeling that would not leave us, yet we had to force ourselves to walk away from it on many, many occasions.

As Kennedy began to cheer at the football games and attend school activities, she was assigned to different people to help her navigate and get around. She was enrolled in a religious school class called seminary. This is a class that students are able to take during the day who are part of the LDS church. Once a day, this class teaches them different values, principles, and religious aspects. It was a huge blessing to both of our daughters during junior high and high school.

Kennedy would sit quietly in this class and could only hear voices. As she did, she heard the voice of a boy named Jaden. Now Jaden was not your typical normal high school kid. Jaden was a star athlete, star student, very popular, and also involved in many religious activities. Jaden was considered to be one of the best-looking and most popular boys in school. Jaden and his girlfriend, who was a friend of Kennedy's her whole life, had decided to sign up as aids in seminary for the special needs class. And it was here where "the start of something new" happened.

Kennedy could not see him, but from day one, she felt his presence. She asked her friends in the class to describe him to her. "Wwwhhat dddoes he llook like?" she would ask. They would describe his blonde hair, hazel eyes, and muscular physique to her. She would laugh and say, "Hhot, hhot! He's hot!" Everyone would laugh, but she was serious, dead serious. She began to come home each day and as we would take her off of the bus, the first thing she would talk about was Jaden. And it was not just the first, but the last. I swear I think that we heard the name Jaden over 1000 times before ever meeting him. Yet, each and every time she brought up his name, we felt something, and as cheesy and weird as it sounds, we felt something special.

We wanted to meet this Jaden since he was all too important to Kennedy. We will never forget that day on October 10, 2013. Kennedy and the cheerleading team were cheering at an away football game at Weber High School in North Ogden, Utah. The day was beautiful, but cold. And that cold turned to a pouring and pounding rain, one you would have thought could have even canceled a football game.

The rain beat down like a drum in a rock band that night! It did not let up and it was a heavy, large dumping type of rain. It was cold, it was miserable, and as parents we were dreading going and sitting in it at a football game.

We were also worried, protective, and curious as to how Kennedy would handle the rain cheering with the Fremont High cheerleading squad, it being only her second game. As the night wore on and the rain grew thicker, the clouds grew darker and the drench began to soak through our coats. We began to hear screams, and we saw the rest of the cheerleaders surrounding Kennedy. Was everything all right? Was she ok? We ran out to the track and into the circle of these amazing girls, only to find Kennedy reaching out with her hands on her cheeks and screaming, "fun, fun, fun . . . rain, cheering in the rain!"

She ignored the cold, she ignored the wet. She ignored the misery of a night that really was that—cold and miserable! Instead, she chose to embrace the rain. Many of the cheerleaders commented on this and have since reminded us of that night. Her coach told us that several of the cheerleaders wanted to go home until this moment. It was a night that put a smile on all of our faces. As we were all complaining, she was gleaming! She was living her dream of being a cheerleader come rain, sleet, snow, or hurricanes! She just did it how Kennedy always did, with love.

Toward the end of the game, Kennedy began to scream out "Ddad, Ddad, Ddad!" Her screams were definitely with good meaning. I had told her that I wanted to meet this Jaden and soon. So when I heard the screams and knew they were of serious intent, it was well worth the wait. There, standing in the rain in a hoodie, was the amazing Jaden. He came down from the stands and stuck his hand out. "Hello, Mr. Hansen. I am Jaden." I shook his hand and then reached out and put my arm around him. "The famous Jaden," I replied. "Finally, I get to meet you."

His eyes did not light up, his demeanor did not change. For you see, Jaden was already lit up and charged with an inner spirit of happiness, kindness, and genuine greatness from a mile away. I thanked him for being such a great friend to Kennedy and a support to her. I told him how important he was and is to her. He simply smiled and said, "Kennedy is the best, Mr. Hansen. I mean that. I truly feel something special when I am around her. Thank you for letting me be part of her life." As we were having this little conversation, it was suddenly interrupted with the happy screams of Kennedy and about 10 mauling cheerleaders who brought her over to his side. She was beaming and I had never before seen her like that. It caught me off guard and it caught me by surprise. I think that as her dad, I probably knew and had seen her more than anyone else other than her mom. But, I had never seen a look on her face like that one before. She did not just hug Jaden, she basically attacked him.

She could not stop hugging him, saying his name and saying, "hi," "you're hot," and "thanks." I stepped back and leaned against the railing with the rain just pouring down on us. I had every reason to be so unhappy at that moment. I had more bills than I could pay, I was struggling in a new job, I had a daughter who was dying, and, yes, it was raining. But instead, I just sat and my tears mixed with those raindrops. This was surely "the start of something new" and everyone there knew it and could feel it. After the game, Kennedy only asked for one thing . . . hot chocolate! We gladly bought her a cup and she slurped it right down. She was wet from head to toe, but she had a smile from ear to ear.

And more than anything, she showed her true self which in turn was touching people like Jaden. When we got home that night, she told us that she was going to ask Jaden to the Sadie Hawkins dance. We really did not know how this would work out. But it did. Kennedy asked him to the dance with the help of her mother, sister, and Jaden's girlfriend. They got it done and he said, "Yes!"

The next couple of weeks were crazy to say the least. At that time in our lives and in those weeks when we would arrive home, it seemed we spent countless hours going over medical equipment, changes in our home, future planning for care, and so, so, so many great events for Kennedy.

Our only real free day was Saturday. And Kennedy's Sadie Saturday going to a girl's choice dance with Jaden finally came. We helped her get ready and then spent the remaining seven hours of our day going through a completion of a life documentary that we were making of Kennedy.

Our "moments" seemed captivated by her "moments." We were so inspired to catch these "moments" and live them at that moment. We were being blessed to have time stop and to have peace and happiness with that time. It is hard to explain. We had a friend tell us at that time, "You guys are just so busy, you never have time to do the things that you used to really, really enjoy." Well, from a worldly perspective that is true, but we were enjoying "moments" that otherwise would never have come. And our new "moments" were more enjoyable than any other worldly experience we could buy.

After that Saturday was over, Heather was flat out exhausted and sick. She lay in bed all night, being so tired from being up each night late with Kennedy. We wanted to get some rest, but she could not because Kennedy was coming home from her first girl's choice dance and neither one of us wanted to miss the "moments" we would get with her excitement telling us all about it.

So, around midnight she was brought home and we experienced some wonderful "moments" with both of our daughters sharing all about their great date night. We could see "the start of something new" with

Jaden and we were beyond grateful.

It quite frankly is hard to have your life change, but having those "moments" is a time we were trying to enjoy, endure, and face with utmost courage, forward thinking, and positive attitude.

"Moments" continue to come and more than anything, we would enjoy these "moments", hold on to them, and look to the future with hope. But at that time, our feeling was that "moments" would not be much longer with Kennedy. She was declining rapidly in her communication, her nights were shortening, and her memory was fading.

We were trying to enjoy the "moments" and all in all we were just remembering that "moments" are all you take with you when this life ends. "Moments" are real, "moments" are special, "moments" are important. Enjoy the "moments!" was becoming our motto.

That night I recorded in my journal, November 2, 2013. "I felt something that I had not felt in a long, long time today. I felt the Spirit whispering to me that Kennedy will be going home SOONER than LATER. It was an overwhelming presence that could not leave me. It is now to the point where when the Spirit speaks, I just believe. I could not bear the thought of losing her this soon. We will lose her sooner than later."

As we each are hit with "the rain" in our lives, do we embrace it and learn to deal with the darkest and most miserable parts? Or do we run from it and hide from the track that we have been assigned to, to cheer on in our lives? The rain will always come. It may dump some days, it may sprinkle on others, and at times it may pour. But, if we choose to change our perspective, our attitude, and our minds, if we choose to share in the rain versus run from the rain, sometimes, not all the time, the result may just be as Kennedy said, "Fun, fun, fun . . . rain, cheering in the rain!"

http://goo.gl/o76U4l

Scan to view post

CHAPTER 50

Party or Preparation?

Dear Christ, Thank you for never giving up on me. Thank you for me on earth. I love you so much! Thank you for my Mom and Dad too. Thank for hair, eyes, ears, nose, legs, arms, feet, hands. I love your comfort. I always go to church. Love it and love you. Thank you for seminary and my birthday and Jaden. I love Coke. Thank you for all friends. Thankful for my heart. Thankful for my bones. I love you. Love, Kennedy."

Kennedy's sixteenth birthday was right around the corner and she was beginning to express herself in different ways. Her discussions were turning to eternal, and heavenly discussions and "so many lasts" were going to happen that she was telling us about. Her gratefulness to those around her and especially her Heavenly Father and Jesus Christ was paramount as we would have so many different experiences to share that they were having with her. Her "Letter to Christ" was her own words done in her own way and written by a dear friend for her during her church seminary class. She truly was grateful for all of the simple things in her life, when she could have been so ungrateful for so many other things.

We were all feeling the emotions of enjoying "so many lasts." Kennedy was deep into cheerleading and making friends all over at her high school. Her cheer coach told us that many times during cheer class, the team would stop and focus on Kennedy. She felt that those days may not be as effective for cheerleading skills, but were all to worthy of life skills. One morning the cheerleaders showed up to class and were in some trouble for missing a bus to a game and other things. The girls were not very happy that morning until Kennedy walked in. The cheer coach asked Kennedy if she wanted to cheer that day and Kennedy said she wanted to have girl's talk instead. So, the cheer coach gathered this team in a circle, feeling like this was a perfect day to talk since some of them were in trouble. The cheer coach told Kennedy what a great cheerleader and example she was to the team and how much they all loved her. Kennedy asked why. The cheer coach then told Kennedy that was a good question and turned it over to the team. She asked each of the girls to tell Kennedy why they loved her, what they had learned from her, and why it was so special for her to be on the team. Each of those girls went around that circle one by one as they shared their feelings about Kennedy. Suddenly the room went from a bunch of girls being upset to a bunch of girls being full of love. Tears streamed and we were told that some of the responses were "I have learned not to take anything for granted," "I love how Kennedy just loves everyone and hugs everyone no matter who they are." "I have learned to be grateful for what I have, because you never know when it could change." The coach then asked about the challenges that these girls face. She turned to Kennedy and asked Kennedy if she had any challenges. Kennedy looked at her and simply said, "No!" She asked her again, "Really, Kennedy, you have no challenges?" Kennedy immediately responded, "No, Fun!" Kennedy then told her team that she loved boys, friends, her family, school, and cheer. The room fell silent and many of the cheerleaders were in a bit of shock. The question was then asked by their coach, "Can anyone tell me why Kennedy has no challenges?" One of the girls raised her hand and said, "Because she doesn't see them that way." The coach relayed this experience to Heather and I and told us that Kennedy had taught them more in those few moments than she as a coach could have ever taught them in years.

Was everything a party or preparation for Kennedy at this time in her life, or both? It seemed that every day was filled with magical visits, wonderful activities, and endless stories of how happy Kennedy is and was making everyone else feel. She was at the pinnacle of her life. She was cheering through every single football game. And not just through them, I mean all the way through them, EVERY SECOND of every down. She was screaming for those two hours and moving, cheering, and executing the cheers. There was no sense of her dying. No sign to so, so many around her that she physically would be leaving us soon.

Yet, when you were around her, it was beginning to be a party FOR the preparation. So many people would spend time with her and then ask or meet with us privately to know "why they were feeling the way they were feeling?" and "What was going on?" How could so many be getting feelings that she truly was preparing to leave this life and leave all of us when it felt like such a party?

Through all of this, Kennedy had told us that she was going to have a HUGE Sweet 16 party. It was a never-ending discussion with her daily. She experienced her sister Anna having her Sweet 16 party earlier that year and loved every minute of it. So she kept telling us that she was going to have hers and it was going to be HUGE! Weeks after receiving her diagnosis in June, a dear friend of ours and her husband came to visit our home. During that visit, she shared that she had felt impressed and inspired to coordinate and hold a party for Kennedy. A party that, yes, would be to raise funds for the costs of her disease, but also would be the biggest party of Kennedy's life. This party and planning eventually became Kennedy's Sweet 16 birthday party as the stars aligned with the date. We were not allowed to know details of the party as it drew closer, only that we were to attend and were asked specifics about some of Kennedy's favorite things.

Saturday November 16, 2013, truly felt like Christmas Day!

For days, weeks, and months, Kennedy had been gearing up for the party of her life. One that we knew little details about other than to get ready for her dreams to come true.

We only provided favorite colors, food types, friends list, and so on for the party. We were told for three months to just be ready for a HUUUGGE BASH.

When we arrived at the event, Heather immediately took Kennedy up to the ballroom at Weber State. I was busy unloading vehicles and helping bring things to an elevator provided for transport. After loading the elevator a few times, it was time to ride to the top. I rode up alone and all I could feel was a bursting of love inside my chest before I even arrived at the room.

After exiting the elevator, I turned the corner and entered the room pushing Kennedy's wheelchair we had brought. I staggered. I fell toward the ground and the only thing that held me up was the chair. I immediately broke down. Before my eyes lay over 10,000 square feet of balloons, tables, a stage, a HUGE Kennedy sign, a photo booth, a cotton candy machine, an ice cream booth, a chocolate fountain, a dessert bar, a pizza bar, a drink bar, a cupcake station, tables loaded with silent auction items, and on and on and on. I was so overcome. I literally had to leave the event and go into a back kitchen room to compose myself. THIS WAS HUGE! I could not believe what everyone had put together and done for Kennedy. I had to get it together. This was way too big of a night, way too important, and way too special. This was Kennedy's night. So I said a little prayer, pulled it together, and re-entered the room.

I will never, ever forget from that moment on (four p.m. until midnight). We estimate over 1,000 people showed up. There were people from California, Montana, Idaho, Wyoming, Colorado, and Hawaii. We were surprised to see old neighbors from when Kennedy was a baby on the planning commission. Old work friends from past jobs, old friends from high school and college, hunting buddies, best buddies, aunts, uncles, cousins, schoolmates, cheerleaders, and on and on and on and on. There was a line formed to visit with Kennedy and she hugged every guest.

The cheerleaders did cheers, music was playing, and people smiled, cried, laughed and just had a great time. We had amazing photographers who donated their time and resources. And so many came just to support our family.

A program occurred recognizing major donors to Kennedy's Hugs and honoring Beau and Anna as siblings.

The night wound down and then heated up with a dance for the hundreds of teenagers who showed up. It was as if time stopped for a moment as I watched Kennedy dance with all of her friends. She was in her element, her moment, her time. People were having such a great time and could not get over the feeling there. So much had happened and so much had occurred in the last few months for this party.

How could we ever repay everyone?

A huge scrapbook was put together with everyone making a page and putting down their favorite memories of Kennedy and pictures and so on. A video of her life was shown that we had made.

And as I sat there as her dad, tears welling up as I looked over this scene of almost perfection, a friend of mine came over and said, "Well, Mr. Hansen, what can you teach me from all of this?" I looked at him and said, "If there is one thing I have learned from tonight, it is that when you give out without asking for anything in return, you will always get back ten-fold from those whom you helped. This is the village effect. This is what it is all about."

I was right. It was perfect and I did not want it to end.

As we walked out to the car, Jaden allowed her to kiss him on the cheek. This, as weird as it sounds, brought tears to this dad's and mom's heart and eyes. It was priceless to see her feel normal. To feel like she had everything perfect on her Sweet 16 night. She looked out toward me and said, "DDDDad, iiiitt,tttt wwwwas on thee ttthhhhhe cheek, not lips!"

"I am proud of you Kennedy," I said. "You made it! You made it to Sweet 16 without a kiss!"

* * *

The party was definitely over that night, yet the preparation was in full swing. It was so evident that the feeling we had relied on so much (of listening and knowing exactly what to do) was around us in a great capacity. We did know what to do! We were being directed, we were being blessed, and we were being guided. That party provided so much for us in so many ways. A MIRACLE had occurred. Our daughter experienced normality. Yes, normality. And what is normality, you might ask? Well, normality is all of the things that we as parents hope and dream for our children from all aspects of life. And for years, we had dreamed of our Kennedy Ann Hansen not only making it to Sweet 16 without kissing a boy, but also making it with all of her hopes and dreams in hand. To have a party with preparation.

http://goo.gl/nZFp1t

Scan to view post

CHAPTER 51

Letting Her Be Happy?

November 17, 2013—

> Well today will be the start of Kennedy's official decline in a rapid, major way. I have not enjoyed carrying this inside and knowing that the worst is about to come. But, I am so grateful for the last almost 6 months of magic. Now, the worst is to come and it will be the toughest, most grueling of our lives. I AM READY. (From my journal.)

It was so apparent the decline that Kennedy was experiencing. Her ability to talk still existed but she was becoming tougher to understand each and every day. And all we wanted to do was let her be happy. Part of Batten disease is dementia, memory loss, and disorientation. There were some frustrating moments for sure.

Kennedy at times would suddenly become angry and lash out, telling us that she was not a cheerleader or was not going to go to school. She would become so agitated that she would begin to yell, scream, and swing her arms around trying to hit the air. She would try to tell us something and at times we could not understand her. This frustrated her even more because she knew what she was trying to say but could not say it.

So we would rub her back or try to console her, yet at times she would strongly oppose us and scream and push us. Those times were the worst. Because we knew that was not Kennedy, that was Batten. And after these episodes, sweet Kennedy would look toward us and say, "Sssorrry, ssso so, sssory, Mom and Dad. Nnnot mee! Nnnot me." She would then put her head down in her lap or on the counter top or on her bed and cry. She would feel horrible for her behavior, yet she did not understand it. Her body was doing one thing and her mind another.

At times she seemed trapped inside knowing that this was not her, yet not knowing how to truly be her. And she was more than aware of the disease that plagued her and this part she simply ignored. Whenever we tried to talk to her about Batten, she would say, "I know. I know. Dddon't like, dddon't like. Have fun, Mom and Dad, . . . fun!" She uniquely had figured out how to control her inner anger and frustration against this disease through simply loving, having fun, and serving others.

Again, Heather, Anna, Beau, and I found ourselves dedicated to giving up all and making sure that Kennedy was happy. This meant that each of us had to do hard things. It meant that each and every day, our lives revolved around Kennedy, what was going on with Kennedy, and how we could simply let her be happy.

As Thanksgiving arrived, there were so many invites given to us to celebrate this holiday. Looking back, we really did not know or realize how hard traveling was on Kennedy. We traveled over 5 hours to Kennedy's grandparents' home for Thanksgiving. The trip was very hard on her. We did not have her van at this time, nor the ability to lay her down in a vehicle. She became antsy, tired, agitated, and uncomfortable quickly. She needed to stop many times more than usual and she was also in pain. It was definitely a very hard trip for her to make and even harder for her family to make. She complained about pain that weekend. Lots of pain. Especially in her head and her legs. She was evidently in pain but did not want to ruin Thanksgiving. We did the best we could to help subdue her pain in several ways, but it was not going away. And on top of this, the stresses of life were insurmountable. We were still trying to run our nutritional supplement business and black Friday was always our biggest weekend of the year. With two retail store locations, we were up to our eyeballs with phone calls, emails, texts, and social media posts. I was also still working my full-time job and although it was going well, it also was not. I had just been told that I needed to step up in a major way or I may not have a job. Our debts were piling up both for the needs of Kennedy over the years and the needs of the business. The business needed money to keep operating, yet without us there to run it, it was taking a hit. All of these stresses seemed to crest as this holiday arrived. The fear of losing Kennedy, losing my job, losing our business, and holding it all together were so much to bear.

We were up all night every night on that Thanksgiving weekend. We went a few places, but I found myself at my parents' home trying to hold down the business with the sales we were promoting and financially figuring out ways to help it survive. As the family would go places, I offered to keep Kennedy with me. She was not well. She did not feel well and really was miserable. She kept telling me that she just wanted to go home. "Home, home, home!" she would say. And that did not make it any easier.

We went to a play that weekend at a famous play set and the whole time Kennedy was miserable. She had a major absentee seizure and sat helpless in pain, throwing up and in agony in a wheelchair at this event. All of the other kids were gone seeing Santa Claus, but Anna and I sat rubbing her back, her feet, and her head. She kept saying, "home, go home, home!" She also was becoming more agitated with her mobility and walking. As we pushed her in the wheelchair, she did not like it. Yet, everyone expected her to have fun because they would see her at her best. For the half hour or hour or fifteen minutes they would see her. So this was hard, very hard. We were just doing all we could to help her all day and every day to be able to function for those small moments she would have. Looking back we had handled everything just about as darn perfect as we could and for once we showed some unsatisfactory emotion. We left early that weekend to get Kennedy and ourselves home. Upon arriving home, it felt so, so, so good. Kennedy was back in her comfort zone, her element, and her happy place. She was so happy to be back where she could be comfortable and at peace.

Later that week, I found myself meeting with an amazing counselor who now has become a dear family friend. He helped us to see our strengths and the good in all that we have. He helped us to realize that there were those around us called "rescuers" and all they wanted to do was help us. But, with rescuing, sometimes there are those who want something in return and there are others who do not. He taught us to face our fears and, more important than anything, to understand one another's feelings. He taught us to accept the realities and face those head on. And he helped us understand that we had every right to be going through a struggle as he educated us that our family was enduring some of life's most grand challenges all wrapped into one big moment.

From that week on and moving forward, we never looked back; we looked forward. We possessed a new attitude as we were taught that we were in the grieving cycle even prior to losing Kennedy, because we were losing Kennedy. And the best part about it was that Kennedy was oblivious to the entire thing. She was just having fun and living up to her reputation of being Fremont's Angel and giving out Kennedy's Hugs. Our faith grew and our love as a family grew. We were letting her be happy and that made us happy.

CHAPTER 52

The Choice to Ignore

Kennedy's will far out weighed her limitation. Basketball season at her high school was well underway and she was cheering at each game, even sometimes two nights in a row! She was trying so hard to just be Kennedy. To share her love with all and be a normal high school cheerleader. And it seemed the harder she tried, the more miracles came her way. Her choice to ignore her disease was more than evident in her face, her body language, and her efforts. Kennedy was aggressively moving forward socially. She was interacting, laughing, screaming, and having more visitors over to the house than one person could handle.

Her agenda was simple. She had made the choice to ignore Batten disease with all of its ill effects and was going to live out the rest of her days by enjoying every second she had and allowing those seconds to prick the hearts and souls of all those around her. I think one of the most touching things that was happening then was seeing the physical and outward support from the community. We also made the choice to ignore all of the hardest parts of her disease and to FULLY focus on her and the most important things that would help keep us going. So our days were full of me working very hard at my employment and Heather spending the majority of her time with Kennedy and the rest of the time helping to keep our business running. And we saw blessings and miracles. Some that were apparent and some that were silent until they conveyed themselves to us at the perfect moments.

Yet, as we watched Kennedy become happier and happier and

happier, there was a part of us, as her parents, that we began to experience. This was sadness. We found ourselves so happy as we watched Kennedy live out her final days in a dreamlike fashion, with all of her dreams coming true. Yet, when the days would end and the silence would fill our home for just a few moments, Heather and I seemed to find ourselves already experiencing the grief. You see, the choice to ignore the disease and the bad parts was fairly easy with Kennedy leading the way. But, what would happen when she ultimately would have to leave us and go home? Who would be there to lead us, guide us, and help us?

Although our faith was strong in a God who loves us, the realities were setting in. We have always been organized people and so we had to begin facing the great responsibilities of making sure ALL was planned accordingly for Kennedy's exit from this life. Her body was dismantling and yet we were watching her go on dates, cheer at games, and go out for ice cream. She was so, so strong during these moments and it seemed that her choice to ignore now was benefiting those moments. Yet, the redness in my beautiful wife's eyes and the tiredness in her step was not going unnoticed by many.

Heather was spending the majority of her life just caring, managing, and helping Kennedy to enjoy all of these moments, and part of that process was getting no sleep at all. There were nights where Heather was up and down so much that she really never could sleep! Yet, with the disease, Kennedy would somehow sleep very deep, experience a night terror along with a seizure, and then fall right back to sleep. She would sleep inconsistently and without a full night's rest, yet she got more energy and possessed more physical ability during the day at all of the high school events she was now a part of.

As this was all going on, all too often we would hear people comment or ask, "Is she really terminal?" "Do you really think she is going to pass away within this year?" "She looks fine to us, she seems like she is as healthy as a horse!" All of these comments were true. Yet, the public did not see the pain at home, the all-night terrors for Kennedy, and the digression that we could see. The public would only see her for one or two hours at a time. But, those close to her in her school classes or in her cheerleading group began to see the digression and the different parts of her diminishing.

It was at this time that we began to get phone calls from her school resource department telling us that she was falling asleep in class and having a hard time staying awake. Many, many medical trials, tests, and processes have been attempted for Batten disease. Yet there was nothing available to help Kennedy other than medication for seizures, medication for pain, and different types of equipment available to help her with her physical mobility and needs. We continued to become Kennedy experts and not Batten experts.

We had decided early on with her diagnosis to surround ourselves and Kennedy with the best experts on Batten that we could find and let them focus on the disease so we could focus on her. And with all of our experiences, we had learned early on that *"You always listen to the Spirit, which is a higher power, and if you do, you will know exactly what to do."* We had not only followed that counsel but also lived it, experienced it, and seen it guide us up to this point in Kennedy's journey. On December 13, 2013, we had to endure and experience one of those tough, tough moments. The following is from my journal on that day.

> Today was by far the most tender day of our marriage. We had to go to Lindquist Mortuary to complete the funeral planning for Kennedy. It was very real and very emotional. Reality hit and it hurt. The planning of your daughter's end of life without knowing the date? That is by far the hardest part. But, I do know that her salvation is made sure, her life for eternity is going to be important and going to be critical. I feel that her spirit is reaching out and ready to go home. I feel that we now need to accept this and then she CAN go home. That is how I feel and what we need to prepare for. Because Kennedy and our family will always be TOGETHER FOREVER and she will always be right there with us. So . . . onward and upward in everything. Hopefully, we can have some PEACE continuously.

That night a piece of her parents died. A piece of us left a hole very, very deep. A hole that could never be filled with money, friendships, possessions, or time. This hole was one that we could not ignore and for us the choice to ignore some parts was impossible. *We had just experienced a date night planning our daughter's funeral! Planning our daughter's funeral,* I thought to myself as we drove home and said to Heather, "Who does that? Who does this? Who has to plan their daughter's funeral and then drive home and hug her in the same day as she stands before us, breathing, walking, and smiling?" And I do remember us getting home that night, when we both seemed to rush to Kennedy and wrap our arms around her. That piece within us that died was the ability for us to have the choice to ignore.

As that weekend wound down and the following Monday came, I went back to work. I had my boss ask me how my weekend went. He asked if I had done anything fun and if Heather and I had gone out. It stopped me dead in my tracks as I answered. "Yes, we planned Kennedy's funeral for our Friday night date night. We planned her funeral." I immediately found my emotions taking over and I had promised to keep them at bay while at my employment. The tears began to come and my lip began to tremble. My boss simply said, "Jay, I am so, so sorry. I, I really do not know what to say." Suddenly I found myself, at that moment, trembling my emotions into a smile where I simply conveyed that the choice to ignore the worst parts could be accomplished while at work, but I could not avoid them as I traveled home. He offered his support and his concern for me and my family and told me if there was anything he could do to let him know.

I believe that day was when I really, really changed. It seemed that all moments now were, without question, the last. And I looked at each one that way. Whether it was helping Kennedy put on her shoes, brush her teeth, or getting her a treat. I treated each and every moment as if it were her last. Because the preparations were being made and the realistic emotions were being portrayed. Kennedy was going home and she was going home quickly. From that moment on, I allowed the choice to ignore to be a cat and mouse game that we played well. Yet, Kennedy only played one side. The side of the choice to ignore all of the bad and entertain all of us with the magic of so, so much good.

http://goo.gl/uyhscX

Scan to view post

CHAPTER 53

I Believe

The choice to ignore was one of the great blessings that Kennedy provided us. She would ask us deep questions, mainly about heaven, Heavenly Father, and living forever. Many times she would tell us, "It's ok, I'm going home to be with Heavenly Father and Jesus, and they will take good care of me." Her choice to ignore the scary parts of that thought process were not completely gone. She would share with her mom that she was afraid and scared of leaving us and our family. And she would share with us that she was scared of dying. Not of going to heaven, but what dying would be like. She would ask if it would hurt or if it would go fast? At times she would say, "Die, die, scared, scared. Don't want to die, ddddon't want to die." You see, as much as Kennedy understood the spiritual side of her journey, the physical side was like it would be to any of us. I mean, who really wants to know they are going to die or who wants to die? Kennedy still experienced and maintained the same feelings that anyone would have when it comes to dying. But, one of her differences was her ability to believe that in dying, she would be living.

CHAPTER 54

An Awakening

"Jace, I can't do this. I just can't do this." Heather said. She was kneeling by the side of our bed and weeping. It seemed that most of our conversations, if they were face-to-face, always took place late at night by the side of our bed either before or after we prayed. She was exhausted. Her face looked tired, her body looked tired. "I cannot just sit here and watch her die. I have done this before with my mom and I cannot watch Kennedy suffer. Every day she gets weaker and weaker and weaker. I just wanted and want her to be normal, Jace. I do not want to see her suffer. I can't! I just can't! She is my little girl and I love her so, so much."

As I sat there and looked at my beautiful wife kneeling in agony across from me, I could see how physically tired she was. Yet . . . she was also beaming! I was beyond emotion since I did not really know how to answer this question for her and knew inside my heart that the effects of the disease on Kennedy were completely out of my control. I wanted so badly to pray for a miracle, a cure, and a complete reversal of her disease. I wanted so badly for our daughter to be whole. Yet, I could not.

I had already had my experiences and knew what Kennedy's role was. She was to touch the world with her story by sacrificing herself to leave the world. She knew it, I knew it, and her mother knew it. But, that knowing did not make it any easier.

It was a cold December night. I can remember just staring at Heather in awe and then without knowing what to say, asking her to say our nightly prayer. For once . . . I was speechless. That night, she pled with Heavenly Father that Kennedy would not suffer to the extent that she truly could suffer. Heather kindly and lovingly asked Heavenly Father to "gently," not "aggressively," take Kennedy away from us. Her prayer was so sincere. Her prayer was so real. Her words and her voice were so poignant, so loving, and so full of faith.

When she was done praying, I was so, so emotional and had some true feelings of inspiration hit me during that prayer. I simply looked at her and said, "Heather, you will miss taking care of Kennedy one day. I challenge you to enjoy every minute you have taking care of her. I promise you that you will miss it one day."

"Miss it?" she questioned. "How in the world am I going to miss the night terrors, seizures, throwing up, headaches, screams, her losing her ability to talk, walk, and function? Watching our daughter die? How am I going to miss that?"

I arose from where I knelt and walked to her side. I knelt down by her and wrapped my arms around her. Together we knelt and together we cried. It seemed that even though we were in the midst of a great trial, a real living hell, one that was robbing us of so much good, we also were growing, expanding, and lifting one another like we never had before in our marriage. Again, we found ourselves growing closer to one another yet. at the same time, feeling the distance deepening of the realities that lay at our feet. We were all in and had been all in, yet it was time and we both knew it. All we could do was rely on our Heavenly Father, rely on each other, rely on the spirit continuing to whisper to us, and rely on laying our burdens at the feet of the Savior.

We found ourselves at Kennedy's bedside a short moment later. Both of us were in tears and both of us were smiling. Great comfort, great peace, and great sorrow engulfed that room as we sat and just stared at our beautiful creation. She was stunning and she was ours! That night, it seemed as if a transition occurred and an awakening was happening. We both were not quite sure exactly what that awakening was, but we both felt that there was a difference in the air. Kennedy even looked different. She seemed more at peace, more angelic, and more radiant that night. It was something that we could not figure out until two days later on December 19, 2013.

As mentioned and shared, we are very devout to our faith and our beliefs. Part of our beliefs within our religion is that God has placed his authority to act in his name again on earth through righteous men. This power to act is called the priesthood. As a worthy member of that priesthood, I have been ordained as an elder to enact and use that priesthood to bless others lives and my family's life. Part of that priesthood is the gift to administer father's blessings to our children through the laying on of hands when indicated by invitation or by the Spirit to do so. And those blessings are for the purpose of healing, comfort, direction, and revelation given from Heavenly Father to direct our children's lives. It is a great responsibility to hold this priesthood and it is something that truly forces you to live as good a life or as even a better life than you would normally.

There had been many times where I used this priesthood to give Kennedy blessings, but one thing was for sure, Kennedy was strong, very strong, and she was preparing to go home and go home quickly. Back to her Father in Heaven who sent her to us and back to live, work, and serve Him in order to serve others. She kept telling us that she was having dreams about heaven, and she kept telling us that Heavenly Father wanted her home and that she was ready. I had felt many, many times that her spirit was silently communicating to mine that, spiritually, she really wanted to begin to visit, prepare, and travel to the spirit world before dying in order to be prepared.

You see, on the other hand, she, mortally, was scared and had told us that she was scared. She was scared of death, because death in movies and the world had always been portrayed as something scary, painful, and so dramatic. These thoughts, emotions, and things weighed heavily on her mind, her mother's mind, and my mind as her father. I again found myself wanting to fix what I could not fix and wanting to help what I could not help.

So, two days after Heather's fervent prayer, where she pled with Heavenly Father to take her "gently," a miracle occurred. It was close to 1 a.m. and we had all gone to bed. Typically by that time, Kennedy would have already woken up several times with outbursts, seizures, screams, and night terrors. But on that night, the night of December 19, 2013, she slept like an angel. And at around one a.m., both Heather and I awoke at the same moment and time. That feeling hit us both instantly that I have mentioned so many times. *"You always listen to the Spirit, which is a higher power, and if you do, you will know exactly what to do."* We both woke up and Heather said, "Do you feel that?"

"Yes, yes I do." I answered.

"It is time, isn't it?" She asked.

"Yes, Heath, it is." I said. "It's time her spirit is released." We both had been feeling through the priesthood that the appropriate time would come when one day we would release Kennedy from this life and we knew that day was quite far off. That day would be the hardest and the worst. That would be the day that she would physically and fully be released. We also knew and felt that we would be prompted for another day, when we would be directed to release her spirit to begin to travel back and forth from her body in order to be prepared.

We both were wide awake and we both felt it and a still small voice had whispered it. We sat up and both knew it was time for her spirit to be released to travel as it needed to and prepare to go home. We walked hand in hand into her bedroom, where I will testify that the feeling there was beyond description. It felt so powerful, so heavenly and so peaceful. It looked as if Kennedy was an angel lying there before us and I testify that she glowed! Heather told me that she wanted to write down the blessing that was about to be administered to Kennedy in her journal and so she sat down on a chair and the following was transcribed and recorded in her journal. I laid my hands on Kennedy's head and this is the blessing recorded:

"Blessing to Kennedy" 12-19-13

> Kennedy Ann Hansen, ...BEGIN THE PROCESS TO RELEASE YOURSELF from all of the worldly cares and burdens that you would face or have faced. I bless you that your spirit will come alive and be quickened in the Lord and will be exalted in the Celestial Kingdom when the time is right. Be whole in spirit, so you will know what Heavenly Father will have you do. I bless your Spirit to pass to and from the veil with peace and understanding, so that you can fulfill your mission.
>
> Heavenly Father loves you and is aware of you and is grateful for your willingness to be available to him. This blessing comes from him. Many great joys will be yours. Don't be afraid of anything from Heavenly Father. Be at peace and may your mind be quickened. Kennedy, another blessing will be given to you where more clarity will be given. Things are speeding up quickly and are happening for so many reasons for you. Many will be blessed from them. Your time is limited and your spirit is ready. I bless you that your spirit will respond. You WILL NOT suffer greatly. This will be a massive blessing.
>
> You will be known as one of great joy, happiness and love. You will be this up until the day this life ends. Don't give up, but let your spirit dictate you. You are elect and chosen. You have been prepared from the beginning and there have been people that have lived from knowing you.

> I bless you to have a sense of normality for a time. You will feel mortal pleasure of others. You will be tempered and be able to handle Batten disease. You will not be a burden, but a blessing to everyone around you. Pray here and in heaven.
>
> You will understand this blessing with and through the Spirit. Your Parents love you, you are most precious. Now, go with faith, understanding, and no fear. Your time has been amazing here. I seal this blessing upon you in the name of Jesus Christ, Amen."

Kennedy was asleep during the entire blessing, yet as it ended . . . she smiled. Kennedy knew—she knew it all. And this blessing and revelation from our Heavenly Father would become all too important and true over the course of the next six months. The bells were ringing in all of our ears. They were loud and were being rung from the watch tower of our Heavenly Father as he ushered in one of his greatest and most choice spirits . . . Kennedy. And yet as we listened, heard, and began to witness their chimes, it was all we could do to sit back and try to enjoy the sounds and not run for safety behind the great walls of heaven. For you see, we needed her a little longer. The bells were ringing and calling, but we just needed to listen. Yes, all we needed to do was continue to listen and witness the sweet music that was being played from heaven on earth through Kennedy.

http://goo.gl/VfP5gR

Scan to view post

CHAPTER 55

Our Time

It was Christmastime and this was by far Kennedy's most favorite holiday and time of year. We were so involved in Kennedy's everyday life and it seemed that every day we now had visitors, friends, new friends, cheerleaders, neighbors, and family visiting and spending time with Kennedy. To be candid, as this was all going on, Heather and I were struggling.

We wanted to share her with the world, yet we also wanted our time. And in a sense this felt like a selfish request, yet it felt like a simple one. Our existence here on earth as a family unit was coming to an end shortly and we both felt it, knew it, and recognized it. Early in the month of December 2013, I can remember us having a discussion about what we could do in order to get our time with Kennedy and our little family. We wanted something more, we wanted something different, and we wanted something memorable. And yes we had seen magic moments that year. The trip to Hawaii, the school year thus far, and the miracle of cheerleading, dating, and friends. Yet, this was something that was different. And, yes, it was a want more than a need at the time.

We talked and talked and talked about this for the first couple weeks of December. We had already decorated, hung lights, and begun some traditional activities. We were excited for Christmas as usual, yet we were also disheartened. We knew that our time during Christmas would be the last that we would ever have with her. We knew this and believed this. So, as we were planning, discussing, investigating, and looking for things to do, we began to find that nothing was working out. And, as all of this was circling into a great tornado, Heather simply let me know that Christmas was going to be simple that year. She told me that, more than anything, we could not afford to go and do anything extravagant or memorable. Out of nowhere, I was hit so hard with that same feeling, *"You always listen to the Spirit, which is a higher power, and if you do, you will know exactly what to do."* Simply put, my mind and heart was told, "Do nothing. Just wait. Do nothing."

It was strong. I felt comfort, I felt peace, and I felt more love then I had felt in a very, very, long time. As I arrived home from work one day, I found my little sweet Kennedy with friends in her room. She hugged me and began to sing me some Christmas songs. She began to tell me how excited she was for Christmas and that she loved me. I felt such peace, such love, and such emotion all throughout my body. It resonated and I just had this feeling that Christmas was going to be beyond special. Kennedy began to say, "Special, special, Christmas, special!" I was overcome and found Heather and conveyed to her that we were to do nothing. That this Christmas would be the most special and our time would be granted completely to us. As we were sitting there, the doorbell rang. Kennedy and her friends went to the front door and sitting on the doorstep was a basket with a gift and note within.

We brought the gift inside and opened it to find the remarkable gift of an evening out with our family to experience a horse sleigh ride, a dinner, and a night on the town. And this was in downtown Salt Lake City. Not only was this an amazing gift, but there was also a letter from this gift giver that announced that for the next 12 days, our family would be given a special gift each day that would compel us to have our time together during this last Christmas with Kennedy.

It was as if the skies had parted and we were in heaven. For suddenly peace entered and peace stayed. The magic of our time began at that moment and we knew again that we were not in control of our time left together with Kennedy and as a family.

The 12 days of gifts given to us were more than material, they were our time together. We attended a special Christmas performance, we received Kennedy's favorite movies that we watched and we received her favorite treats to enjoy. Each day we looked forward to our time together that allowed us to spend each night from December 13 to Christmas Day. There were so many amazing gifts, moments, and feelings that as we look and think back, it hurts and is beautiful all at the same time.

It is like a beautiful rose with all of its thorns—such beauty yet such pain as you experience its entirety in your hands. We went to many cities of lights and wonderful eateries, and, of course, even with it being winter, we still went to some favorite ice cream places of Kennedy's. And there was a truckload of Coca-Cola and Butterfingers given to us. Enough that every night and at every activity, we seemed to find our pockets full of both as we gorged on them until we were full. These were our last Christmas moments! This was our time and whoever it was that did this for our family had nailed it.

By December 21, Kennedy was exhausted. She was experiencing everything that she should be experiencing, along with the toll the disease was taking on her body. We began to let Kennedy completely dictate her schedule and she began to sleep much more. She would sometimes sleep so much and so long that we allowed her to attend school for just part of the day. With all of this going on, we still were trying to also do normal things like Christmas shopping, continuing family traditions, family parties, neighborhood parties, work parties, and so on. Through it all, for the first true time in our lives, we began to feel the peace that should come from Christmas.

And when the day came when her Hugs, smile, and voice would be gone and the physical presence of her disappeared from our view, the greatest feeling we would have as a family is that Kennedy's peace will always live with us, be within our midst, and fill our hearts.

http://goo.gl/gm9Adu

Scan to view post

CHAPTER 56

And Then . . . There's Jaden

Amidst all of the wonderful gifts, moments, feelings, and wondrous Christmas activities, Kennedy was still completely twitterpated and in love with her Jaden. This young man was so good to her and to our family. As Jaden spent more time with Kennedy, with our family, and in our home, we could not help but fall in love with him. The thing that probably impressed us the most about him was not the fact that he was taking time out for Kennedy, but that we never heard him utter an inappropriate word. We never heard him speak an unkind, poor, or harsh word about someone else. And more than anything, Kennedy and her disease did not intimidate him one bit.

Simply put, Jaden got it. He understood it. He felt it and he knew his role. He was a beacon on a hill that sometimes we could not climb. He shined so bright that even Kennedy could see his light with her blindness. The week of Christmas was busy. And with Kennedy being out of school, her usual visits from Jaden changed that week. All we could hear about was Jaden and the questions of "Is he going to come over? Is he going to bring me a gift? I want to give him my gift." And on and on and on. She was relentless in her love for this kid. As Christmas Eve came and we celebrated that night, we had many family members over who wanted to be with Kennedy on that night, her last Christmas Eve. We also had many friends who visited, brought gifts, and showed up to surprise us. Through all of these visits and events, Kennedy consistently asked if he was coming. Where was he and would he come? We had texted him and told him that she had a gift for him and that she really, really wanted to see him. He texted back and said that it may not work out due to some family plans. We completely understood this. Yet we had to relay this to Kennedy. She was pretty upset and more than anything quite down the rest of the night. You could tell that she truly wanted to see Jaden.

And as the night drew on, so did her anticipation. She told us that she knew he would come. And her faith never wavered. It always seemed that whatever Kennedy said would happen, did happen. And she was not letting up on this one. About an hour passed after she told us this and then the doorbell rang. She felt her way through the hallway, touching the walls and feeling her way to the door as she scurried her little feet. She rushed to the door and swung it open. Without any hesitation, she knew who was standing there. You got it. The wonderful Jaden and his family. They had come to visit Kennedy. You could see her heart ignite. Her smile seemed to light the earth and she was complete. Her Christmas was complete.

http://goo.gl/1DWF6p

Scan to view post

CHAPTER 57

SEEING IS BELIEVING

During Christmas that year, there were times where there was so much peace in our home that you could hear a pin drop. Other times, there was so much going on and so many people visiting that you could not even hear yourself breathe. There were so many that wanted time with Kennedy and so many that gave time to Kennedy. I admit that there were times where, behind closed doors, Heather and I had some serious discussions about how much time we should allow or give of Kennedy to the rest of the world. Many, many parts of us wanted to hog her all to ourselves and our family. But, the answer was simple: "Share her with the world. Share her with the world!"

And this answer was the right answer. Yet it was hard sometimes to stand back and watch as others wanted to take her every day and let her do just what our answer was: "Share herself with the world!" It was as if there was a tug of war within Heather and me, allowing this to happen but wanting her all to ourselves. Many, many times, I would race home from work during this time to see her, hug her, and just tell her that I loved her. And as I would arrive home, I would find her in her room with a large group of visitors. I would tell her hello and then be promptly invited to leave by Kennedy.

We would all laugh when she would ask this of me or her mother. She wanted to feel normal and we wanted her to feel normal. We had prayed for that for years and it was finally happening! She was becoming so popular, yet she did not know or understand the effect that her popularity had on others. There were times when she would ask us to leave that I would sit outside her door with the door closed and just listen.

Sometimes Heather would join me and we would embrace or hold hands and just listen to Kennedy laugh and scream and joke and talk.

Earlier in the year, we had received a phone call from a very fine artist. He told us that he had been commissioned by a private party, and then he told us a white lie. He told us that he needed permission to create a painting of Kennedy and the Savior for a religious magazine. As we began to discuss this with Kennedy, she immediately told us what she would always tell us. In her stuttered and now broken words and voice, she again said, "Jesus will heal my eyes when I go to heaven!" She had said this so many times before. She then said, "Picture of that. Ppppicctturre ooff fff, th, that! Sssseeeing J,JJJeesus. Seeing Jesus!" We immediately knew what she wanted. She wanted a picture of herself seeing Jesus after her eyes were healed. This request and thought process touched our hearts and souls deeply. We knew that this request was something she felt strongly about.

When the artist arrived, it took some work, positioning, and, more than anything, some relaxing on my end. I felt so inadequate portraying as the Savior for this art piece. Yet, as this photographer positioned us and we began to pose for pictures, something changed. Kennedy and I began to feel a father daughter bond that was so deep, so real, and so peaceful. She kept hugging me and laughing and giggling. She was having fun, yet at the same time she was feeling the spiritual nature of this moment. Finally at the end, the room went silent and she peered up and into my eyes. She completely froze that room in that moment and slowly she moved her fingers toward my face. I simply kept my hands frozen in position on her where they were at and she slowly reached up and gently touched my face and said, "Ssseee. I, I cccan sssee yyyour fffface, Ddddaddy! Lllike JJJesus, lllike JJJesus."

The feeling in that room was overwhelming. The emotions were beyond description. Heather, myself, and the artist all could feel this moment. She was blind and yet she could see! Her faith was so real, so simple, yet so powerful. The moment was caught perfectly for this artist to create his masterpiece.

When Christmas arrived, we were blessed that year. And on Christmas morning we heard a knock at the door and standing before our eyes was this most beautiful painting of Kennedy and the Savior, portraying the day that she would be able to see him again and receive her sight back. This picture made us all stop, pause, and reflect. It identified perfectly the desire within Kennedy to see physically again. There was no other gift that day, no other moment or feeling that could top that moment. We learned that, for Kennedy, seeing is believing. She sat from a distance and just stared toward the picture with a deep inward look of satisfaction. She walked over and hugged the people who delivered it to our home. After they left and we sat the picture down on the ground, she sat in front of it and just stared at it, telling us that she could see it. The peace in our home that day topples any up to that moment. And the piece of art that now sits in our living room on display proudly displays the caption, "Seeing is Believing!"

http://goo.gl/ytYXdf

Scan to view post

CHAPTER 58

Celebrating Her Tragedy

What is so interesting about tragedy is that you have two options. The first option is you can let tragedy be just that . . . tragedy. You can simply look at all of the bad with a tragedy and let it consume, destroy, and hurt everyone around you. Or you can turn tragedy into triumph. What was so amazing about Kennedy is the fact that she was celebrating her tragedy! It had been seven months since the absolute and definitive answer had been given to Kennedy, and to our family, and now it had been shared with the world about Kennedy. And all we could do was try to keep up with this celebration that Kennedy was experiencing.

By the time New Year's Eve came that year, Kennedy was still celebrating and having the time of her life. New Year's Eve consisted of many, many friends and visitors coming over to the house to visit and spend time with Kennedy. You would have thought with now only five months left to live that Kennedy would be stuck in a hospital bed with a feeding tube, oxygen, massive medication, and tireless medical assistance. But Kennedy was doing the opposite. Her role and her purpose was to celebrate her tragedy by living life on this earth to its fullest. She was completing her purpose and was doing things that no one thought could be done by a terminally ill high school girl.

That New Year's Eve, Heather and I were exhausted. I literally felt like that entire year had busted me to pieces. New career, changes in our business, massive financial pressures, and the news of Kennedy all seemed to tirelessly catch up to me and I was beat. I fell asleep around 9 p.m. that night, While everyone else was laughing, playing games, watching movies, and eating good food, I quietly snuck out of our family room and into our bedroom where I literally crashed and went to sleep. I remember laying my head down and hearing Kennedy in the other room as she laughed, played, giggled, and even screamed. The most beautiful part was the fact that Kennedy had been celebrating her tragedy and teaching all of us. Tears slowly rolled down my cheeks and my spirit was broken in some ways, yet so strengthened in others.

This year had been one of the best of our family's life, if not the best. Yet, how could that be? How could this tragedy of losing Kennedy have made this one of the best years? I tried to understand as my heart hurt and my body and mind were so tired. As my mind drifted and flowed, I began to have a movie of 2013 replay through my mind and my heart. I fell asleep seeing all of the scenes, all of the moments, and all of the things that had happen on replay. It made me happy, yet my pillow was wet. I was exhausted with emotion and I lay there and cried.

Eventually I fell asleep until right around midnight, when two giant arms embraced me and woke me up. I looked up to see Kennedy at my bedside. "DDdddad, wwwhhhaaat yyyyou dddoing?" she asked. "Nnnnew, yyyear, NNNeeewwwwww Year. Yay! Yay! Yay!" She had a smile from ear to ear and had all of her friends with her. I got up and joined the fun for a bit. I had more fun watching than anything as the New Year rolled in. Kennedy was screaming Happy New Year and people were banging pots and pans and blowing horns that Heather had purchased.

Celebrating her tragedy was definitely something that overflowed to everyone around us. Heather and I prayed together that night and simply thanked our Father in Heaven for an amazing year. I then can remember just laying there and holding one another, because we both knew now what was coming. The year 2014 would present the hardest part of celebrating her tragedy. It would present the ending of her physical presence and the passing of her life.

Neither one of us wanted to face it and neither one of us wanted to go through with it. We wanted to celebrate her tragedy forever. The sweetness in the air that night could have cracked even the most bitter man. And although we both were so worn out, so tired, and so emotional from 2013, neither one of us slept much. We held one another and then tossed and turned. Not because we were necessarily worried, but because we internally wanted every second of every day to be magical, meaningful, and memorable with our angel. For the time would come where we would wake up and want to celebrate, yet she would not be there to celebrate with. And that time was coming quickly.

http://goo.gl/W8u1cX

Scan to view post

CHAPTER 59

UNAWARE

The year 2013 was such a year. It was not just special, it was monumental. Kennedy had made her mark. And her mark was spreading quickly. Thousands of people were beginning to follow her story on Facebook, through the media, and at her school. She was unaware of her great influence, yet was so aware of the love that she possessed and could give out to people. We were receiving hundreds of messages of support, love, and thanks from people from all over the country as her sweet story was spreading throughout social media. And yet Kennedy was unaware of all of the attention. To her, it was all part of her plan. Looking back, we now know that she knew the whole time in her heart how this was all going to go down. She was on track to experiencing some amazing things and was not going to miss a heartbeat doing them.

There were times where Kennedy would become physically unaware of what was going on around her. With Batten disease, many times the child becomes unaware of his/her surrounding or environment. The brain does not know how to socially function at times and emotions dictate a falsehood of who the person really is.

Kennedy began experiencing this many times a week in public. The unaware for her was not remembering things, people, places, or sometimes even who she was. At times, the unaware became a trial greater than any in her life. The unaware also involved not being able to see surroundings or navigate pathways. This became a group of obstacles that became increasingly tough, but also increasingly understood. As Kennedy continued experiencing the unaware scenarios, there was one rescuer, one hope, one voice, and one touch that always gave her back her awareness. That is her MOM. Heather has been and will always be the shadow by Kennedy's side, the listener at her call, the caregiver, and of course the MOM.

When the unaware crept in, Kennedy wanted MOM. When the unaware took over, MOM was the calmer. And as the stormy sea had arrived and would continue to toss and turn, Heather was the keeper of the storm and the protector from a drowning path. We were all so grateful that the two of them had each other, recognized each other, and loved each other.

For Kennedy, the unaware played Dr. Jekyll and Mr. Hyde with her. Some days she would lash out and say some mean terrible things to us as parents. She would say things so uncharacteristic of who she was or how she was. Yet, at the same time, she would take her hand and began beating it endlessly against her forehead, screaming, "no, no, no, no!!!!" She then would say, "Sssssorrry, ssso, so sorry! Love you both so, so much. Not me, not me!"

We were so far from being upset with her and were understanding of her. We knew! Yes, we knew that this pathetic thing called Batten disease was the culprit of her behavior. And so did she. All she could do was her best. This became increasingly difficult over time as we would be so patient, so loving and yet this was so hard to watch. Kennedy's disease would at times make her unaware of so many things that just were not her. And to be candid, we were and are so grateful that those parts of her were not seen by the rest of the world. With this behavior would come the absentee seizures and also the pain. She began to complain about the pain in her back and her neck and her head. She did not understand why it hurt so bad and what was happening. We really wanted to limit the medications that could become addictive or that could make her become unaware of even more of who she was. We officially had began her on a medication to help her sleep better at night and also to help manage her hundreds of seizures. And yet somehow, somewhere deep within Kennedy, she always knew about the unaware in all of us. For we were struggling with the unaware of what we would do as the truth of her disease was beginning to show its ugly head and not one of us were liking that at all. Yet the unaware that Kennedy possessed was such a blessing, such a miracle, and such a strike force against all of the bad that accompanied her journey and all of us just needed to hold on!

http://goo.gl/gmxH2T

Scan to view post

CHAPTER 60

Surreal

The great necklace full of keys was now well beyond our capacity to wear. This necklace had been given and had added so many keys to it, that it now was to be placed around the thousands of followers of Kennedy's Hugs. And with that necklace being shared with the world, there were times where we felt as if everything around us was so surreal. Our dreams for Kennedy had diminished in our hearts and minds. Yet, her dreams had emerged and it felt so, so surreal to all of us.

The miracles occurring with Kennedy, with Kennedy's Hugs, and with the world were mind blowing. The cheerleaders, their involvement, and their love for one another was crucial for Kennedy in her journey. The team early on had been searching for something to bring them together, to bring them closer and complete them. And that something was Kennedy. The team created the slogan, "Do it for Kennedy!" And that slogan would become so important to this team, because they had been struggling. Kennedy's cheer coach had told us that at the beginning of the year, the team had set goals but had struggled and not really bonded as a team yet. The coach told us that the team had set the goal of wanting to be the team that every other team would want to be a part of. She told us that the team wanted to also be the best and number one like most teams. The coach told us that she taught the team that being number one was not always the most important thing and was a pretty generic goal. She told us that they decided to set their goal to be the team that would have no deductions or penalties while competing. This coach was also coaching her team to put the needs of every other girl ahead of themselves. She was always teaching them to show selfless love, which she believed would make them unstoppable and allow them to grow immensely. So, when Kennedy became part of the team, it was an easy decision to make her part of the routines. Her coach told us that she knew Kennedy would not be able to perform all of the skills necessary for their entire competition and performance routines. So, this team would lovingly escort Kennedy out onto the floor, where they would place her in her spot until they would start. Upon hearing those cheers and that music, Kennedy would instantly pipe up and begin cheering. Her coaches would sit on the mat in front of her and they would shout out the cheers to her and describe what she needed to do. This was so special to watch, since we would see this unspoken connection occur between the team and Kennedy. Kennedy was nothing short of a true champion. Her coach told us many times that she was able to see past her disease and into the heart of a true competitor. The team would help Kennedy off the mat once her part was complete. Kennedy would then sit or stand on the edge of that mat and stare towards her team, screaming, chanting, and cheering them on. She would constantly sing the words to each and every song that they would perform to and was the team's biggest cheerleader. Once it was her turn to go back onto that mat to perform, she would almost jump at the opportunity as one of her teammates would escort her back into her position front and center on that mat. It was so special to see how this coach put Kennedy right in the middle and front and center in these routines.

We would sit and watch silently, emotionally, and so proudly before these competitions as these girls would include Kennedy in everything. Before competitions, they would always form a circle and would mentally go through all of the words, cheers, and routines. It was amazing to watch Kennedy as she would participate in this without ever having seen the routine before with her physical eyes. In fact, it was a miracle. But, the biggest miracle was watching how these cheerleaders and their coaches were able to include and do all of this with Kennedy while knowing the whole time that she would be leaving them and going home. And that part, to us, was the miracle of the moment.

The team did "do it for Kennedy!" We found ourselves finding comfort at this time during basketball games, assemblies, or cheerleading competitions. Kennedy found herself sitting quietly and patiently by our front door each and every day as she would wait for different cheerleaders to visit her at our home. Her body was getting tired, very tired. She began to fall asleep often and was becoming more agitated as her mobility was weakening. Her schedule was the same each day, though, and she knew it by heart.

After coming home from school, she would immediately do her chores. With her mobility lessening, we thought we would have to take this part away from her. Are you kidding? That would mean that she would lose her allowance. Kennedy loved her allowance. I do not know of any kid who could save more or be more frugal than Kennedy. Her piggy bank was always full and she would save, save, and save! So, she continued to do and even attempt to do her chores right up until the week that she passed away. After her chores were done, it would be about 3:45 p.m. and then it was time for the cheerleaders to come. At first it was just two of them or sometimes one of them. The intent was to teach Kennedy the cheers.

But, by this time, it was rare to see just two of them. Typically 3 or 4 or 5 or even as many as 10 would show up to visit her. She would know when they would arrive, because you would hear her squeal! Her way of knowing that they were coming was from hearing the sound of a car pull up or a car door closing. Her ears were so sensitive and she learned how to use them well. She would clap her hands and jump up from where she was kneeling by the front door and would wait with her hand at the ready on the handle of our large front door. The minute that knock or doorbell would be heard, she would swing that door open and would rush forward into the arms of those sweet girls. They would instantly catch her and hug her as well. They were truly "doing it for Kennedy."

Each one of these girls became an important key on this key chain. There was no stopping this love that still exists today. For the rest of our lives we will never forget them and we promised to be there for them like they were there for us.

There have been many late night phone calls, texts, and knocks on our front door. There have been graduations, weddings, birthdays, events, and monumental days we have shared with them. And more than anything, there has still occurred the feeling of surreal. For that "only exists with the most special and heavenly moments here on earth." And to us, these girls are just that. HEAVEN ON EARTH.

http://goo.gl/vhCHHM

Scan to view post

CHAPTER 61

It Will All Work Out

One minute Kennedy could be as healthy as a horse, literally galloping around her room and completely full of joy and the next we could have her flat on her back in confusion and pain and leaving us for periods of time with her absentee seizures. We had met with the Palliative End of Life Care team at Primary Children's Hospital on several occasions. Those meetings were so resourceful, so loving, and so helpful. Yet, those meetings were also realistic. In those meetings, we discussed those things which really could not be discussed in any other setting. With Batten disease, you truly do not have a time line and our doctors had told us at best that they felt Kennedy could have close to two years left to live. Yet, no one really knows. Well . . . no one except for that greater power on high. And suddenly, toward the end of 2013, all of those feelings that Heather and I had experienced were now transmitting to us more powerfully than we expected.

We had felt that we only had a year left with her and as 2013 came to an end, both Heather and I felt strongly while in these palliative care meetings that we needed to place Kennedy on hospice in January 2014. The feeling was overwhelming to us in these meetings. We both felt it and we both were passionate about doing this. As we consulted first with one another about these feelings, we decided to take the decision to our knees, where we again prayed for guidance. The answer was clear. PLACE KENNEDY ON HOSPICE NOW! We consulted with the palliative care group, worried about the response from them. I mean to look back now and to think, "Who wants to go and push to put their child on hospice?"

Yet, we needed their support, the doctors' support, and the hospital's support in order to do this. I will never forget the day that we met and requested this. We even had Kennedy with us that day in the hospital and she was in another room with an aid doing activities while we spoke to them. As we relayed our feelings on this matter, it was as if another power engulfed the room. And their response was, "No one knows their child better than a parent, so we trust your intuition and will support this decision." As we left that meeting and returned to Kennedy, she was all smiles and hugs with the staff. She was laughing, giggling, and smiling. I looked at her and saw the bright glow in her face, the strength in her soul, and the resilience in her body. I could see everything that she was and could feel everything that she wanted to be. She looked so healthy and she seemed so healthy. Still, we all felt 100 percent sound and confident in our decision. She needed to be placed on hospice and she needed to have this step taken in her life. And that decision would become paramount from that day moving forward.

Her bathroom was completely remodeled and we were now able to wheel her wheelchair right into the bathroom and even the shower to bathe her. Her wheelchair was used more often and she hated it at first. Yet, she was now adjusting to it and beginning to use it more frequently as she would become tired, agitated, confused, or in pain. When we would go different places, we would bring it if we had to wheel her long distances or for long periods of time. We would load her "Bubblegum Pink" wheelchair in the bed of the truck and strap it down and then lift her into the truck. As her daddy, I enjoyed and to this day will forever remember and enjoy lifting my princess into that truck. But, for her Mom, it was impossible to do that. So, we would drive two cars to most places that we would go. Over time, this was becoming increasingly difficult for everyone. With me working so far away and with so much going on, we needed to somehow fix this. We had been looking into purchasing a mobility van or vehicle for Kennedy. We had gone and looked at and driven these vans on a few occasions. Pressures began mounting even greater in this area as Heather was transporting Kennedy one day. Kennedy was struggling and needed help moving. Heather lifted her to transport her from one chair to another and unfortunately her back gave out and they both fell to the ground. This fall injured Heather and completely changed everything. There was no way that she could lift the wheelchair.

As I sat at work one day, I began to analyze the great amount of debt that we possessed and that was piling up. I began to look to the future and feel the great weight of the costs that would come from Kennedy being put on hospice. I also was being told that our business needed more money to operate and pay for things. I went to the bathroom, where I knelt in prayer and pleaded for some miracles to happen on that cold January day. The world felt cold that day, I felt cold, and our situation felt literally frozen in time. As I stood up from that bathroom and went back to my office, I began to think of Kennedy and our situation and simply tried to listen intently to my feelings. As I listened, the promptings came on strong, and that day, the feeling overwhelmed me! "*You need to get a van now to transport Kennedy!*"

It was so powerful that I called Heather to discuss it. As I did, she ironically said that she had been feeling the exact same feelings that morning. Heather, suddenly became worried and asked, "How are we going to afford this? How are we going to get a van for such a short time period?" We had been looking at vans with wheelchair lifts for 6 months and could not find anything used . . . anything! We ultimately found what we wanted and needed available in one brand new van. The only problem was the van was well beyond our budget, over $50,000. As we talked, I told Heather that I had to go to meetings and asked if she would call one of our contacts in Salt Lake City. I said, "Just call, I feel like you should call them. I have a strong feeling, IT WILL ALL WORK OUT. I promise."

After my meeting was over, there was a voice message from Heather. All it said was, "Call me ASAP." I called her and she said the following, "You are not going to believe this, but I called that company and yesterday they received a 2001 Chevy van that has a lift. The owner of the company told me that it is rare to get vans like this in and that this one is in great shape! He also told me that we better get there quick, because it will be gone quickly. So, can you go and look at it tomorrow?" I asked Heather where the dealer was located. She told me 2100 South and West Temple.

I said, "You have got to be kidding me."

"Why?" she asked.

"I just got out of my meeting and I am literally at 2100 South State Street." There was a silence for a minute and then we both knew. We knew that IT WOULD ALL WORK OUT and that this was completely meant to be. I pulled into the dealer no more than 5 minutes later, where I sat inside the van, looked at the owner, heard the price, and simply said, "We'll take it!"

We drove that van for the last 6 months of Kennedy's life. It was literally one week later that she began to use her wheelchair full time, lose massive navigation and coordination abilities and we were in great need of it. The van fit our budget, our needs, and our time frame perfectly. It was a miracle! IT WILL ALL WORK OUT is what we said, have said, and have trusted so many times. How did that happen? How was it that it happened to come one week before Kennedy ultimately would need it for good? And how was it that I was sitting less than a mile away from this van at the moment I knew about it? I am confident that our incessant and endless prayers and all of the prayers from all of those around us were heard. And lastly, I am confident that the faith that we showed and presented that it will all work out" proved all to true with this and so many other things that we experienced throughout Kennedy's journey.

http://goo.gl/zdscqw

Scan to view post

CHAPTER 62

Fremont's Angel, the Miracle of Cheerleading & the Storybook Ending

So much was happening and so quickly. Kennedy was officially on hospice and was now receiving visits from nurses, staff, and her doctor on a more regular basis. Her ability to touch lives was broadening as her physical body was diminishing. And we were witnessing the simple things begin to be taken away from her. Most of us get up in the morning, go throughout our day, and do not pay much attention to the small things around us: the shoes on our feet, the coat on our back, the ring on our finger, or the bed that we sleep in.

These small things became significant things to Kennedy as she lost her sight and ability to utilize all that was around her. One of her greatest comforts was her bed. It was always there when she needed it, and acted as social atmosphere for friends.

These friends and so many others gave Kennedy the nickname of "Fremont's Angel" at Fremont High School where she attended. Kennedy had become an inspiration to so many as she dealt with her disease in positive ways. She would go to school with excitement, with great anticipation, and with high hopes of being a normal teenager. More and more students were finding their way to our home, where they wanted to spend so much time with Kennedy. She was fighting to be normal and was fighting to be their example. Internally and spiritually, she knew that her battle would be over soon with this disease, yet physically she was fighting it every step of the way.

Cheerleading was so important to her and the competition season was coming to an end. Her coach was aware and in tune with these feelings and these moments and was an angel sent to Kennedy whom Kennedy loved so much.

The cheerleaders first competition was a regional competition in January and they had another in February. The day of the second competition, Kennedy was not doing well. She had missed school and we did not think she would even make this competition. We took her to the competition in her wheelchair and were worried that she may not even make the first five minutes. But when we arrived, she transformed. If I could describe this transformation to you, it was almost like coming out of a long coma. The minute she knew she was around her girls, it was go time. She performed flawlessly and gave it every amount of energy she had. By the time the team's region competition rolled around, the team felt that this may be the last performance with them. Kennedy's health was still spiraling and the team had to place in the top three to advance on to state. There was a lot of attention on the team as the community, media, and many others watched them. The cheer team just wanted to make this wonderful for Kennedy, so if they did not win or qualify, they quite frankly were fine with it. They wanted to show the judges, parents, and world that day that through their experiences of cheerleading with Kennedy hearts could be touched. The feeling in that room was magnificent as Kennedy helped lead this team onto the floor. The room fell silent as onlookers watched them start their routine. The routine was going perfect until suddenly one of the girls tripped and fell, causing other cheerleaders to trip and fall. The crowd let out an "Oh no" type of moan and parents put their hands over their mouths. But the team just recovered and kept going. You could hear Kennedy screaming, undeterred from what happened. In her mind, they were going to win no matter what! When the competition was over, most thought that Fremont was done. The announcer announced third place, then second place, and then unbelievably announced Fremont High as the regional champions! The crowd went wild, the parents and fans stormed the floor. Heather and I found Kennedy and embraced her. She looked at us and said, "Ttttold, tttold you! We won! We won!" Kennedy was awarded the trophy and put right in the middle of the celebration circle. Earlier that day, she had said a prayer and in that prayer she had asked that they could win. As she said that prayer, we knew that they would win due to her faith. The cheer coach was baffled and asked the judges to see the score sheets. Those sheets indicated that there were no penalties or deductions. The team had the highest score and because of the quick recovery and the fact that they did not fall during a stunt, they could not penalize them. Due to this win, the team went to state. State was the last competition that the team had together. That day, like all the others, was magical. The team did not win, but they took second place. But, in their minds, they took first place. After the day was over, many of the teams honored Fremont High, Kennedy, and her team by giving her fun little gifts, notes, flowers, and hugs. The winning team that day surrounded Fremont High and the moment and the trophy was for Kennedy. Everyone whether close or not close to Kennedy knew that this was the end. But her cheerleading sisters knew that it was not the end, but the beginning. The storybook of cheerleading had and was feeling like it was coming to an end on that last day of competition. We sat in those stands and just wept, Heather, Anna, and myself. That year, that journey, and that legacy now seemed like it was over, yet it was not. For looking back, we are still living within that storybook. We attend the graduations, the weddings, the celebrations, and the highlights of these girls' lives. And every time without fail, we see a little bit of Kennedy through and in each of them. We feel of her through them. We see her in them. And we know that just like the day they reached out and handed her a set of pom-poms and were cheering her on, she now holds multiple sets of pom-poms and cheers them on from heaven.

About a week passed and Kennedy's team needed her. They set up a cheer party at our house. Kennedy's dementia and seizures were worsening. She was becoming agitated and even confused with who people were. That night, it was heartbreaking as Kennedy could not remember many of the cheerleaders including her coach. This scared and confused many of the girls. Where was their Kennedy? What was happening and how were they going to get her back? The cheerleaders gathered in her room and this sweet cheer coach had each of these girls began to tell favorite memories of Kennedy with her. At first Kennedy was very resistant and did not want them there. She was saying things like "not a cheerleader and ddddon't care!" As one of the cheerleaders was sharing a memory about a date she helped Kennedy get ready for, she knelt by Kennedy and held her hand. Kennedy suddenly took her hand and slowly raised it to her mouth, where she kissed it. The girls kept telling her stories and she suddenly was back. Her confused look turned to smiles, laughs, and screams. She remembered. They helped her remember who she was and they never gave up on her.

http://goo.gl/w5QXIV

Scan to view post

CHAPTER 63

My Girl, My Heart

Those first couple of days after the cheerleading competitions were over seemed overwhelming and proved to be difficult. So much had happened with the experiences of cheerleading. And yet, the hardest part of all was telling our beautiful angel Kennedy that it was over. And you have to do that when your child is dying. You do not have a choice. It is your duty, it is your responsibility, and it is one of the crosses that you have to bear as a parent. And I knew as her dad on that last day of her competing, that would need to happen. She had lived her dream and she had done it. Completed her physical mission of cheering as best as she knew how and could at these games, events, and competitions. I had to tell her, I had to be honest with her, and I had to carry her as much as I could in letting her know that her last time to cheer and compete had come to an end.

At her last competition, after all the dust settled, I had the rare but hard opportunity to explain to my little beauty queen that the season of competition was over. "Oooooover???" She said. "Yes. You did it, Kennedy, you made it to the end of the season, when many thought you would not! I am so proud of you! And you got 2nd place in State! How awesome is that?" All she could do is put her hands on my chest and lay her head on my shoulder as I sat there and cried. "Whhhhy over, Dad? Thhhhhhhhis is mmmmy laaaaast competition?" she said. "Yes, Dee, Dee, this is and NEVER, EVER, forget this moment." As I sat there crying and holding her and never wanting to let go. The tables turned and she began to console me. "Ddddaddddy, yyyyyooou aaaarrrrre crying. It's ok, Dad," she said. " Wwwwwe won!!"

We were so worried that Kennedy did not understand that it was over. Yes, over. Her cheerleading year would still have some games to be at, some parties, and a few assemblies. But, essentially she had done it. She had made it through an experience that many thought she would not. Our only prayer was that she would be able to understand this. As we loaded her in her wheelchair after that competition and took her to the van, you could almost instantly see that something had changed. Her demeanor, her physical nature, and her charging personality was diminished in moments. We loaded her in the van, strapped down her chair, and got in. I turned on the ignition and then gripped the wheel. All I could do was look back at her for a moment and then look over at Heather. Tears welled up, feelings welled up. Emotions and memories began to flood from this magnificent year of triumphs for Kennedy.

Suddenly, Kennedy sat up and reached out like she always would with her hands as she began to talk to us. "So, ssso, tttired, ssso tired. Mmmmy bbboddy is ttttired, Mom and Dad. Dddddid mmmy bbbest, mmmy vvvery best. Llllove cheerleading. But, Ddddad sssaid cccheeer-leading nnnow is over. Sssoo, tttired, ssso tired. We won! We won! We won!" She silently sat her head back against the wheelchair's head rest. Her body slumped down and her hands lay gently on her lap. She looked tired, very tired. She instantly fell asleep and we instantly cried. We drove away from that mat that Kennedy left everything on that year and that day. She had no regrets and now had no hesitation in just resting. She had given it her all. She was a true warrior and one that without question had never given up. In my estimation, if there would have been ten more competitions that year, Kennedy would have found a way within herself to show up to each one of them and to give it her everything. But, she had. She did. We won! And from that instant and that exact moment moving forward, Kennedy physically plummeted. For physically she had nothing left to give. To stand, to cheer, and to do what she needed to do on that mat was a miracle that she did anyway. As we drove home that day, I will never forget that Heather and I reached over and held hands in that van. We just held hands and soaked in the quiet moment of peace . . . until it was disrupted by the sudden snoring of Kennedy. And she was sawing some logs I'll tell you. We both began to laugh and laugh and laugh. She always had a way of making us smile even in the hardest of moments. Those moments so hard were softened by her sweet blow.

http://goo.gl/NdD8sQ

Scan to view post

CHAPTER 64

Twitterpation and Love

The cheerleading season was over and Kennedy was officially tired. Very tired. EVERYTHING CHANGED. That week Kennedy went to sleep and really never woke back up. What I mean by this is that she was physically done, yet physically being changed. You see, with Batten disease, the pain can become so overwhelming at times, that some kids have to be induced into comas to avoid the endless pain and onset of seizures.

With Kennedy, her day-to-day routines completely changed and she literally became a sleeping beauty. She still was up many, many times each night, but her ability to jump out of bed with the excitement and thrill for each school day literally vanished. We just let her sleep. In fact, we let her do whatever she wanted! On one of these mornings, I was rushing out the door to work, only to find our sweet Kennedy dining on M&M'S and Coke for breakfast! I stopped, set down my bag, and wrapped my arms around her in a giant bear hug from behind her. She could not see it, but I had tears streaming down my face. It was not because she was dying, it was because I knew, yes I knew that those little moments of M&M'S and Coke like that, would be leaving us shortly, very shortly. In fact, in less than ninety days.

Kennedy began to lose her sense of time, and even after sleeping in, she would still get ready for the day thinking that she would be going to school. Yet, the mornings now were becoming ever increasingly more and more difficult as Kennedy just kept sleeping longer and longer and longer. It almost was as if Kennedy was placed in a deep sleep during those morning hours until 3:30 p.m. And without fail at that time, with or without a knowledge of real time, she would be sitting by the front door waiting for her daily visit from the assigned cheerleaders for the day. Our house was magical from about 3:30 p.m. until midnight every night. And almost every night, sweet Jaden would come to visit. He always had a card, a treat, or a stuffed animal.

That week Jaden asked Kennedy to go out on a date with six other kids including her. He called and asked if he could use the van in order to take her in the wheelchair. He said that night was a big night for Kennedy and him, because they would be going to the F at Fremont High. I had no idea what that meant, until I went home and asked Kennedy. She immediately began screaming "F, F, F, FFFFFFFFF, kiss, kiss, kiss!" The other girls at our house explained to me that when a boy takes you to the F, it means that you are going to get kissed!

As I sat frozen for a minute, I simply stared at my daughter. She was glowing! She was illuminating a light that I had never before seen on a human being in my life. Time did not stand still, time went into slow motion as I sat and looked at my daughter. She was not feeling just some high school moment, she was not feeling some crush, she was feeling love. I for a moment literally could see her spirit. It was pure, it was whole, and it was solid. She was dead set on Jaden and had chosen him. She also was dead set on marrying him, loving him, and kissing him. I will never forget that thirty seconds of my life, because it made me realize that this would be the only few moments in her life that she would have to feel this way. I had to make them the greatest, the most magnificent, and the most magical I could.

I called Jaden back and asked him to tell me whatever it was he needed to make this night perfect for Kennedy. He simply said, "I got this, Mr. Hansen. All I need is your daughter, her wheelchair, and the van." As the date got closer and closer, she got more and more excited, while Heather and I got more and more nervous. Suddenly, our hearts could feel of Kennedy's heart and we knew how important this was to her. I detailed that van from head to toe and got it all ready for her big date. And then the inevitable happened. The van broke down! With only a day to spare, I rushed to my neighbor's home (he was a mechanic). I told him my dilemma and he told me to bring it over to his shop immediately. He went to work on it and told me that he would have it done. Well, the big day came and he called and said the keys were in it and it was ready to go. He told me that they would be going out of town, so he would leave the garage door open and to just go and get it when ready. I had decided to leave it in his garage that day since I wanted it to remain spotless for the big date.

As the time neared for Jaden to arrive, it seemed like we were all so nervous. Why? What was the big deal? What was it that was so special? Two hours before his arrival, two cheerleaders showed up to help Kennedy get ready for the big date. With less than a half hour to spare, feelings of true nervousness and anxiety were shooting everywhere like a machine gun. Jaden finally arrived with three other boys and their dates. Kennedy was not waiting by the door this time. This time, she made a grand entrance into the entryway. Her beauty was beyond anything. She radiated! That same feeling from a few days before entered within me and I could feel what Kennedy was feeling. I knew that she was sincerely in love.

I stuttered with my words as I invited the kids in and said, "L-l-let m-m-me go and and get the van. I'll be right back!" I ran over to my neighbor's home and to my horror, another truck was parked right up against the garage door of the mechanic shop. What was I going to do? I walked home slowly, trying to rack my brain. You see, Kennedy needed her wheelchair at this time, because she was wearing down so quickly and her seizures were also very frequent. She could not stand or walk for long periods of time and in order to go anywhere for any long period of time, it was needed. As I sat looking like a little kid whose dog had just died, Jaden suddenly walked over.

"Mr. Hansen," he said. "I am going to go completely out on a limb, but what the heck. I know that your truck is your baby. But, I also know that Kennedy loves to go on rides in it with you. I also know that it has a bench seat in the front and me and my buddies here are pretty strong. I promise I will take the very best care of it, if you let us take it." I had to pause for a moment and then I looked over at my daughter. Without a word, I walked into the kitchen and opened up the cabinet door where the keys hung. I took the truck keys and tossed them to Jaden. "Drive it like you stole it!" I said. "Now, get outta here and go have some fun!"

Cheers erupted and Kennedy ran to me. She embraced me and wrapped her arms around my neck. "Oh Ddddaddy, thank you, Dddaddy, thank you. Truck ride, truck ride with Jaden. Fast, fast, Dddadddy, fast!" That truck had never been loaned. It stayed in the barn for special things, especially truck rides with Kennedy for Saturday Cokes!

As the truck rolled out of the barn and the kids loaded up the bubblegum pink wheelchair, I will never forget the music blasting and the sight of that wheelchair in the back. They jumped up in that truck and pulled out of the driveway. Six kids (one being an angel), my beloved truck, and the bubblegum pink wheelchair in the back. As they pulled away and pulled up to the stop sign, my eyes began to well up in tears. Until all of a sudden, black smoke poured out of the tail pipe, the engine roared, and the tires squealed. I do not know if those tires or Kennedy squealed more as that truck went from 0 to 90 and disappeared out of our sight. At first my heart raced and I took a step forward, but then Heather slowly reached down and placed her hands on mine. As they disappeared from our sight, all you could hear was Kennedy's scream, the roar of that engine, and the blasting of Toby Keith's country music.

That night, Kennedy received her kiss at the F. It was something that no material truck, no business deal, no title, trophy or material matter could ever trump. And guess what? The kiss at the F was a kiss from Kennedy that she gave to Jaden on the cheek! As she arrived home, the truck arrived home and the wheelchair and kids arrived home all in one piece, I felt the most unbelievable peace for her. Jaden reached out to shake my hand, and I pushed his hand away and hugged him! Kennedy was complete! As I looked at her as she hugged him goodbye and felt the interlocking of my sweetheart Heather's hand clasp within mine, we were fulfilled. She had experienced this. She had somehow, someway been blessed through this earthly young man of an angel, Jaden, to feel twitterpation and love. As we tucked her in that night and said our prayers, all I could do was cry at the foot of our bed and say, "Thank you, dear Lord, thank you, thank you, thank you!"

http://goo.gl/9XRsk7

Scan to view post

http://goo.gl/Sk47ds

Scan to view post

CHAPTER 65

ROLLING WITH THE PUNCHES

Our little family's key chain was finally full! We were at the PINNACLE of our lives. Kennedy seemed to just be a glowing, walking angel. She was literally touching everyone and every heart that she would come into contact with. This was the PINNACLE of our family's life. This would be the greatest chaos that we would experience and also the greatest loss. We really did not have any more room to place other keys on the key chain around our necks. We simply would have to carry the key chain and shortly remove it as Kennedy's time was coming quickly. It seemed that each day, we had things going on from sun up until sun down. And even after the sun went down, we were used beyond our physical and emotional capacities.

Kennedy was able to go to another school dance with a boy, where she wore one of her mother's pageant dresses, and she was able to have the energy to dance and dance and dance and dance. The separation of her brain to flip on and off from the disease was unlike anything even some of the doctors had seen. With her aggressive declination, it would seem that she would be fully bedridden much of the time. Yet, as she was in much pain and experiencing the hardship of her disease one night, a young man whom she had a crush on in junior high school showed up with flowers and knelt at her bedside and asked her to go the junior prom. Kennedy instantly perked up and then sat up and produced a beautiful smile, saying yes. At that dance, the young man let Kennedy dance the first dance with Jaden. It was acts of kindness like this that kept her going, kept her inspiring, and kept her alive in ways unknown physiologically.

We were struggling financially and the business that had once thrived was tanking. It was not receiving the attention that it deserved. I was fully focused on my new career, needing the insurance and income to survive our ordeal with Kennedy. We were getting punched hard each month as sales were plummeting and expenses were rising. We were up to our eyeballs and at the end of our rope. No one was saving us, our employees, or the business. All we could do was survive. And with that survival, we were having to take on new debts, new liabilities, and new challenges. We were the founders and we believed in the success for the business for everyone else but ourselves. We truly would pray and pray long and hard. We would ask if we should keep moving the business forward or if we should just close it and walk away? The answer was always the same. KEEP MOVING IT FORWARD. KEEP IT GOING! We trusted in that and I was turning to my greatest advisor: my wife.

Heather Hansen was the greatest advisor for all of us through this all. She and I were not sleeping in the same bed. We were not going on date nights, we were not able to go on vacations or spend quality time for some time now. Yet, we were growing closer. We were relying on our Heavenly Father first and each other second. As things were worsening with Kennedy, we found out some very important things about each other.

I was able to handle losing Kennedy in ways that Heather was not. On the flip side, I would wake up in cold sweats, sometimes screaming or panting. I would sit up in bed and then Heather would run to my side. I would bury my face and forehead in my hands and cry and scream out, "How are we going to make it? How is the business going to make it? How are we going to pay for everything and how in the world are we going to survive once she is gone?"

Our daughter was dying, our pocket book was dying. Our resources were all but gone. But, Heather was able to handle the business side like a champ. That side did not stress her or affect her at all. It terrified me. She just rolled with the punches. I would at times fall asleep on my knees at the side of my bed after exhausting myself in prayer to my Maker. I would plead for miracles and will openly admit that I saw many of them. If you would have told me five years prior to this that my daughter was going to be dying, that my business would be dying, and that everything I had worked for was literally being demolished and that I would be in this much debt, I would have told you that you were crazy. So, now with our backs against the wall in every way, we were both being punched.

The punches hurt, so Heather and I began to switch out rounds.

We would each get beat up and when the other was getting pounded, we would slap hands and switch places in the ring, never allowing the other to throw in the towel. The bottom line is that we were a good team. We were sensitive, patient, and good listeners to one another. I feel before this time in our life that we knew each other, but now we *were* each other. Our thoughts became one another's thoughts, our words became one another's words, and even physically we began to feel of one another's pain. Although on paper with banks, businesses, doctors, and calendars we were losing everything, within our marriage, our family, and our hearts, it felt like we were gaining everything.

One night as we laid in bed thinking about our situation, I will never forget what Heather told me. She leaned over and hugged me and said, "Guess what? So we lose everything. Big deal! Nothing can or will hurt as much as losing Kennedy, Jace. And if we can lose her and make it, then we can lose everything else and make it too. Let's just keep taking the punches and have faith. None of the things that we have in this life materially will go with us anyway. Look at Kennedy. To us, what we have from her, is exactly that. Her! And she will take nothing when she leaves this earth other than what we have taught her, our sealing love, bond, and eternal family. The rest of her stuff will just stay here, Jay, and does not matter. I promise we are going to make it. I promise!"

As I listened to her, I wanted to believe that we were going to make it. And without question, whenever Heather promised me something, it always did happen.

CHAPTER 66

The Loss of an Angel

It had been very surreal during our journey to become friends with the Nelson family. Their daughter, Charlee, who was the only other living child with Batten disease in Utah, seemed to lead the charge in this journey. They were amazing as they helped guide us through the things that we had not experienced. When Kennedy really began having multiple seizures, they were there to know what to do and how to handle this. When Charlee went on hospice, Kennedy followed suit a short 3 months later. It seemed that we had only known the Nelsons for less than a year, but it felt like a lifetime. Charlee had been in and out of the hospital and was not doing well at all. Kennedy began to ask about Charlee intently. She had not seen her in a while and was asking how she was doing and where she was at. We explained to her that she had not been doing well and that she had been hospitalized. Kennedy was asking to go and see her and wanted to see her desperately. It seemed that Charlee had become somewhat stable and then suddenly took a turn for the worse. Her situation decreased dramatically and caused her plummet quickly. There was nothing more the doctors could do for her and it was her time.

Her beautiful parents brought her home and just decided to make the rest of their time with her the very best they could. Upon hearing this, we knew we had to get the two girls together. We dropped everything, and visited and committed all of our attention to Charlee. Charlee was laying down on the couch in their family room where she spent most of her time. She was struggling and coming in and out of consciousness at this point. Her motor skills were all but gone. She could not talk, she could not walk, she could not chew, swallow, or communicate. And still, she was as beautiful as ever as we entered that home.

On that day as we visited Charlee Nelson, we all knew that this would be goodbye. Kennedy sat with the most concerned look on her face for almost one hour holding her hand and did not move. She was emotional and worried for her little friend and angel Charlee. As Kennedy sat there holding her hand with the most serious look on her face, the four of us as parents were and are still convinced to this day that their spirits were talking. They were making big plans and were getting ready for their next adventure together.

We were humbled, saddened and shaken up. THIS WAS A VERY HARD VISIT AND so hard to say . . . goodbye.

As we got in the car, Kennedy said, "Hhhhheaven . . . Ch charlee . . . hhheeeeaven!" Kennedy knew where she was going and so did we.

Kennedy left Charlee's home on Sunday and just was never the same. She finally went to school one day, but still was just not the same. Her sweet little spirit was so saddened by Charlee's suffering and all she could do was sleep and sleep and sleep and sleep. When she would wake up, she would talk about Charlee and would get very sad. Although the mind cannot always register things, the spirit can.

The next five days were very exhausting as we watched our friends from afar lose their daughter. The whole time, our daughter was silently and quietly slipping further and further into her abyss. We lost sweet Charlee on March 15, 2014 as she peacefully took her last breaths in her mother's arms. As we told Kennedy the news, she became very serious and agitated. Her little angel friend was gone. Kennedy instantly went to her bed and went to sleep. She slept for over twenty hours.

We attended the funeral that week and as we entered the chapel of the church, we sat down close to the front row. After about 10 minutes into the service, Kennedy kept pointing up to the ceiling and began to say out loud, "Charrlllee, Ch,charrlleee, Heeaven, Heaven!" We would reach over and push her hand down and ask her to be quiet as we did not want to interrupt the service. This continued several times throughout the service. As we drove to the cemetery to lay sweet Charlee to rest, Kennedy began to cry. She was in pain and was struggling, yet this cry was a cry from sadness. She missed her Charlee and she now knew that she was gone. As we arrived to the cemetery, Kennedy had fallen asleep. We gathered around the grave to pay our respects. As this ended, I quickly went back to the van where we had laid Kennedy down on the bed in the back. I laid by her and gently stroked her head. I told her how much I loved her and let her know that she would see Charlee again. She quickly sat up and said, "Already have, Dad, . . . aaaalready hhhave. H,hhhhere, ccchurch, spirit!"

Suddenly the van door opened where my wife and kids looked up at Ken and I. I looked at Heather and she looked at me. This was a new chapter, a new phase, a new beginning to the ultimate end. For Kennedy would soon become a spirit and was now seeing spirits and the loss of our little angel Charlee was the igniter to this next phase. For she was near, she was present, and she was one of many whom would comfort, love, help, and not leave Kennedy's side as she would exit mortality.

http://goo.gl/8mRwj6

Scan to view post

CHAPTER 67

Angels and Demons

Almost one year had passed since we had completed Kennedy's final Genetic test with the University of Utah Hospital and Primary Children's Hospital. This test was to be the LAST test that doctors said they could do in order to determine Kennedy's situation. Kennedy, one year prior, could talk better, understand more, and definitely could walk better. Her condition had changed many lives, including her own.

The year had gone too fast. We could not believe that it had been a year since that last genetic test was administered. And never did we dream the outcome would be what it was: Batten disease. But, with the speed of the year came moments we would never trade, experiences we will forever keep, and friendships that we will hold throughout the eternities. With that year behind us, we still had the struggles of demons. Real life demons that were plaguing us, attacking us, and trying to bring us down.

Kennedy's clonic seizures were increasing. We would be talking with her and suddenly she would begin jerking either her hands, her legs, her arms, or sometimes both at the same time. These seizures would not last long, but were becoming increasingly evident when she was awake. And she was having hundreds of absentee seizures. This is where she would simply blank out, or black out for a minute and become unresponsive. She would simply stare into space and leave us. We would rub her hands or give her a hug and tell her that we loved her. At times, these absentee seizures, which could last up to a minute, would seem like an eternity, until she would come back to us. And at night, she was increasingly having seizures followed by night terrors and horrific screams.

Her pain was worsening and we were doing all that we could to make her comfortable. Sleep became a chore more than a help. When we could sleep, we would literally have to force ourselves to get an hour here or an hour there. The feelings of Kennedy changing and not being herself began to wear on us. She was very different and her memory was going quickly, causing her behavior to become out of control, with outbursts of screaming, punching, and kicking the air.

It was so hard to watch this as you could see on her face that she did not want this. She knew that something was wrong that she could not control! She would crinkle forehead and grit her teeth in frustration. She would stop these outbursts and then began to cry and say, "Nnnot mmme, nnnot me. Sorry, sssorryy, sorry." And the pain, oh the pain. She would describe to us and we would ask where she hurt. This description ripped our heart out as she would tell us, "Everywhere."

We received visits daily from our hospice nurse and doctor. We had to increase Kennedy's medications and incorporate a sedative to calm her at night. This was a very hard and difficult time. I could watch and see the demons of this disease with the demons of life and the real spiritual demons plague us as a family. It was flat out tough to watch Heather tire out and go through so much. I felt like a puppy being thrown into water for the first time. I was watching everything going on and somehow, I did not know how to swim through all of this, but was dog paddling.

And as this was going on, I was hit hard right in the gut, with that feeling that I had felt on that day four years prior, where I was told, "I need her home, my son." I could not get over these feelings that became so real. I felt all of those same feelings of the day, when I sat in the shower and cried and cried, accepting that she would be going home. The other hard part was that she was sleeping for hours. It seemed that when she was awake, she was enduring a hell that no one could endure, unable to control her mind or her pain. And yet, when she was asleep we wanted time with her. As I would watch her sleeping I knew without a doubt that angels were preparing her to leave us.

Our home became heaven. You could feel it the moment that you walked into it. Kennedy began to sleep every day for the entire day. She would really only get up early in the morning to eat and play with her dolls for a minute and then she would go back to sleep. People were rallying, visiting, sending cards, and calling. Her phone was filling up with texts, yet she was just sleeping and sleeping. I felt a longing to be with her more each day. This feeling was tugging at all of us every second.

As Kennedy would sleep, there were times where she would instantly wake up for the important things and tell us that she wanted to go. For instance, she woke up one day begging to go to the school for a pep rally that they were having. It shocked and surprised us. She even seemed fine. She seemed like the old Kennedy and went and screamed and clapped and cheered her heart out for her Wolves! Heather and I would look forward to me coming home. I was like a little kid as I would rush home as quickly as possible and literally would run from my car into the house. I would leave all of those demons in that car and in the world and I would return home to our angel.

We were trying so hard to hold it all together as a family. There was heartache within each one of us. As Kennedy would sleep, we would sometimes find ourselves sitting as a family and watching her, sometimes for hours! We just wanted to be together. Her little brother missed his play buddy so much. He missed their laughs, their giggles, and especially their horse rides. He began to become introverted and was unusually grumpy and confused. We would find him in Kennedy's room silently alone stroking her hand or whispering in her ear. His little heart was breaking and there was nothing we could do to fix it. Anna was struggling beyond belief. Her grades had declined severely and her time with us had all but disappeared. She was trying to be involved in things at school, yet she was also losing her best friend. The tension was growing and she was challenging us. How could she not? We could not give her the attention that she wanted or deserved. We had to give everything and were giving everything to Kennedy.

So, all of us had our demons and these demons were real. Yet, all of us also had our angel. We all missed our Kennedy and we all knew what was quickly coming.

Tender mercies did come for each one of us. For five days we had some of the most amazing times with Kennedy as our angel squashed the demons that were around and reminded us of what was most important: OUR FAMILY! We saw tender mercies and we saw our Kennedy come back to us as if she had never had a disease.

One of those days, from the moment that Kennedy woke up until the moment that she went to bed, she was just different. We had her back for awhile. Her speech was very clear; she was laughing, joking, making animal sounds, and eating everything in sight! She was singing and smiling. We limited her visits for those days, but those that visited were lucky. She had few if any outbursts, her dementia seemed nonexistent and things began to feel normal to us. All she could do was smile, laugh, and be happy.

At one point, we could hear so much laughter coming from her and Beau in his room. We went to his room to find him riding on her back like a horse! This had not happened in probably a year and a half! At first, we were a bit worried about this, due to her pain as of late. But, she insisted, so we let them have the time of their lives. Beau thought he was in Disneyland!

The feeling of those days was so wonderful. It was a tender mercy to have her back for a while—to see our true Kennedy.

It was so apparent that we purposely took long moments to talk with her. And her speech, although still limited, was absolutely amazing. She was putting together sentences and explaining herself. As her father, I just wanted to talk with her forever. I talked to her and talked to her and talked to her. We basked in it, enjoyed it, and really felt of it.

Those days would carry us and spill some sunshine over to us.

Our love for Kennedy was the same. Our thoughts, hopes, dreams, and concerns for her were no different. We just seemed to have a little bit of light in the mortal tunnel those days. Because the spiritual tunnel was already decided. We were fine with that tunnel and knew the greatness it holds. Just at times it was nice to get a day to remember.

And I received one such day. It was 3 a.m. and I laid in bed awake again with an empty spot at my side. I reached over to console my lovely wife, but she was not there. I knew where she was. She was with her little girl.

I walked into Kennedy's room and saw this beautiful wife of mine exhausted and lying right by her little girl's side. She was ready to comfort, care and do everything and anything she could do make her comfortable. It was very touching and personal to watch her brush her hair and guide her around our home. You felt as if you were watching a scene from heaven. She helped bathe her, brush her teeth, and get her dressed. There were moments—TOUGH MOMENTS! Ones that even I sometimes do not want to bear to remember. But there was Heather, so willing, so able, and so endlessly full of love for her little girl. She was not afraid of doing anything when it came to caring for her little girl. She missed outings, workouts, family events, church events, and parties to be with her little girl. She got tired, but rarely complained. She knew the outcome, but kept serving. And she did the hard things that none of us wanted to.

I think that sometimes, she would long for the piggy tails, the laughs, races, and tickle parties. The shopping sprees, the movies together, and most definitely the glamorous dress up parties that she and Kennedy used to have. She missed the normal talks, the nice walks, and the old way things used to be. But, she had new things, new memories, and new ways of celebrating life with her little girl. She ignored the blindness, the slow walking, the hard understanding, and just took Kennedy on special little outings when possible. She was trying so hard to hold on to moments with her little girl

That week one of the hospice workers brought a beautiful gift to us. She took a mold of Heather and Kennedy's hands clasped together and she had it plastered. It depicted so much. The never-ending trust of Kennedy with her mother, the clinch of love and care so deeply clenched by Heather's hand. The mold shows the wear on Heather's hands of age and care. It shows the fingernails bitten down to nubs on Kennedy and the small lines and details on her fingers. It shows so much and speaks so loud that this is her little girl. One whom she will never let go of, never rid herself of, and never break a bond so deep that words hardly touch its grip.

Her little girl was changing, and her little girl was preparing. And Heather wanted nothing more than to have another normal moment with her. So, on one of these days, Kennedy woke up, began to get ready, and told her mom that they were going to go on a shopping spree. And they did! Kennedy walked around the stores, she smiled, she felt items in her hands, and requested to buy specific things. Miraculously, she did not even need or use her wheelchair. She was out of pain and was back to herself. Those hours for Heather were not just normal, but were magical. For that was the last time that Kennedy would ever walk through a store, clasping her mother's hand, talking, laughing, and seemingly feeling like life was normal. This was a miracle of a tender mercy that no one expected to happen, but needed to happen.

As that week came to an end, we were both in shock of how well Kennedy was doing.

But, that shock would turn to reality as it ended. This was not our design and of course this was not our plan. We were supposed to be on spring break boating with our 3 kids riding in the tube and screaming and laughing. We were supposed to be going to sporting events and having chaotic times. Kennedy was supposed to be attending school each day and getting ready for cheerleading tryouts. Anna was supposed to be playing lacrosse and dating boys, but she gave this up to spend time with Kennedy. As this all went on, I again felt that same feeling, *"You always listen to the Spirit, which is a higher power, and if you do, you will know exactly what to do."* I again fell to my knees. We were not asking why at this point. We knew why. We just were tired and were beginning to feel the wear and tear like an old tire that had given its last tread. While on my knees, I truly sat and listened after praying at that time for inspiration. I remember it was early morning and I was told to simply go and walk into the kitchen.

As I did, I saw our angel Kennedy. She was glowing. She said, "Sit, sssit, eeeat, Coke, Coke, Ccccoke!" She grabbed my hand and sat me down. I sat there and ate pizza and Coke for breakfast! And as I did, the demons that I felt went away. The pressures we were loaded up with began to disappear and all I could concentrate on was her. Seeing the pizza between her teeth and watching her drink that Coke brought so, so much happiness. We were laughing and joking and I was telling her how crazy she was for eating Coke and pizza for breakfast. Especially at 5:30 in the morning. Suddenly, Heather showed up, then little Beau, and then Anna. We all sat in that kitchen, ate pizza, drank Coke, and enjoyed some heaven on earth. For on that day, our angel squashed the demons. It is my belief that she knew exactly what was going on spiritually and that she knew what we all needed. And for that, to this day I believe is why we still call her our angel.

http://goo.gl/u6gULz

Scan to view post

CHAPTER 68

EVERY LITTLE BIT

Everyone thought that Kennedy was back! For those who were visiting her, texting her, and following her on Facebook, her miracle week seemed to ignite and spark a feeling within us all that she was making a turnaround. And yes, we had witnessed a miracle. We had witnessed some of the most amazing days that we ever would have with Kennedy. So, suddenly her whirlwind became a tornado of sorts. So many wanted to visit her, take her places, and do things with her. But, it was as if a snap of a finger instantly changed her back to the road she had been on. After our morning feast of Coke and pizza, it was as if a light switch just shut off. The next week Kennedy could barely walk. Her weight was dropping.

I recorded in my journal on April 8, 2014, "She is very unaware and she can barely even walk anymore. I feel we have four weeks left before she will not be able to walk at all. We will get through this and more than anything we are seeing people change and be affected by her story."

Her ability to touch people's hearts and lives was simply with her presence in a room. She had not gone to church or school really in three weeks, and we had limited her time to go to school down to one day. She knew that Tuesdays were her one day to go and see cheerleaders, friends, and Jaden at school. She would get up at 4:30 a.m. and give it EVERY LITTLE BIT to get ready to go. It took her until 6:00 a.m. to get the little things done by her mother. And by 6:05, she was exhausted and back to sleep. EVERY LITTLE BIT is what she was giving. She wanted so bad to participate, be normal, and to not face confusion each day.

I recorded the following on Facebook on April 8, 2014,

> Today, she went to school in her wheelchair for 3 hours. She has been so embarrassed in her little mind to have to use her wheelchair, afraid that Jaden will think she is weird! Yes, at times we still see that sweet teenage normal side in her and can get words here or there that seem to resonate with where her true feelings really are.
>
> That is probably the hardest part right now. She is so confused. She is getting lost in her own home, becoming unaware of her surroundings and is going through many struggles as her brain continues to decline and goes through the process of shutting down. When a visitor comes, she will wake up for a minute and try to play, give a hug or a kiss. She gives them EVERY LITTLE BIT that she has and will then go back to sleep.
>
> And as we now see her progressing, digressing and traveling quickly down the path that none of us ever dreamed, wanted or expected in her life . . . all we can say is we are enjoying EVERY LITTLE BIT. When she wakes up, we gather around, when she calls out, we seem to run. When she speaks, we listen more. For it is the EVERY LITTLE BIT that this Mom and Dad will try to remember, will try to enjoy and will try to relish as we move further and further down this journey.

Every little bit of time that we had with her and for her was now adding up. We needed her and she needed us. I recorded in my journal on April 10, 2014,

> I was really prompted that it will be hard but to know that we are getting a small glimpse of what it will feel like when she is gone. How Eternal Families will feel and what forever families are all about. I know that Kennedy is getting frustrated. I know that she is getting so tired of all that's going on. She more than anything is wanting this all to end. She cries so much and hits her head. She screams in pain many hours a day. She began yelling that she just wants to die the other day. I am heartbroken over this. She cried so long and hard yesterday morning that we finally had to administer a medication up her nose that calms her down and makes her sleep. No Father, man or good person, ever wants to have to hold his or her child down physically as they scream, yell and physically fight you. Kennedy would not calm down and we had to do this in order for her to stop. We do not get much sleep, because she is up all night. So, it is difficult to say the least as we fight this and have to do hard things. But . . . I know the Lord will always be right by our side. He walks with us many, many times a day.

To have heard Kennedy say that she actually wanted to die told us that she was definitely in a miserable place. She had been so positive and had never, ever complained. But, the unexplainable, unbearable pain that none of us could understand (including Kennedy) was what really pained us the most. And the pain was now beginning to affect her in ways that we were not ready for. Her Hansen grandparents drove six hours to visit her at this time as they knew that things were developing for the worse. While visiting her, Kennedy collapsed while walking with her Grandma Linda and fell down.

Kennedy could barely walk anymore and she was falling more and more and more. Her agitation was worsening and she actually was becoming irritated with visits. It was not because she did not love her visitors. It was because she could not be herself and participate as usual. Her grandpa and grandma stayed for quite a few days. They took her to Walmart in her wheelchair and to get treats. They helped around the house and in the yard. They truly were angels sent to us in our time of need. They helped with Anna and Beau and more than anything were right by Kennedy's side.

Kennedy slept solid for a lot of the time that they were there. But she would wake up and call out for them. She was sooo happy that Grandpa Doug and Grandma La La were there. She cried many times and we could not understand her. She would scream out sentences that we could not understand. Many times, we would find her grandma lying down next to her just holding her. Her grandpa hugged her, loved her, and caressed her head. He kissed her on the forehead and told her how much he loved her.

And on the last day of the visit, I found them both lying down by her, just holding her, loving her, and talking to her. She was pretty much comatose and not responding until they told her they were leaving. She immediately woke up and then with every inch of strength she could muster stood up and hugged both of them as she cried.

After they left, Heather and I finally figured out what she had been trying to say to them. She was saying, "Grandpa and Grandma . . . I'm dying." She was trying to tell them goodbye. Trying to let them know how much she loved them. Trying to give them the true her before she no longer could.

Every little bit was being given by this girl. She was fighting, yet she also was preparing. But she did not want to give up. I recorded the following in my journal on April 13, 2014:

> She is very sad and understands some parts of this. We were administered the [sacrament] at home today. She was laying there and folded her arms. As she did, reverence entered the room as did the Spirit. The bread was administered to her and to our family. As the water came around, she tried to get up, she WANTED to sit up for respect of the sacrament so badly. Her frame shook, she could not do it. I gently put my arm underneath her back and pushed her to be able to sit up. She trembled, but insisted to sit up. I told her she could just lay down. NO WAY! And she sat up with help and partook of the water and then collapsed back into my chest. What respect, what a testimony, what an example.

I realized that day that if Kennedy could do it, then we could do it. Yes, she was agitated, yes she was showing fits of anger and was out bursting and becoming difficult. But, yet she still never complained about her situation or about dying. Her frustration and her anger were purely from the disease itself and the dementia that followed. So, with every little bit, she just kept moving forward.

http://goo.gl/ZvzYwE

Scan to view post

http://goo.gl/JJwsFT

Scan to view post

http://goo.gl/QL4uqr

Scan to view post

http://goo.gl/sujnmW

Scan to view post

CHAPTER 69

Understanding Last Moments

Outbursts began to pour out of Kennedy each day. She began to say, "I hate you!" And not to anyone in particular either. She would say it out loud and to herself. I recorded in my journal, "When Kennedy says, "I hate you," I believe she is saying that she hates her disease. There is so much to hate. But, Kennedy does not hate people. She really hates the disease."

We had never, never heard her use the word hate before in our lives. But, there was no question in our mind that she officially hated the disease. So much was moving forward that she wanted to be a part of. The school year was coming to an end and she had completely stopped attending school. This was very hard, confusing, and frustrating for Kennedy. Her body was simply controlling her schedule and it was becoming more and more dormant. Many of her friends were reaching out and were so worried about her. They wanted her to come to school and they wanted to have her part of everything.

During this time, she pleaded with us to take her to school. "Of course we will!" we told her. She was sleeping the entire time on the way to the school until we arrived. We wheeled her out of the van and began to take her into the school. As we did, suddenly one student, then another and another and another saw us and Kennedy. They all began to come running to her and surrounded her. She woke up to the sight of all of these friends surrounding her so excited to see her. As his happened and we were wheeling her into the school, she suddenly had an iconic seizure along with an absentee seizure. "What is wrong?" they all began to ask. "Kennedy, Kennedy, Kennedy!" they began to scream out.

Kennedy simply finished her seizure and then was unresponsive to them as she stared into space. We assured them that she was ok and told them she was having an absentee seizure. This really scared and freaked them all out. They had not seen her this bad and it was difficult.

When she finally did come back, she began to smile and squeal and laugh with them all. She went to the lunchroom, where literally hundreds of kids surrounded her, hugged her, and told her how happy they were to see her. She was struggling, yet she was at home. She loved these kids, she loved Fremont High, and she loved the feeling. She was very pale, weak and could not move much, yet she reached out and she hugged each and every one of them that she could. This went on for the entire lunch hour and of course she had to see her famous Jaden. When the lunch hour was over and the kids had to go back to class, Kennedy then became almost like a vegetable and sat in her chair and was drooling from her mouth. She instantly left us and this was hard on those kids who were left and was hard on us and her sister, Anna, to watch. Her digression had become so rapid and so aggressive that many did not expect to see her like this. Many did not know how to act and many did not know what to do. So, all of these kids would simply do what Kennedy would do and that was to reach out and give a hug. Amidst all of her pain, amidst all of her digression, dementia, and seizures, she still was reaching out and hugging everyone. Kennedy truly understood last moments.

And one of those last moments was drawing closer and closer that week. Kennedy had asked Jaden to the girl's choice MORP dance and we were so worried that she would not be able to go. Her situation was worsening with every passing day. We continued to amp Kennedy up for this night and tell her it was coming. As the day got closer and closer, we were worried. But, Kennedy knew what she needed to do. This would be her last girl's choice dance. She was so tired, but so ready when that day came. Anytime that Jaden was involved in anything with Kennedy, she just would try even harder and would magically have a miraculous turnaround.

We were so happy that she felt this little love in her heart. So happy that she could experience what this felt like with no long term feeling available to her. She had never seen Jaden physically, she had never known him before that year.

You see, Jaden loved her too! His love was just different. He gave up dates with his girlfriend. He gave up time from his family, he answered phone calls and hundreds of texts from cheerleaders who send him texts all week. He showed up, picked her up, and pushed her in her wheelchair to that dance. He whizzed her around on the dance floor and made her feel special. His love for her I believe is eternal. Just in a different kind of way. I have told him many times that Kennedy will be his guardian angel, watching over him throughout his life and cheering him on as he becomes the man, the father, and the husband that she would have dreamed of having.

She really loved him. When he would leave, she cried, when she was in pain, she called out his name. When he came, she would push her body with all she had to stand for him. She really loved him.

And when the night came to a close, Jaden brought her home. He carefully helped set her on the couch and he kissed her on the forehead. He could have left, he could have felt weird, in fact he could have just done what most guys will do and done nothing at all. But instead, he held her. Yes, he held her. And she was not well. She leaned against him, she touched his face, she hugged him tight. If she was completely healthy, this may be a bit much for me, but as I watched her, I just knew . . . SHE REALLY LOVED HIM. Kennedy would be moving on and so would Jaden—to amazing journeys, experiences, and times.

And as we sat at a table not too far away and watched how gentle Jaden and others were to Kennedy at dinner before that dance, I became very emotional. I looked at Heather and said, "Twenty years from now, this incredible young man will be sitting at dinner out to eat with his beautiful wife and kids. And I am sure, he will become emotional with joy as he shares with them his amazing journey with Kennedy. How did we get so lucky to have a young man like this come into our daughter's life and journey? I am not quite sure that I ever could have done what he is doing or now is enduring."

After that dance was over, Kennedy's breathing became shallow. Her oxygen levels began to decline and she had once again proven to all of us that she had an understanding of last moments. Her ability to endure was unlike anything we had witnessed. For love was proven that day to be the most powerful prescription that she could have. Because unfortunately there was no prescription on earth that could save her.

http://goo.gl/c84Rke

Scan to view post

http://goo.gl/Cijgau

Scan to view post

CHAPTER 70

Legs Broken

It was as if everything was starting over again: the year, the moments, and the memories. Everyone was astounded that Kennedy even went to that dance. After that and for the first time ever, Kennedy began to tell us that she did not like her life. She tried so hard to communicate over the next several days that she was not happy. She was losing mobility so quickly and then it happened.

I encountered one of the most TENDER moments of my life and of Kennedy's journey. As I hustled out of my car into the house and toward Kennedy's room one day, I saw a sight that will forever be frozen in my mind.

Lying on the floor just outside of her room was Kennedy in her mother's loving, gentle arms. Without even saying a word, you could just feel the love between them. "What on earth are you guys doing on the ground?" I asked. "Bbbbrookeen, broken, leeegs bbroookken," Kennedy said.

She had rolled out of her bed onto the floor and pulled herself into the hallway with her arms. This is where Heather found her. She wanted so bad to just get up and walk. Heather just sat down, enveloped her in her arms, and sealed her up with love. Although so painful, this moment was also joyful.

The look on my sweet wife's face was that of love and a broken heart. My daughter's look was that of determination, sadness, and confusion.

Coming home that day to that scene, although it broke my heart in half like a sledge hammer to granite, also mended it. That day confirmed so much to me about the fact that we really were home. The doorways so wide for her wheelchair, the hallways big, the rooms so perfectly laid out, all had played part in making sure that Kennedy's going home was as comfortable as possible. As I rewind those ten years and begin to play the movie screen in my mind, it is all too clear, why I was told to "buy the home, buy the home." Tens turned into hundreds and, toward the end of Kennedy's life, thousands of visitors came to the home. One thing was constant with them, one thing was always heard, and one thing was always said by all: "we're home," strangers would say. "We're home," 27 cheerleaders would say, who ALL would become Kennedy's other sisters and our other daughters. "We're home," nurses and caretakers would say.

I was struggling with all of this. Again, I found myself as a father not being able to fix this and not being able to know if I could carry my little family through. And yet, I had received promises and had seen miracles, premonitions, and knew the outcome! It was so tough to endure. But, I had to endure it well.

Looking back now, those were some of the sweetest, most tender, and merciful moments of our lives. For you see, although I felt I could not fix it as her dad, we were there. Her mother was there. We were all there. We never left her side and we helped her to know that it was ok as we comforted her and helped her understand that her legs were really not broken. They were simply just resting up for the eternal voyage to come.

http://goo.gl/UlQe2v

Scan to view post

CHAPTER 71

What She Sees

It was not every minute, it was not every second, but every breath that we were with Kennedy. I would struggle each and every day with having to leave for work. I wanted to be with her all of the time. I had wanted to carry her pain, her burden, and the hard parts that were now happening. Heather was there for her every breath and to this day, I am grateful for her for taking care of our little girl. For there is no one else who could have done what she did. And although we were wanting every breath, we also were needing to get away from it all for just a minute. We needed to breathe outside of the cabin fever and just regroup.

So, Anna came to us and offered to watch Kennedy for two hours so that we could go to a movie. We thought about it and decided to go. Kennedy had experienced a good day and was sound asleep when we left. We felt that we just needed to go and sit outside of all of the pressures, stresses, and feelings that we were having. About a half hour into the movie, Anna began texting us and telling us that Kennedy kept calling out for Heather to come by her side. Anna texted us and asked us to call her. Heather got up and went out of the theater to talk to her. Anna told us that Kennedy was singing "Joy to the World" and telling her that there was a vast amount of people who were in her room who came to visit her. She was calling out their names and was singing and putting her arms and hands up in the air in excitement. "She's seeing people. She's seeing kids and is singing and calling out their names? What do I do?" Anna asked. We left the movie immediately and went home.

When we arrived to Kennedy's room, you could feel a presence that was so similar to the presence we had felt earlier in our lives when

Heather's mother, Ramona, had been around us and Kennedy so many times. This feeling was special, different, and yet so powerful. Kennedy was clasping onto Anna's hands, looking straight out and up to the ceiling, and looking far off into distant space. We knelt by Kennedy's bedside and told her that we were there. She surprisingly really did not care at all about us and began to call out all of the names of the people that she was seeing. Anna told us that she had told her that Joseph of Egypt was there and a woman named Shelly. She also had said that a king and a queen were in her room visiting her as well. And the biggest thing was that she kept saying she could see kids. Lots and lots of kids! She would again began to sing "Joy to the World" and as she did this, she suddenly stopped and said, "Charlee, Charlee, Charlee? Charlee!" She reached forward and was trying to hug the air. She told us that Charlee had come to visit her as well and was there. As we sat in this room, there was no question of insanity or of false visions or far-fetched fakeness. Kennedy was the most sincere, honest, and trusting person we had known. We all just sat around her bed for almost one hour as Kennedy looked around the room as if she was looking right through all of us. And she kept looking up at that ceiling. We just soaked in the great feeling of peace that we were all feeling. None of us could see these angelic visitors, yet all of us could feel of them. They were real, they were there, and they were preparing and comforting Kennedy for what was to come.

After close to one hour, she finally called out for me to come to her. I went to her side and took her hand. "What is it, Dee Dee?" I asked. "Ppplease tttell tthem ttto llleave," she said. "Ttttired, ttttired, ssssso tttired," she said. I asked kindly and politely out loud that whomever was visiting Kennedy would leave so that she could rest. Suddenly, you could feel the room change and the feeling of those presences disappear as fast as they came. As I asked those present to leave, Kennedy slowly laid her head down and closed her eyes and said, "Work, llllots and lllotsss offffff, wwwwwork!" I thought this was an odd closing statement to the scene which we had just witnessed. So I asked, "What do you mean, Ken?" She then opened her eyes and explained to us as best as she could that these angelic visitors who had visited her were there surrounding all of us and were telling her that she needed to get ready to arrive to heaven where there was lots and lots of work for her to do.

After falling asleep, Heather, Anna, and I just kind of looked at each other like, "What just happened?" We sat together in that room for quite a long time in an embrace and did not say much. We just soaked.

Over the next several days and the weeks leading all the way up until the day that Kennedy passed away, visitors to Kennedy from the other side were regular and would come every night. It was such a sacred time in our home and was one that I wish the whole world could have experienced. The following is from my journal entry on May 9, 2014.

> "She is having some amazing spiritual moments right now. She is seeing things at night. Things that only her little heart can understand. She cannot talk a lot, but will open her eyes really, really wide and will tell us about all of the people who are coming to visit her. So, we began asking her questions and would say, "Squeeze my hand if Grandma Mona is here. Squeeze my hand if they are wearing white. Squeeze my hand if you see Gold. Squeeze my hand if Charlee is there."
>
> As we asked Kennedy seemed to have a sight of mainly female visitors that were older. However, Charlee was there. We then asked if Heavenly Father was there? No squeeze. When we asked if the Holy Ghost was there, she squeezed like crazy. It was very special, interesting and emotional to watch. When we were sitting there, I then asked the question, that was the very hardest of all. "Is Jesus there?" She squeezed the hardest on this one. She tried to reach to the sky and even get up. She was trying to talk and describe things but could not. We had to ask her questions and ultimately what we figured out is that she was seeing Heaven. She described many people there and said, there were children and babies. She described the word, NOW. She described that they had white hair and white and silver clothing. She described that Heaven itself was white and gold. She also described that Jesus was there with the Holy Ghost working. She kept saying, "NOW, NOW, NOW!" She did not want to go, because we asked her if she wanted to go. She kept her eyes wide open like this for almost 45 minutes. I HAVE NO IDEA how she is my daughter."

Amidst all of the wonderful and spiritual things, these moments were so needed. They were the only calm moments of each day. Kennedy's bowels began to shut down. Her brain just could not tell them to work and she was in so much pain. She would scream in agony as her body would try to digest, but the brain was not relaying the message. She was still eating, but began throwing up, many, many times a day. Heather began to give her enemas on a daily basis so that she could digest and function. It was so sad to watch and see. Everything was getting tougher and tougher. Kennedy developed her first bed sore and her ability to move was diminishing. The physical demands were wearing on all of us and hospice was telling us that the time was shortening quickly.

We all could feel of these spirits present but could not see them. And that helped us to understand how and what Kennedy had felt with the loss of her eyesight for so, so long.

http://goo.gl/sxMsMR

Scan to view post

CHAPTER 72

Not Much Time

We were trying to do everything right. We became so worried how we were going to be or what we were going to do when Kennedy would be gone from us. I was really worried about Heather and her health, both mentally, physically, and emotionally. We began to feel how hard this was going to be and yet so rewarding for Kennedy to leave us. Kennedy had carried so many and would be able to carry many more from the other side. Each day we began to be saddened, knowing it was one less day with her. The following was recorded in my journal on May 13, 2014:

> I am so happy that she is able to be touched and helped by people who really, really care. I am positive that she is being kept alive spiritually by many of them. She really struggled to talk or even breathe at all tonight. We were scared. We were in her room together by her side, helping her to get in bed. We felt very strong that she was very, very different. Her breathing was [sporadic] and extremely separated. Her speech was so slurred and garbled that she could barely even talk. We were right by her side and she was in so much pain and was so unaware. I was holding Heather's hand. We both knew that she was very, very different and very close to almost passing away. It was and is a moment that I will never forget. I almost felt as if were in a different world, a different place and a different realm. I was very grateful for our relationship and more than anything for our daughter Kennedy. She has brought us so much joy!

It was so odd to be writing about the end of her life. To be simply accepting this and to be at peace with not much time left. Our little family felt it, we knew it and we believed it. Everyone else on the outside, including friends, family, the cheerleaders, and classmates, could feel it, but not how we could feel it. It was different for us. Many others were telling us that "she would have a great turnaround, or a miracle of healing, etc." There were also those that told us that they knew that this was just a hard bump and patch in the road and that she would be back to school and cheerleading the next year. That night as I lay holding my wife, as hard as it was, I had to be grateful. I had to be grateful for the last four years of amazing inspiration, miracles, and more than anything that feeling, *"You always listen to the Spirit, which is a higher power, and if you do, you will know exactly what to do."* Kennedy was going to be fine! She was going home and she was now going to be able to touch the world with her love, her story, and her great spirit. My mind began to shift to what I needed to do for Heather, Anna, and Beau. Each of us were handling this differently.

Everywhere we went that week, we were reminded of Kennedy. It seemed as if the whole world knew about her and was rallying around her and cheering her on. The following is from my journal on May 14, 2016:

> I went to the bank and the tellers were asking me about Kennedy. They asked me if there is any "Good Part" to this journey? And that is when it hit me. I looked at them and said, "Yes, actually there is. I am so blessed, because I am 1/3 of the way there with my kids. Kennedy has already made it to Heaven and I will not need to worry about her anymore. I now have 1 down and 2 more to go. I still have to take care of Beau and Anna and make sure that they make it and that we raise them right. But, I feel so blessed to know that at least 1 of our children has made it and will be there for us when we go.

With not much time left, there were moments where the spirit of Kennedy would take over. As odd as it sounds, but I believe it with my whole heart. I would feel her with me in spirit even before she had died. She was already working and already doing things for people as her time wound down. And with not much time, we were learning that thousands would be touched by her story long after she was gone and it would be our job to be in tune in order to do this.

http://goo.gl/hl9Wro

Scan to view post

CHAPTER 73

The Last Cheer

Kennedy was wearing down, Heather was wearing down ,and I was in survival mode. There was no way that Heather could help Beau and Anna, so I officially took over. I found myself not sleeping except maybe 1–2 hours per night, arising extremely early and getting everything done for the home in order to leave for work. I would start work as early as possible and work my guts out so that I could come home to pick up Beau and take him to his baseball and soccer practices and games. Anna was driving on her own and so she could drive herself to school and different activities.

We were all living each minute as if it were the last, trying to endure it well. The end of the school year came and with that, we knew within the walls of our home what was coming. Kennedy had promised us that she would make it through the end of the year and especially that she would cheer all the way to the end. When the last assembly arrived, none of us knew if she really would be able to go and cheer. We knew that this would be the very last time she would EVER take that stage as a cheerleader in her life. This would be the very last time that she would be in a cheer. Yes, this would be the last cheer.

All we had to rely on was our feelings which we did believe were being helped from a greater power. It was the year end assembly at Kennedy's high school: Fremont High. So many had asked if she could be there. Earlier in the week, Kennedy adamantly had said no. She was not well and had a very hard week and did not feel like going anywhere. We asked her several times to go and the answer was still no. With nothing to lose, I sat down as her dad and explained to her as lovingly as I could, that this would be her last assembly and opportunity to cheer with her squad . . . in this life. That one was hard. It cut deep. Surprisingly, she paused looked right at me and said."Ok . . . go."

But, I will say confidently, that day was the last cheer for Kennedy.

It was part of the "fairy tale ending" to a journey that few people would ever believe REALLY happened except US, because we had lived it.

So, here is what happened. She went to that assembly, she came out of her almost nonreactive state she had been in, and she cheered! She moved her hands, she tried to scream, and she cheered! She gave the last cheer in her wheelchair and the girls surrounded her.

After they left the stage, I was able to thank the school, the students, the faculty, and of course the cheerleaders and the principal. I could not contain my emotions. I immediately let loose, the tears began to run, and the entire year from the first walk down that track at a football game where a cheerleader noticed Kennedy until now flooded my mind.

"A lot will happen in your lives," I said to the assembly. "A lot of things will come and go and you will see a lot of things. But, this thing, this year, this moment, and moments that you have given Kennedy are something to remember and something that we will all remember. Never forget it and thank you! I can say with confidence that Kennedy will not cheer next year, she will not be here. . . . So never forget, never forget. Thank you for all you have done and we thank Kennedy for sharing herself with you as well!"

The auditorium went silent and you could have heard a pin drop. We put the microphone to Kennedy's face and she said, "Thank you" and "Jaden." This experience, this journey, this time with her at that school all culminated to this moment, and then they stood. All of them. Every last person in that auditorium stood and clapped and cried and honored our daughter. The girl we dreamed of being a cheerleader, a normal high school girl wanting to fulfill her dreams. That was the last cheer. The cheer from all who were involved. The cheer from those who reached out, spent time, raised money, visited our home, sent cards, gifts, texts, or called. The last cheer was for everyone. And as they cheered, Kennedy rose her hands as high as she could and waved to everyone. The principal came on stage and we embraced. I thanked him from the bottom of our hearts for being a good man.

As we left the stage, the cheerleaders went into the hallway and surrounded Kennedy. The mood changed. The spiritual silence of Kennedy entered that hallway and for a couple of minutes, they all just sat, cried, and felt of her and this moment. Nothing was said, there were no words. Kennedy silently reached out her hands to all of them, but more importantly her heart. It spoke and it spoke . . . LOUD!! It was so hard to watch. We all had known, we all do know and we all knew that this day would come.

Yes, this is the last cheer. . . . Something told me I was right and as my wife and I embraced and looked at our daughter, so innocent, so perfect, so full of light, love, and life. We realized, accepted, and had to forever remember, ALTHOUGH SO HARD, this was . . . the last cheer!

http://goo.gl/QhtgRq

Scan to view post

CHAPTER 74

Lucky

We all knew and we all dreaded the moment that now laid in our path. There was no way to climb over, around, under, or through it. We had to simply endure it and swim right through the middle of it. Kennedy began to experience pain that truly none of us could understand or endure. Her head was in so much pain and she would scream. She would point to different areas on her body and scream. This was agonizing for all of us to watch. Her nurses and doctor were doing all they could to mitigate the pain.

She had also began to have days where she would literally throw up for the entire day. She would begin to throw up early in the morning and would not stop until sometimes the middle of the night. A constant action for her of trying to rid the pain from her body. The doctors were now recommending that we place a port in her stomach in order to administer pain meds. Her nurse at one point mentioned that she had never experienced anything like this and did not know how to help with the pain, because no one could pinpoint the location or reason for it.

During one of these tough days, Kennedy's cousin took her, along with a friend, on a walk in her wheelchair around the block. We found that the fresh air for a longer period of time helped to calm her body and allow her stomach to have a break. But this time, for whatever reason, it did not. This walk was a disaster because she threw up the entire time in a bowl and just became worse with the pain. She had nothing left in her and after arriving home, the pain was so great that there was nothing mortally that was giving her the peace, comfort, or help that she needed. While they took Kennedy on this walk, I had to go outside and work in the yard for a bit. I needed to pull some weeds, I needed to think, and I needed to let out some emotions of anger, frustration, sadness, and grieving that I was already experiencing. I was out back pulling weeds, and mixing sweat with tears, trying to learn to cope with this part of the journey. As this was happening, I silently spoke and whispered gently to Heavenly Father, "please, please, help Kennedy. Please help to send us something or someone to help her with this pain. Please, Father. We are willing to let her go, but are asking that somehow and in some way we can help with this massive pain."

I suddenly felt a warm feeling come over me that was so new and yet so familiar. I felt and heard in my mind that same feeling, *"You always listen to the Spirit, which is a higher power, and if you do, you will know exactly what to do."* I stood up and looked at the house and then heard Kennedy scream. Suddenly at the gate to our backyard, I saw an image from heaven appear: Heather's uncle and aunt were standing at the gate and had come to visit us out of the blue. I knew that the answer I had prayed for appeared not within weeks, days, or hours, but minutes. I ran to them. I took off my work gloves and said, "Your timing could not have been better, Uncle. You are an answer and a miracle to my prayers." They did not understand until I took them inside of our home, where they witnessed Kennedy in the most pain yet of her journey.

I knew what we needed to do. We had done it so many times, but now it was time to truly exercise great faith in administering a priesthood blessing to our beautiful daughter. I have spoken of the priesthood in earlier chapters and want to touch on it again. In our faith and church, I am an elder and have been given the priesthood as has my uncle. Worthily, we are able to administer priesthood blessings through the laying on of hands on the sick, the afflicted, or those in need. We laid our hands on her head and simply blessed her to be without pain and to be comfortable. Without hesitation and within seconds, she gently laid her head back and through her heavy but shallow breathing was able to calm down and stopped screaming.

Our uncle was speechless and our aunt was in tears. Kennedy was grateful. This experience calmed me and I was able to set everything to the side and simply be right by Kennedy's side from this moment on until she died. That day was a roller coaster, as the pain would come back. She asked me to give her a blessing three times that day. Each time, it calmed her and allowed her to have peace. And each time she fell back to sleep. I recorded in my journal that day, "This little girl has so much faith in the priesthood and in the truthfulness of the Gospel. I was so impressed with her Faith and her ability to believe. I am so LUCKY to be her Father."

The emotions were so raw and so real for all of us, yet we felt lucky. It almost felt like when Kennedy was first born, other than the illness was really taking its toll on all of us and exhausting us all. But, during this time, I began to see how really lucky we were and close we were as a family. We had the young men and women from our church come and visit Kennedy that week and bring her happiness, support, and love. They sat and played dolls with her, sang her songs, and brought us meals they had made. The young men from the community and our church worked outside on our yard with many of the men, doing all that I could not do on our large acre lot. There was a giant spirit of love that surrounded and accompanied these youth and the service that they were giving and rendering to Kennedy and our family.

Her friends and family were visiting incessantly. She was lucky to have them there for her and with her. Every moment that we had was by Kennedy's side. We were lucky. So, lucky to know and to feel of a loving Father in Heaven at that time. And although the stresses, the problems, the disease, the anxiety, the finances, and the business problems were all still there, one thing was certain. No matter what, we all loved each other and we loved Kennedy. And that part was lucky. Anna would come home every day and would simply put her arms around Kennedy or sit by her side. Her love for Kennedy was so strong, so apparent, and so real. Because the one thing that kept us together and to this day keeps us together was that. We were lucky to have an angel like Kennedy who was, is, and always will be such an example to us of what it truly means to love one another.

As Kennedy worsened, she began to ask for priesthood blessings every few hours. The following was recorded from my journal May 20, 2014.

> She was in so much pain and asked for a blessing every few hours. This is the 4th or 5th blessing I believe in 2 or maybe 3 days. She has so much faith. We gave her a blessing and administered consecrated oil this time. In the blessing she was told that her body would need to adjust to the pain. She was told that she would need to "Endure it Well." She was also told that she had a Savior who is the only one who can understand what pain she is going through. She was told that he will be here for her through this entire journey. I truly believe that and I know that. I am so grateful for the Priesthood. It is real. It works

> through Faith. I am even more grateful for the faith of Kennedy. She is so faithful and is one of the most simplistic spirits on earth in my opinion. It is getting very hard to move her. It is extremely difficult. All we can do is take one day at a time.

It was amazing from that moment on to watch Kennedy adjust to the pain and to endure it well. It seemed as if Kennedy's faith was all she had left to help with the pain and miraculously it was helping.

Just one week before she would pass away, Kennedy woke up on the last day of school and told Heather that she wanted to go so bad and see everyone and attend the yearbook signing. And with just one week left in her life, we were so lucky to witness another miracle as she for the last time fought through the pain and visited her school: Fremont High.

Heather brought her and although Kennedy was incapable in many ways, she was so capable in others. Heather said that she took her out of the van and instantly Kennedy was surrounded by hundreds of kids. They wheeled her away and Heather sat in the van at a distance and watched as Kennedy was surrounded and mauled with love by so many. EVERYONE wanted her to sign their yearbook and she did! Heather was very emotional as she just watched and let the kids take her and help her hold the pen and sign. And Kennedy signed away! This was her last day of public school and last day to sign a high school yearbook.

When she got home, she crashed and literally slept the rest of the day and night. So many texted or called or sent messages thanking us for having her come. She was in so much pain and so much grief, but was able to fulfill her goal of finishing the year as strong as she could.

Friends were coming to visit Kennedy like crazy. She had completed her mission and she seemed to be physically done. She was not going to stop fighting, but her abilities were all but vanishing before us. Many were coming to visit her and say their goodbyes.

May 24, 2014, I recorded in my journal,

> Today, EVERYTHING changed with Kennedy. She can really no longer chew. Her swallowing ability is all but gone. She had the hardest time getting any food in her body today. Heather and the nurses increased her meds, she was much more sedated and out of it, it seemed. She was very comfortable and that is exactly what we have wanted and needed for her. She was out of it, but I am confident that she could feel of us. But, it is getting harder and harder each day with her. Her decline is so severe.

Yes, we were lucky to have so many wonderful and amazing people whom had sacrificed so much of their time, resources, love, and energy for Kennedy. But, it was time to officially prepare to let her go. Now it was reality—now it was real. All of it, so real and so lucky. For we had only five short days left to savor. Five days to feel, love, and be lucky enough to share and spend with her.

http://goo.gl/Enx1kI

Scan to view post

CHAPTER 75

The Comforter

We knew that the day would come and we thought that we were ready for it. But you are never ready for the day the Comforter comes. It would be hard for some, great for others, and difficult for all to accept and understand. But the Comforter officially entered our home and Kennedy's life on May 25, 2014.

Kennedy officially could not chew. Her ability to swallow was limited, but thank goodness for Icees, shakes, and Popsicles! Those were life savers. To watch her suffer from not eating was one of the hardest things we have ever gone through.

We were to the point where the sadness and some despair set in and then . . . we felt the Comforter arrive.

It is unlike any feeling we had ever felt, unlike any gift we had received, and unlike any material possession or spiritual feeling we had experienced. Our goal was mainly to keep Kennedy comfortable and at peace. And this goal was being accomplished!

I believe the Comforter comes directly from our Father in Heaven as a person nears the end of their life. But I also believe that the Comforter is sent to us through others. We had best friends, family, cousins, neighbors, and many close to us come and visit and comfort Kennedy. Some brought newborns and some came from far away. Some had known her her whole life and others for just a year. The feeling of the Comforter was something that we knew was present.

It was humbling to feed Kennedy with a dropper. We were feeding her protein shakes and mandarin oranges at this point. We would tilt her head back and she could swallow very little at a time. They would kind of slide down her throat. She still was wanting to eat, but could not. She could not tell us what she was feeling or what she wanted, so she began to communicate through hand signals and squeezing our hands. The signals were clapping for a movie or hitting her palm for the table. She would move her fingers like rain for a drink. It was the saddest thing thus far. It was all going so fast, but was all so real. We understood that she was unable to communicate. However, when she heard us, she would groan or wave her hand to let us know that she knew what was going on. She just could not tell us through words and that was the hardest.

We tried to make it fun, having Kennedy's Hugs colors in her cups and telling her about the bright pinks and greens. Many came and told her stories or read to her.

We had promised to make her comfortable, yet she still cried out in pain. We could give her a feeding tube, but why? All this would do is prolong her pain, her decline, and her suffering. And she had asked us long ago to not do this. We knew that the Comforter was very near.

It was so hard when Kennedy was able to ask, "Why can I not eat? Why?" Heather's response was just lying by her and stroking her head and comforting her. I think that she truly did not want to leave all of us and none of us wanted her to go yet. But I could not stand to see her suffer, to see her mom suffer, and to see her brother and sister suffer. The entire thing was just unfair. I never asked until now, why? Why does she have to go through this and suffer? Why is her body so frail and does she have to endure the pain? At this point, it took two people to move her anywhere. Heather could no longer do this alone.

And Heather was becoming agitated and very upset. She was becoming extremely tired and very frustrated, without answers. I know Heather well enough to know when she is done. And I also know that Heather is a fighter but can only take so much. We are only given what we can handle and she was at her max handling point.

MANY hard things would occur over the next week. We knew Kennedy would now go quickly. I thought we had three months, but now believed we had less than 1 week. It was time to be prepared and prepare for her to leave. I contacted Weber State University at the request of Kennedy. She had said so many times that her funeral would be held in their basketball arena, the Dee Events Center. Her funeral would be large and we wanted it public. We also contacted others to let them know they better come and see her. If she could not eat, we would lose her sooner than later. I felt like the only other person I could contact was our Heavenly Father. How much more could I petition him? How much more could I beg? Was he sick of me? Did he really continue to bless us or were we becoming a nuisance?

Heather and I would kneel in prayer for a very long time. Probably over a half hour. It was very emotional as we prayed together and as we let our emotions out. I was to the point as we thanked Heavenly Father, and prayed for comfort and peace for Kennedy. As we knelt, I invoked the power of the priesthood to shield our home in peace and to allow the Comforter to be present. I also pled with the Lord to be present with each one of us, so that we could and would be carried, lifted up, and consoled. More than anything I pled for Kennedy that angels and ministers would come to her aid and that she could be gently taken and pass very peacefully. The Comforter came and we wept.

It was so very hard, so very real, and so very emotional. We held each other tight and we knew that the time had come. Her journey, her work, and her influence had made its major mark on us and the world. Heather and I began to formulate in our mind who we needed to contact to come and say goodbyes. All of it was real—angels were among us, people were around, and we had so many blessings.

Heather and I had probably slept 4 hours in 48. Yet, we were being carried. The Comforter was something we had heard of, yet had not experienced. Having the presence of the Comforter was something that we wish every human being could experience. For it is so surreal, yet so real. Our time line of less than three months quickly now turned to less than three days. And yet, amidst our broken hearts and minds, we were also clear. Probably more clear than we had ever been at this point in Kennedy's journey.

The Comforter, which was with us, was giving us the comfort to calculate every move, decision, word, and feeling. There was no instruction manual for what we were going through, no schooling, course, or book. We solely had our Heavenly Father who had sent the Comforter and we had each other. But, more than anything, we still had Kennedy. And although she could not say much, although she was in so much pain, although she was not able to eat or drink and was at times completely bedridden, she still was our leader, our guide, our hope, and our comfort, and the one whom we all to this day would turn to in the hardest of times. And we were committed to keep our promises to her that we had made. For she was still in her own unique, but loving way, showing love, giving love, and exuding love through her spirit. And all who were around not only could feel of it, but knew it. Yes, the Comforter was real.

http://goo.gl/jXqswq

Scan to view post

CHAPTER 76

The Last Ride

Many came to tell Kennedy goodbye. Neighbors, cousins, friends, church members, and close family. We were and still are to this day so grateful for the support. But the Spirit kept nagging at me. I was being told to take her on a truck ride—the last ride: the ride that now goes down in my heart as one of the most special moments of my life and a monumental part of my life. So, as everyone was visiting, caring, and talking with our sweet Kennedy, I could not take it any longer. We had so many over at the house. Many outside helping to do yard work and the inside packed with people. But, ultimately, I could not handle the spiritual, the emotional, or the physical pressure any longer. So,I followed that prompting and interrupted the visits so that a daddy and his daughter could experience their one last ride together. So I could see the smile on her face, the thrill and sound of the diesel engine. Kennedy screaming "faster, Dad, faster" and then the two of us singing Toby Keith's "Who's Your Daddy" and "Beer for My Horses." These rides would take us different places, but we always would end up at a gas station and would buy a Coke. This was our special thing, and it was our little ritual that happened every Saturday or when it needed to happen. And it needed to happen one last time.

I came home one day, looked at my wife, and said, "There is only one more thing that I want to do with her and we NEED to do it today. I NEED to take her on our last ride, while she understands."

Kennedy perked up and groaned out a little groan. She wanted to go, she loves these rides and as of late, we have not been able to have them. So, I fired up the truck and pulled it around front. I WILL NEVER forget the feelings in my heart or hers as I scooped her up in my arms and we both began to cry. I gently lay her in the front seat and with every ounce of courage had to whisper in her ear that this would be the last ride. As she cried, I cried and all who were there knew that these cries were not for pain. . . . She absolutely knew and understood the event taking place.

We brought Heather to take pictures and to be there to help hold Kennedy in place. We rolled down the windows and blasted our favorite two songs. Kennedy gently reached over and motioned for my hand. We clasped as tight as we could. The MINUTE that the song "Beer for My Horses" came on, Kennedy reached her hand in the air and tried to act like she was riding a horse with the other hand. The funniest part about that song is that when she used to be able to sing, she would say "root beer" for my horses! She was trying to sing, and she was trying to smile.

We pulled into her favorite gas station and I asked her what flavor of Icee she wanted. She motioned with her hand—none. Then she reached over toward me and tried to pull me to her. I completely lost it and she held me. Heather had to get out of the truck and take pictures. Kennedy kissed me and tried to rub my arm. She understood and understands that there is something so special about our truck rides and about a man and his truck and his daughter.

We began our drive back home and played the songs again. She put her head back and let the wind hit her face and her hair. Heather and I were sobbing. I did not want to go home. I just wanted to drive and drive and drive and drive. But, I knew that this was the last ride and that I needed to get her back to her comfort zone and the many visitors at our home.

We pulled in the driveway and many came out to our aid. All were offering to lift her and help transport her out of the truck. But this was Dad's moment, this was our ride, our time, and my little girl giving me the last ride. I gently told them that I wanted to do it myself and scooped her up in my arms and held her tight. I did not want it to end. I did not want it to go away. I KNEW right there and then that was the last ride. Kennedy took a big breath and again gave me a kiss. Many watching were in tears. I gently set her in her wheelchair and had to walk away.

The day of the last ride was something that I really knew would come, but never wanted to come. It seems as if this last year that she has been on the last ride. She has taught so much, given back ALL that she has had in her, and has reached as far as she has known how.

I woke up several times that last night, breathing heavy and crying in my sleep. My tears and sobs woke myself. But, what is amazing is finally at about 3 a.m., my little boy, Beau, heard my cries and came and crawled into bed next to me and laid his little head on my shoulder. He snuggled against me and wrapped his arms around me. As I felt of his comfort, I began to realize how much we still have to live for and how much we still have to do. Heather was asleep in Kennedy's room and Anna downstairs. I thought of each of them and I thought of our future. It then occurred to me that from here on out and as we lose Kennedy shortly, that we will then have the last ride within our family. A ride that if we participate, if we jump in and experience, live, love, and try as hard as we can to live right . . . we will all be reunited together as a family.

Time to get ready for the last ride and that brings us so much peace and joy!

As I composed myself after that ride and again entered our home that night, we had many, many dear friends and family still visiting us. Kennedy had given her daddy everything she had on that ride and believe me when I say that she had nothing physically left to give. But she did!

The next day, while Kennedy's room was occupied with probably over forty people, I was nudged greatly to write and post about the last ride. I snuck away for a few minutes into my office so that I could record such an emotional yet wonderful event. After writing this post, I will never forget as I walked out of my office and looked at Heather. I said, "Well, I just wrote a post about our last ride together. No one is going to want to hear about that. What was I thinking?" Heather simply looked at me and said, "You have no idea how many people that will touch, Jay. You are not thinking at this point. You are following exactly what we are supposed to do as a family, and that last ride is something that will touch many, many lives."

At the time, those words comforted me. Amidst the pain, and still to this day amidst the pain, all we and Kennedy wanted to do was touch other's lives with her story as we knew that she was leaving us and she knew she was leaving us. That little story, that little moment has now been read by over eight million people. Over half a million people have commented, shared, or reached out to us about the post and its effect on them continues to spread all over the world.

http://goo.gl/WCRFyr

Scan to view post

CHAPTER 77

It's All Real

I want to say that we were sad, and I know we were. Yet, we were also being carried and it seemed we were celebrating her rather than memorializing her. The hardest thing for us was that, there was so much that we still wanted to say, to do, and to discuss with her. Not just tell her, but have her communicate with us. During the last few months of her life, Kennedy and her mom would have endless talks in her bed, where Heather would embrace her and snuggle up to her so tight. Those talks were theirs. Much of them no one will ever know. But our talks were on the back deck, in her wheelchair where we could feel the sunshine, wind, rain, or even snow at times. Kennedy wanted to feel all of those feelings before she left. And I just wanted to scoop her up, put her in her wheelchair, and take her on the back deck away from everyone and everything that was going on and have one of those talks. Furthermore, I wanted her to assure us that we were going to be ok. Even though we were being carried, we still were relying on our own faith and our own selves to believe that all would be ok. There were so many pressures and we just really needed some assurances.

One of the special things happening was that we had a few select individuals, including my father, come to us and tell us that Kennedy's spirit had already come to them and relayed some sacred messages to them. Many will not believe that is possible, but I am no longer merely a believer in if it is a possibility, because it happened. Her body at this point was simply a house for her spirit to come and go from. She was already leaving it and doing some wonderful things that were so sacred for many whom reached out that day and since her passing away to share with us. As Heather and I discussed this part, there was no doubt that the stories we were being told from others were true and we ourselves felt like Kennedy's spirit in her body was only with us when her spirit would allow it to be.

After everyone finally left that day, the feeling in our house was again a different one. It was so overwhelming and we were able to get Kennedy under control enough so that she could peacefully rest. We did not know when we would lose her and so we were not leaving her side for a second.

Heather laid down next to her on another bed that we had slid next to Kennedy's medical bed. She reached over and her arm was around Kennedy. Kennedy's breathing had been shallow and we had been suctioning out her saliva, along with giving her oxygen. I could not sleep if my life depended on it. I sat in her black wheelchair at the foot of her bed and just stared at her and my eternal wife. As I sat there, I was not tired, I was simply basking in the greatness of the scene before me, but withering inside wondering when it would go away. I began to long for Kennedy to talk to me, to communicate with me. All of the realities were compounding in my mind and I just seemed to scream out inside that I just wanted her to communicate one last time with me. As this was happening, I suddenly heard her voice as clear as day come into my mind and say, "Dad, get your journal and write down what I am about to tell you." I looked at her and then at Heather. Kennedy was sound asleep. But, again I heard her voice inside of my head say, "Dad, get your journal and write down what I am about to tell you!" Once more, I looked at her as she was sound asleep and I gripped the handles on the wheelchair wondering if I was losing it. Finally a third time, I heard, "Dad, get your journal and write down what I am about to tell you." With me, many things have happened in threes, so this time I knew it was real. I quickly went and got my journal and at 1:30 a.m. on the last physical day of my daughter's life May 29, 2014, I recorded the following. (Please keep in mind that I will not share all that was shared since some is too sacred.)

(Kennedy's Spirit Came to me and relayed everything) 1:30 a.m.

> I am sitting here in Kennedy's room and it is all real . . . all of it. I am looking around at her newspaper clippings, her cheer trophies, her letters, necklaces and dolls. I am sitting here and her spirit is talking to mine. It is telling me very specifically the following. It is telling me, "Dad . . . I am tired. My body is tired. My Spirit is ready Dad, but my

body is done . . . right Dad?" I am looking at Kennedy sleeping, her body is asleep but her Spirit is not. It has just spoken to me as if she were speaking like a human. She just told me that it is ALL REAL, ALL OF IT. She also told me that I will be o.k. with

1. My Business
2. My Job

"Dad, the business will be taken care of. You will be taken care of is what she is telling me right now. Heavenly Father says to quit sweating the small stuff and go to work. Especially take care of Beau Dad and regrow your relationship with Anna. She is going to need you. Be: LOVING, KIND AND UNDERSTANDING. She will be the BIGGEST BLESSING of your life Dad, outside of Mom. Stay close to the cheerleaders Dad. They were there for me and you need to be there for them. Go to the games, have them over to the house. You will be one of their largest blessings and I will be a <u>guardian angel to each of them.</u>"

You and Mom have some things to do. Continue to share my story Dad. I think that you should write a book But . . . keep your head on. DO NOT EVER let it get to you.

Dad, enjoy your life. Go and hunt, ski with Beau and Anna. Play a lot of sports with Beau and be very involved in the Gospel. You will be asked to speak many times and very frequently. Use your Priesthood to touch lives. Many callings will be coming your way with Mom, Dad. LOVE HER! She is my Mommy forever. I know that you love her, but you need to know that she already has a place reserved in Heaven for her. She is and will be a great leader there. Dad, your Grandpas are very present and near you. They are working hard in your behalf. Love them. They have been so good to me! Dad, your biggest worries shall become your least worries. Survive for just a bit longer. You will be able to pay everything off and you will be able to enjoy your life debt and stress free. I PROMISE TO BRING YOU MIRACLES WITH THIS PART DAD. Own your mistakes and just work smarter. Your business will stick around and it will bless many. USE YOUR SUCCESS TO SHARE MY STORY! I promise that you will not tire from it and you will long to see me again, every day for the rest of your life. Store knowledge, store food and store savings. Be peaceful. You have changed Dad. Listen, serve, obey. Dad . . . it's OK. It ALL is OK. You are going to be just fine.

Dad, I chose this. Do not ever forget that.

On a fun note, take truck rides for me and with me. I will be there. I will be laughing & giggling and drinking a Coke. Dad, go and buy Mom a new trailer or something to get you guys out. It will take a little time, but it will all work out.

Now, for the hard things Dad. So, here it goes.

I will pass away this weekend. If you can, have my funeral on June 5th. If not, it is o.k. That will mark one year since my diagnosis and I think that is pretty special.

Make sure and take care of the cheerleaders when they come to tell me goodbye. They will struggle and so will you. But, after that visit, I am going Dad. I cannot stand it any longer. It is so wonderful over there. It is too hard to explain. And everything that you taught me is real. I have been there many, many times in the last year. You are pretty popular up there Dad. Do you know where you are different? You actually listen and so many do not.

Dad, I'll be waiting for you! I promise to! Thank you for teaching me, thank you for loving me, and believing in me. . . . I promise you truly are the coolest Dad on earth. I will never, ever understand it all Dad, either. The year, the journey, etc. Just know that YOU DID IT! YOU literally sacrificed everything, put everything on the line for me. ALL FOR ME. And now the miracle and blessing will come. You will witness it in the next month. And tomorrow, you will witness a miracle with the cheerleaders. Well, Dad that is enough for now. I have some things that I need to do today. I am already about my Fathers business.

Dad, one more thing. . . . I LOVE YOU! I have to go now. Be strong, take good care of me like always. The funeral will open many doors. It will be the crowning event of my earthly journey. Many are going to come and many are going to be watching you and Mom. Remember to love her. Little Beau will be o.k. I will come for him many times. I love him so much. He will grow into a fine young man. Oh Dad, one more thing, I am your little Dee, your Kenners, your Princess. But, more importantly, I am the Daughter of a King.

Love,

Kennedy

I will not convey exactly what I saw that night, but will convey that it's all real. Everything that I had and have been taught is real. For I saw and experienced things that night that to this day are sometimes hard to believe. Things that happened to a normal kid from little Bountiful, Utah, who now was sitting in his daughter's wheelchair staring at her lifeless body in the middle of the night and waiting for her to die. Yet, I had just been given clear, ultra clear direction and promises on many,

many fronts. And those promises, those communications have almost all come to fruition.

As I stared at the lifeless body of my daughter, I soaked in the presence of my real daughter—my spiritual angel who was there with me at that moment, at that time that I so needed to communicate with me. I learned that night that heaven is real. I had always believed it, but now knew it. I learned that night, that we are sealed and we are bound together forever with our precious Kennedy and that no matter what, she had a much greater work that she would not be doing, but was already doing. I woke Heather up and gently sat next to her on her bed. I conveyed and read to her through tears what Kennedy had just revealed, communicated, and promised to us. I told her that we now had our time line and our direction and that we would be fine. Heather, was not really emotional at that point, she was not dramatic or overly energetic. She simply placed her hand on my hand and then her other hand on Kennedy's hand and said, "Thank you, Jay, for being so in tune, and thank you, Kennedy, for coming to your daddy and telling him what we need to do and what is going to happen. I love you both so, so much."

http://goo.gl/GqqafD

Scan to view post

CHAPTER 78

Kennedy's Hugs

We had listened to that feeling, *"You always listen to the Spirit, which is a higher power, and if you do, you will know exactly what to do,"* for sixteen and a half years. We had followed and we had built the key chain of a life that was beyond any life that any of us could imagine living. Kennedy had completed more in her lifetime in sixteen and a half years then most would in ninety years. The last mortal day of her life was paramount. It was to this day, the longest, most sacred, and most special day of our family's life. We had not just lived a million lifetimes with Kennedy in her short life, but we had just received clear and direct promises through her from a loving Father in Heaven who loved us and wanted and to this day wants us to be happy. The emotions, the experiences, and the order of events of her last day on earth were so powerful, so magnificent, so hard, and yet so wonderful. The events of that day are pretty raw and are emotional. The only way that I can describe them is to relate exactly to you what I wrote in my journal about that specific day (May 29, 2014) and into the middle of the night of May 30, 2014.

> We awoke this morning and Heather, once again, did her hair. After she was ready, she wanted to go outside. So, I wheeled her outside and let the wind hit her face. There was just enough of a wind, everything seemed perfect. The birds were chirping and the sound of bugs, buzzing. I put my hands on her shoulders and rubbed them. She was so tired and at this point, the sorrow had set in. Before leaving her room, I had leaned forward and told her that we would need to have one last arm wrestle. I grabbed her hand and we placed our elbows gently on her legs. She still was surprisingly so strong, the little bugger! Of

course she beat me! And that is when I told her how big her muscles are and how strong she still is. She actually lifted her arm up a little to show me and Heather how strong. And that is when I lost it emotionally.

I had given her a blessing the night before and right there she motioned for another. I again blessed her with peace to her soul and love to her heart and that she would be comforted. I then told her that today would be the day that she would have to say her final goodbyes. She had told me the night before that she would go on the weekend, and it was Friday. So, she began to sob and I began to sob. She was so sad and she knew. She knew at that moment that it was time. And then an even STRONGER comforter entered our home and her room[—] so strong that we felt as if we were in a different realm or world. As we were out on the deck, I had a chance to feel her beautiful hair, her strong shoulders, her arms, and her back. I caressed her face and I felt her ears. I hugged her so tight. I went and got her dog Aggie and she jumped into her lap. Aggie sat faithfully by her side. And then the day began. The doorbell rang and the 3 musketeers came. These 3 seniors had pretty much led the way to start Kennedy on her remarkable year and journey. It was so tender and so hard, yet so rewarding to watch them and see them gather around her on that deck and just love her. We were right there watching. I had met them at the front door and told them this would be their last goodbye and visit. They cared for her and each one of them said their own little personal things to her. I had to walk away as they told her their own little things. Kennedy just cried and cried. Her cries were different now. They were out of sorrow and mourning versus physical pain. I felt so inclined to try to help her to stop. At first I told her it was o.k., but then I told myself to let it go. She deserved and had earned every right to have her earthly sorrow and pain. I could see that she was fading quickly and knew it was time to get her into her bed. We moved her inside where those 3 girls comforted her until many others came for the last time. Many, many people came from that moment on. We were heartbroken as we watched her experience sorrow and pain. We had increased her meds and at this point, she was on an IV site line that went into her stomach. We pretty much had her pain under control. But, the emotional pain was the hardest. Jaden had shown up and was right by her side. She knew he was there as he took her hands in his and held them tight. Each person or group of persons knew that would be the last time that they would ever see her alive again.

We had arranged to have the cheerleaders come from 4–6:30 p.m. We knew that this would be her last time to be with them and so we wanted it to be special. We allowed the remaining kids including her cousins and very close friends to tell her goodbye and to be alone with her. Then we had the cheerleaders all come into the room at one time.

As they did, the mood and spirit changed. I asked a cheerleader to say a prayer. She did and the spirit entered into the room even stronger. Their cheer coach talked to them and she let them know that they had made it. That their journey and that this whole year had now been fulfilled the right way. I read to them what had been revealed to me by Ken the night before. That was so hard and they all broke down and just wailed and cried. It hurt so bad to hear this and to see Ken. She was sobbing as well. We had to get it together for her. We then told them that each one of them would be able to have one on one time with her and tell her goodbye.

Each of them began to sit by her and tell her things that they needed and wanted to. As this went on, we could just see her getting sadder and sadder. Her congestion was becoming worse due to the crying, so we sat her up several times. I could tell that she was suffering in many ways. As she was suffering and feeling so much sorrow and pain, we knew it was time.

I had told the girls that she knew it was time, but that the only way they would be able to help her is if they LET HER GO! It had been brought to mind earlier in the day, that we would want them to sing "Let it Go" from the movie *Frozen* at her funeral. A good neighbor of ours had brought the disc over to our home as a gift to Kennedy that morning. I knew it was time and at every competition these girls had sang this song before competition. They gathered around her and held hands. One of them held her in her arms. I have never felt so much love exude in a song as that day. It instantly calmed Kennedy down and the room down as they sang that song. Oh there were tears, lots of tears, including my own. The spirit of these girls began to allow her to understand that it was o.k. to go.

As this happened, the sadness turned to almost a feeling of happiness and joy. Each of them continued to tell her goodbye. Heather's parents showed up and they were ready to tell her goodbye. We had to get her to her room. The spirit was telling me to get her there quickly.

Heather and I knew that her pain was to a point where things were getting very, very close. The time was almost 7 p.m. We took her and transported her one final time. I was as gentle as I could be. I needed to feel her warm body against mine. We took her on one more wheeled ride down the hallway to her sacred room. One of the most sacred places in my mind on earth. Heather's Parents came in and completely loved her, cared for her and told her goodbye. They were so loving and faithful. She was just still shallow in her breathing. As it neared closer to 7:15–7:30, it was time for Jaden to tell her goodbye. He knew it and so did we. I put my arm around him and walked down the hall with him. I told him that they needed to be alone.

For five minutes, I sat outside the door, knowing that this one was going to be tough. Kennedy cried and cried. She was almost wailing. It was so hard, so emotional and so difficult all wrapped up into one experience. She was trying so hard to say, "2 years." I could not take it any longer. I slowly opened the door and went in to her room in time to hear Jaden telling her that she had to let him go. She had to let him go! She was trying to say, "No." Tears were streaming down both of their faces. She could not and would not let go of his hand. She truly was in love with him. He had to pry her hand off of his. He walked toward the door and said, "I'll be back in the morning." I did not have the heart to tell him that there would be no coming back. As Kennedy continued to decline, she was still so adamant that she would marry Jaden in two years after high school and would have 11 kids. They would be married in Hawaii and have a dream wedding and than live Happily Ever After. She told everyone about this and as her time neared the end, she would constantly say."2 years, 2 years."

I ran to Kennedy's side and began consoling her, holding her hand and saying, "2 years, 2 years." It was so hard, so, so hard. Jaden's heart was broken. He walked out with his head down and his shoulders sunk. For the first time ever, I saw his heart break. He knew and I knew if he did not say those words, that she NEVER would have let go. "Two years" will always be a time frame that I will cherish and we will cherish. It kept a little girls heart alive as did Jaden. HARD THINGS were done by this Young Man and he never complained, acted like it was not real or was non sincere. His love for Kennedy was proved through his actions and in many ways, she kept herself alive by loving him. Many have called it kindness, many have called it being genuine and many have called it being nice.

But, what I call it, is LOVE. I helped Ken breathe as best as I could by sitting her up and by helping Heather use a tube to suction her out. I immediately texted my brother . . . who was bringing his son . . . and told him that he needed to hurry. Her cheerleading coach's family was outside waiting for their turn. They told her goodbye and then her coach had her alone time with her. A scene that I just have to feel crushed about. Seeing this coach, this friend, on her knees at Kennedy's bedside just weeping. They loved each other so much. We shut the door and let them have their alone time. I do not know what was said or how it ended, I only know it was sacred.

I re-entered her room and helped Heather give her more medication. She was now very congested, and her breathing was so hard to listen to. It sounded like she was drowning in her own mucus and there was nothing we could do. Her tongue was sticking out and she did not have the energy to put it back in her mouth. It was so hard to watch and so very painful. We were trying everything we could. We tried to push her tongue back in her mouth and even open her mouth, but we could not. We were sponging out her mouth and continuing the suction. She was just still so sorrowful and sad. Her cheeks were red and yet she still looked so beautiful and peaceful.

As I turned around to stand up, my beautiful sister KeriLyn was standing in the doorway. I was in complete gratefulness. We needed her and she would be critical. I hugged her and then saw my brother . . . and his son. . . . It was nearing 8:30 p.m. and the spirit was telling me that the time was getting shorter and shorter. [Our nephew] loved and talked with her. He had been such a great cousin to her and she loved him. My heart began to sink. The spirit testified that I would need to release her soon. I was so worried. I had texted my Dad and said, "If you want to say your last goodbyes, you need to come quickly." I was feeling the anxiety of not wanting to release her, but knowing I had to. I just needed others there.

As I walked outside, I immediately saw my Dad, my brother . . . and the doorbell rang. My brother in law, Allan was there on the front porch. They came, the ARMY of righteousness came and I would need them! I told my brother . . . he needed to say goodbye. He entered so peacefully and held her in his arms. He shut the door after his wife took a picture and he then began singing "I am a child of God" to Kennedy. He held her and he said that she tried to sing with him. She tried so hard he said. He sang to her and he was trying to comfort her and love her. His family then entered to tell her goodbye.

KeriLyn came in and hugged her and loved her. Everyone was coming and going so quickly it seemed. They were all trying to get in to see her. They all sat in the Living Room and were waiting their turn. I immediately felt the spirit tell me it was time to prepare. I went to my closet in my room, where it was quiet. I knelt down in prayer and bowed my head ever so gently in respect of my God and beautiful daughter. I thanked him for giving her to me and I thanked him for letting us have her for a while. I then asked for strength and asked for peace. I asked if it was time and it was confirmed. I then changed into my best suit, my best white shirt and put on a pink tie. (Kennedy's favorite color) I put on my best belt and my nicest socks. I made sure that my hair was combed perfectly and brushed my teeth so that my breath was fresh and clean. I sprayed on cologne and exited my room and walked into the family room. Everyone looked at me in shock and asked where I was going? I did not respond. I simply walked to the garage, where my shoes were at. I found my very best pair and shined them.

I placed them on my feet and walked back to little Beau's room. He was all alone and seemed so confused, yet so at peace. I brought him into the Living Room and I told him that it was time for Kennedy to go. He asked me, "where is she going?" Right then Heather walked in. We held his little hands and told him that she was going home to Heaven, back where she came from. We told him that it was time to tell her goodbye. We told him that her body would be free from pain and that her spirit would be free. He was ready and he traveled down the hallway to her room.

He entered and knelt by her bed and laid his little head on her shoulder and chest. "I love you Kennedy, bye, bye Kennedy. I will love you forever," he said. She tried as hard as she could to hug him. Her tears flowed and she cried hard. Her breathing was still so tough. I had told Heather to have someone get Anna. Anna came in the room and we asked to be alone. We all gathered around the bed and joined hands. The spirit was so, so strong! I asked that we say a prayer. We did and we thanked Heavenly Father for allowing us to be a family. We thanked him so much for Kennedy. I than looked at my little family and I said, "We did it! Guys, we did it! Kennedy, you did it! We made it! We committed to make it and we did!" The spirit entered and I knew it was time. I had to soak in the moment, but Kennedy was ready to go. I took Heather in the other room, our room and briefly told her it was time. She said she wanted her time. I told her she would get it. We left the room and walked into the Living Room. Many family members were sitting there and waiting for one on one time with Kennedy. I entered and said, "I am sorry, it is time. Please leave your children in the Living Room and only adults come into her room." I had to do this. It was time. Some asked, "Time for what?" I told them, "Time to release her." They all understood. The older kids came into her room. Her breathing at this point was the worse yet. I asked Allan, Dad and [my brother] to join me.

I laid my hands on her head and could not pronounce the blessing. I could not get the spirit present. For some reason, it would not come. I removed my hands and stood silent. My Dad asked if I needed him to do it? I told him No. I again put my hands on her head and said a prayer. I asked for strength and I asked for the Spirit. I also asked that it come immediately. It came and I pronounced a blessing on her.

I released her spirit from this earth and commanded her body to be at peace and free from pain. I closed the blessing and IMMEDIATELY after she laid her head back and was at peace. Her breathing instantly changed. I laid my head on hers and felt her Spirit leave. "She's gone!" I said. I could not hear her breathing. And then my Dad said, "No she is not!" She began breathing again. We all sat for several minutes. I sat with my head next to hers and my hands clasping hers. Heather had been by her side the whole time as promised and was clasping her hand when the blessing was given.

My Dad at that moment announced that he thought it best that everyone leave except for Heather and I. Everyone left and the peace entered ever so sweet. We sat by her side for 2 hours as everyone waited. We laid by her, held her and were there for her. As time went on, her breathing became more peaceful, but quicker and faster. We administered her meds, one final time in order to keep her comfortable. At this point, family began to come in. They were there to support us and help us. We brought a chair in for me and we slid the bed next to Kennedy where Heather had slept for almost 3 months. We continued to be by her side for a total of 3½ hours. We were tired, but we were not going to leave her. By 1 a.m., she really had changed her breathing. She sounded so peaceful, yet so full of fluid. She all of a sudden sat up instantly and tried to jump out of bed? She took a big cough and finally the fluid went down her throat. She laid back down and at this point sounded so, so peaceful. We told her it was OK to go.

We told her to go toward the light! We told her to be at peace and just go if she could see it. We told her we loved her so much and that it was o.k. that we would let her go. She still had a strong pulse and she was so, so peaceful. We were trying so hard to be with her and stay awake. We each had one of her hands. I had promised her that I would be there with her the whole time til the end. Somehow, we both were put into a deep, deep sleep. Anna had come in right after 1 a.m. and was on the floor asleep, but Heather and I both were put into a very deep sleep. We call it the "Kennedy Dust." We were just out!

At 2:47 a.m., Heather tapped me on my shoulder, "She's gone," she whispered. "Jay, she's gone!" I somehow had ended up on the floor. I jumped to my feet and grabbed her hand. I buried my head in her chest and sobbed. I wanted to be there, I wanted to be awake. "I failed her, Heather, I failed her!" I screamed. I fell asleep. Heather's hand was still clasped in hers. Heather had held her hand all the way til the end. But, Heather said, "I fell asleep too Jay. It is o.k., she could not go with us being awake. This is what she wanted." We sat holding her. We woke up Anna and let her hold her. We all cried, but we were all at peace. Our sweet Angel had gone home. She graduated. She was finally free and able to be herself in whole form. We sat for almost 45 minutes just relishing in the peace of the Comforter. Heather went and woke up my beautiful sister Keri and we brought Beau in to see Kennedy. He could not wake up. He was too tired. KeriLyn hugged and kissed her. She was supposed to be there. As hard as it was, it was so peaceful. Heather called the mortuary and Hospice. We sat in her room and looked at her and she had a smile! Her smile was so peaceful and so beautiful. She was finally free. She was finally home. We knew that she had been taken home by many on the other side if not by the Savior himself.

She had taken "The Last Ride." A ride so amazing that we had to be asleep because we could not see. The mortuary came and the mortician said his daughter knew Kennedy and went to high school with her. He was very emotional and he said he had followed her story. He began to cry. I put my arm around him and said, "You got to get it together, so we can go and put Kennedy on the gurney." He laughed and I laughed. As they wheeled her body away and Heather kissed her on the forehead, I could only stand on the front porch and did not move an inch as they loaded her and drove away. There are only two times, I have ever felt like that in my life. So helpless and hopeless, yet so happy. 1. When Kennedy was born and we brought her home. And 2. On that night. My baby was gone, yet she was living forever.

After Kennedy was gone we tried to go to sleep but all we could do was cry. We kept thinking that we were hearing her voice calling out for us, or many times I thought that I could feel her hand in mine. We finally just got up and knew that we would need to be there for Anna and Beau. Little Beau was trying to sleep in his room with KeriLyn, but he could not. He was staring at the ceiling when we found him in his room. He had wrapped himself in one of Kennedy's blankets and was just trying to figure it all out. I went and scooped him up in my arms and held him. Keri told me that he had snuggled her all night. As I snuggled him, Heather and I had to tell him that she was gone. We laid him back down where he could rest. He had such a look of sadness on his face. His little lips were puckered up and he looked as if he were to cry. We left his room and went back to ours.

After we left, Beau got up and went downstairs. We gave him a minute and I then went downstairs. We found him all alone lying on the couch crying. We asked him what he was doing? He told us that he was looking for Kennedy? "Where is her body? Where did she go?" he asked. We told him that her body was o.k. and that it was taken by the Mortuary to a safe place. Beau asked why we did not wake him up to see her? "We did! We did!" we said. He was upset. "I wanted to see her one more time. I wanted to hug her. Why did you not squirt my face with water?" This just melted us and we were so sad, yet he was so cute and sincere. We just held him and let him, let out his feelings. It was a moment we will never forget. As we went upstairs, my phone rang at 8:31 a.m., it was Weber State University. My contact left a voice message and said that she had got everything approved for Kennedy's funeral and that she would send over a calendar we could start to select future dates, etc.

You have to understand that Kennedy had told us for a very long time that her funeral would be where the Imagine Dragons concert was at Weber State. And furthermore, the mortuary had already told us that there was no where large enough to accommodate the amount of people that would attend. Though it seemed impossible due to approvals, we asked Weber State if it would ever be a possibility to hold her funeral there.

It was supposed to be there. It was amazing, because our contact did not even know that Kennedy had passed away. I called her and she began to tell me about the arrangements, etc. She said, "I know it is hard to talk about, but. . . ." I interrupted her and told her that Kennedy had passed away early that morning. She went silent and then cried. As she cried, we knew that this was to take place at the Dee Events Center. I was so very excited, yet so sad. Kennedy had taken care of everything. Kennedy had told me that she wanted her funeral to be on June 5th. That date was miraculously available! As we hung up the phone, I had to tell Heather what was going on. She did not know if she felt good about the Dee Events Center. I was very adamant that it all came together for a reason. As the spirit took over, Heather completely knew that is where we were supposed to hold the funeral. We both knew and she finally got her confirmation. It was confirmed that the spirit would and could reside there. We really went through the day and received so many messages, texts and calls. . . . Kennedy's Facebook site went nuts! She was most definitely doing the work she had always set out to do. It was mind blowing.

We went to the mortuary, and the floral shop. We had not slept at all, but the Lord was sustaining us. As we met, it seemed that ALL things were coming into place for Kennedy and her funeral. She had told me that she did not want to leave anyone out and by holding her funeral at the Dee Events Center, we would not. As the day wore on, we had more and more visitors and people show up. But, after the florist, we drove home to a beautiful sight of Kennedy colors, balloons, ribbons and butterflies. We had the entire yard decorated OF COURSE by the Cheerleaders. Wow! It was so amazing and so very exciting, yet so sad. The yard looked just like Kennedy would have wanted it. Her own little Paradise! We finally got home and inside thinking that we might be able to get some rest.

But, Oh no, not a chance! Our friends, family and probably over 400 people showed up. And all were wearing pink and green. They all lit their cell phones and Kennedy's wheelchair sat silently on the front porch. The song, "Fix You," by Cold Play was being sung by my brother . . . and his son . . . , as my nephew was playing it on his guitar. All were swaying back and forth and were there as we watched. Kennedy, I feel was there as well. She was there in spirit. A beautiful golden clad/blue and multiple colored sky was beaming in the horizon! Kennedy was there. The spirit was there! Anna walked up the path to our house and the 3 of us embraced! It seemed that Kennedy was already fixing things, already beginning to heal us as a family.

We watched the cheerleaders who took out probably 100 balloons and released them. A note, was attached that stated, "Hug Someone." In loving memory of Kennedy Hansen. The balloons were released and they went every which way. It was one of the most beautiful sights I had ever seen in my life. I was so moved, so touched and so aware. We hugged, we cried and we just loved. Many came into the house. I sat outside and spoke with my very best friends. They all were there and they all were very, very aware of Kennedy's spirit. Many experiences were being shared about Kennedy. My long time friend and trainer whom I consider my brother, shared with me a miracle that happened with one of his clients. One of his clients was driving home from St. George, Utah. It was 2:30 a.m. as they arrived home. They were coming around the corner by the school and the city offices, near where we live. They saw a bright almost illuminated light coming out of the top of a home. They did not know whose home it was? They were stopped dead in their tracks. It looked like a funnel going to heaven. She said it was at 2:30 a.m. If you remember, Heather and I were awoken at 2:47 a.m. Many accounts were shared from many people that a bright light was seen over our home at that time. That light in our opinion was Heaven taking her home. Home to the Father whom we had trusted. Home to the next chapter of Kennedy's story.

http://goo.gl/PTdFMl

Scan to view post

http://goo.gl/0m1sqV

Scan to view post

CHAPTER 79

The Ride Is Not Over

That week we thought that we would be in mourning. But who had time for mourning with the great celebration that we were planning for Kennedy? She had promised and foretold when she visited me spiritually that night two days before she passed,

> If you can, have my funeral on June 5th. If not, it is o.k. That will mark one year since my diagnosis and I think that is pretty special. The funeral will open many doors. It will be the crowning event of my earthly journey. Many are going to come and many are going to be watching you and Mom.

It seemed from the moment that Kennedy revealed those promises to me that night, that Heather and I were ok. From that moment on, we were carried and we carried everyone else. Yes, we missed her, yes, there were tears. Yes, she was gone. But, only for a moment. For she would not allow us to focus, dwell, or even hint the negative. She wanted us to celebrate her life, her journey, her miracles, and her story. Millions needed it and millions would know of it. That week was anything but normal.

You would have thought that a bomb hit our house. We had a pipe break and ended with a partially flooded basement. Shortly after the break, our water heater went out, and then our air conditioner! The week was very hot and so we sat in our home with no water, no air conditioning, and no Kennedy. But guess what? The crowning event would be upon us soon. We did not even care. We showered at the neighbors, we drank bottled water, and we just dealt with the heat. Over 6,000 people came to her viewing and her funeral. There were people that never got to see her or us at her viewing due to the long line that wrapped around the outside of the mortuary. We were all smiles, all hugs, and all so happy to love, care, and thank all who came. Her funeral was as she stated. Many did come.

She filled the seats at the Dee Events Center stadium at Weber State University as she had predicted, with the many who came and were, yes, watching us as her parents. I was told that only 3 funerals had ever been allowed in that stadium and that the streets that were shut down by the Ogden Police to transport her to the cemetery, had also only been shut down two other times in history. As we rode to that cemetery and took in the scene. I had to truly ask, "Is this happening? Is this real? Is this over?"

After we dedicated her grave and had white doves released at its side, We said our goodbyes. We made the long climb into the limousine and drove silently away. Little Beau climbed up on the back of the seat and looked out the window as we drove slowly away from her grave. I was looking at his little face, at Anna's face who sat next to her mom and at my beautiful wife's face. It was all I could do to notice that they were all smiling. I asked myself again, as I took in this moment. "Is it over? IS IT OVER?" I peered at the flowers, the showering sun and the perfect blue sky overhead. A simple voice was heard that I have never shared with anyone before. It was the voice of Kennedy who said, "No, Dad, no. It's just begun."

Her funeral did not just touch many, it touched millions. And it was real. . . . It was all real! She was gone physically, but oh how she was with us spiritually.

There are critics, there are doubters, and there are unforgiving people who simply have stated it was not real. That the fairy tale story of Kennedy never happened. But it did and it does. And as Kennedy promised, it had all just begun.

She promised that after the cheerleaders came, she would be ready to go. And she did go as promised after that visit from them. But, not without miracles happening and promises fulfilled. When all of those cheerleaders came, they each were able to go to Kennedy's bedside and tell her goodbye. Heather and I watched lovingly as each one of them sat by her bedside, held her and told her goodbye. Out of those twenty-seven girls, we only saw one time where Kennedy sat up and spoke. And the one time she did, was with Lexi Velasquez. Lexi asked her something and we saw Kennedy sit up and whisper something in her ear. We always wanted to know what she said to Lexi and we were always curious, because she was the only one that Kennedy spoke to.

For the next month, we truly were on pins and needles, wanting to know what the great miracle and blessing would be that was to occur in the next month. In all honesty, we thought it would be financial. We were buried. We have to laugh now, because there were days where we would walk out to our mailbox and look to see if a check was there. But, guess what? No check ever came. But, what did come was a phone call from Lexi's dad, Lance. He called and asked if I would meet with him. He told me that some things had happened and he was having feelings that he had never had before and he did not know what to do? I told him, I would be honored and would love to meet with him. We knew each other, but it was simply casual at that point.

We met and Lance simply looked at Lexi and said, "Tell them." Lexi proceeded to tell us that the last day Kennedy was alive and when she came to visit her, she had asked her, "Kennedy, did you choose this?" Kennedy sat up and whispered in her ear, "Yes, I chose this. I'll come for you." We finally knew what had been said. But, what happened next, completed the miracle.

Lexi, told us that she left our house and went home completely heartbroken. She ran to her bedroom, locked her door and broke down. She said that as she laid on her back in her room with her arms rested at her side, that she sobbed for a very long time. And then she said, "She came." "Who came?" we asked. "Kennedy." "Kennedy came to you?" Heather asked. "Yes, yes," Lexi said through tears. "I was still crying when I felt pressure next to my side, like someone was sitting on my bed. Then I felt weight on my hand, like someone had just put theirs on top of mine. There was no squeeze, just enough pressure to make me aware that someone was sitting with me on my bed. I stopped crying and knew immediately it was Kennedy. To be honest, I was scared. Her back was facing me and I could see her long brown hair as clear as day and see her hand on mine. At first I went cold and did not understand how she could be there? I mean, I did, but I didn't want to. I think she knew I was scared because nothing happened for a while. And then she talked to me without talking. I could hear things in my mind that she told me were going to happen and needed to happen. "Lexi, missionaries are going to come and you need to listen to them. You need to have faith and be strong. Especially, you've got to help your Dad." "I felt the pressure come off the bed and my hand. I started to cry again and I thought she was gone. But then I opened my eyes and she was there standing at the foot of my bed. "It is up to you now. Be strong . . . ," she said. "I wiped my tears away and when I looked again, she was gone."

The next morning my Mom woke me by putting her hand on my shoulder and saying, "Alexus." I looked at her and started bawling because I knew what she was about to tell me. I screamed "no, no, no." But, she told me that Kennedy had died. I was embarrassed to tell anybody, but I just kept thinking about it all the time and then a few days later, those missionaries came and that is why we are talking with you today."

Heather and I sat in silence and in tears as we heard this from Lexi. Lance then proceeded to tell us that he had been diagnosed with pancreatic cancer and had lost his faith. He told us that he had lost his belief in God, in miracles, and he didn't want to have anything to do with God. He told us that he could see the concern in his wife's eyes when he said this, because she was such a God-loving person. He wanted to know how God could be so cruel to give him such a terrible disease, the same disease that had already taken his mother away from him and his family? And how could God give Kennedy such a terrible disease where her parents could do no more than watch her die? He then told us that everything changed with a random knock on their front door and his wife inviting in two missionaries. At first Lance was angry that they were there in his house and his demeanor and body language portrayed that. But, before he could say anything, his wife, LaTaschia, said, "Lance, just listen to what they have to say." Lance said he could see the sincerity in his wife's eyes, so he agreed to sit down and listen. Lance did not have time for a lot of fluff or a "one size fits all" teaching session. The missionaries must have sensed his uncertainty because one of them finally said, "Lance, we were not just randomly knocking on doors when we found your home." The missionary's candidness caught Lance off guard and he really didn't know what to say. At this point, Lance said that his mind started churning through responses and he believed they may have not been randomly knocking on doors, but they were aware of the Velasquez home and aware that he had fallen away from the Church. The conversation shifted gears at this point and Lance explained the anger he had toward God and explained that if there is a God, how could this God bring so much pain to his family? Lance could feel the anger boiling inside of him. And then the young missionary responded with a response that would change his life forever. He simply said, "Lance, the adversary has you exactly where he wants you." The irony of what he said literally stunned Lance. Lance looked at Heather and I and said, "Had I been so angry at God that I let the devil slip in and position him right where he needed to be? Had I been won over by the greatest manipulator of all time? Heather and Jason, what the missionaries brought to my family that day was extraordinary. The fog had lifted and things seemed so much easier. My wife has decided to go through the lessons with the missionaries and see what will come from it. And with Kennedy's situation I have often wondered how it would continue to impact my family and I. So, here we are one month after Kennedy is gone, bothering you and your family. Yet, [we] have felt so inspired to reach out to you in hopes that what Lexi has gone through might be of some comfort to you and your family. But, more importantly, we want to know if you would be willing to be with us while we take the missionary discussions? Furthermore, I really do not know how to take and handle all of these feelings and emotions that I am feeling."

All Heather and I could do is move from our chairs where we sat and hug Lance and his family. Kennedy had told us that within the next month after she would die, there would be a miracle happen. . . . This was it. A few weeks later, the entire family was baptized and Lance returned to his faith and the Church. That was the miracle and that was the mission for Kennedy—to touch, love, and share the goodness that she believed in in order to better others.

Since losing Kennedy and for the last two years. I believe we have experienced more hardship, more loss, and more difficulty than when she was alive. We were carried and carried smiles on our faces for about six months after she died. And then one day, I shook my fist at God. It finally all caught up with me. The loss, the financial burden, the weight of sharing her story, and the challenge of helping my family heal. But, God did not shake back. He simply reminded me of the promises that had and have been made from him through Kennedy to us. The promises made on that sacred night two nights before she died. She promised and said,

> Heavenly Father says to quit sweating the small stuff and go to work. Dad, your biggest worries shall become your least worries. Survive for just a bit longer. You will be able to pay everything off and you will be able to enjoy your life debt and stress free. I PROMISE TO BRING YOU MIRACLES WITH THIS PART DAD. Own your mistakes and just work smarter.

Guess what? It all has happened the way she said. Our business has somehow been taken care of and has blessed many. My employment has been one of the largest blessings in my life. When Kennedy said go to work, that is exactly what I have done. And yes, I have owned my mistakes. Some that were chosen and others were not. We are not debt-free and will not be for some time. But, the MIRACLES that I have seen to get us there, are without number. I have seen Kennedy help with this part and we are not out of the woods yet. But, somehow, someway we have avoided pitfalls, catastrophes, and scary situations that could have destroyed us, but have not yet. To say we are "surviving a bit longer" is not only true, but has been a hallmark statement in this category.

She told us that we would *"be asked to speak many times and frequently."* This has not only happened, but continues to grow as we share her story. In the last two years, we have spoken over sixty times to different groups about her story.

Kennedy was most concerned with her family and she revealed, that I needed to

> Regrow your relationship with Anna. She is going to need you. Be: LOVING, KIND AND UNDERSTANDING. She will be the BIGGEST BLESSING of your life Dad, outside of Mom.

I can honestly say that outside of Heather, Anna has become the biggest blessing of my life. Yes, there have been struggles, trials, disagreements, and Anna even moved out for a time. But, all of that has needed to happen in order to strengthen, build, and grow a bond with Anna that is now stronger than ever before. Her ability to help us with our business struggles, personal grief, sharing of Kennedy's story, and family unit has been and will be paramount forever.

When it comes to Little Beau, Kennedy promised,

> Dad, enjoy your life. Go and hunt, ski with Beau and Anna. Play a lot of sports with Beau and be very involved in the Gospel. Little Beau will be o.k. I will come for him many times. I love him so much. He will grow into a fine young man.

Out of all of us, I think that Beau has excelled and recovered the quickest. I have done what Kennedy asked and taken him and spent a lot of time with him in those areas. But, the reason he has excelled is because as Kennedy promised, she has come for him many times. Shortly, after she passed, Beau told us that she came to him and comforted him. On many occasions, he will come and get us and tell us that she is there. He will point to her room, outside or out on the deck and say, "Can't you guys see her? She is right there." We will look, yet cannot see. For that special gift is his and his only for the rest of his life given to him from Kennedy.

Kennedy promised, stated, and asked,

> USE YOUR SUCCESS TO SHARE MY STORY! I promise that you will not tire from it and you will long to see me again, every day for the rest of your life. Many are going to be watching you and Mom. LOVE HER! She is my Mommy forever. I know that you love her, but you need to know that she already has a place reserved in Heaven for her.

Since losing her, I have hung up most of my hobbies and refocused on sharing her story and healing our little family. I have not tired from doing it. I have loved my wife and love her more now than I did when I met her twenty years ago. And the goodness that comes from Heather and what she endured in sending Kennedy home could only be rewarded with a place in Heaven. For no earthly reward is great enough.

So many times, so many days, and at so many moments, I have jumped in the truck and driven to the castle, to our Riverdale home, to the soccer field, to that hunting spot, to Fremont High, to the gas station, and now to her grave. And on every ride, I play in my mind as if it is the last. One thing my daughter taught me is what she said in her promise:

> Dad, I chose this. Do not ever forget that. I'll be waiting for you! I promise to! Thank you for teaching me, thank you for loving me, and believing in me. Dad, one more thing. . . . I LOVE YOU! I have to go now. Be strong, take good care of me like always. Oh Dad, one more thing, I am your little Dee, your Kenners, your Princess. But, more importantly, I am the Daughter of a King.

To that I say, "Kennedy, the ride is not over. It has just begun."

http://goo.gl/hSmhJq

Scan to view post

Scan to visit

www.kennedyshugs.com